CRACKED MIRRORS: EMMETT TILL TO BARACK OBAMA AND MY PATH TO AUTHENTIC ISLAM

CRACKED MIRRORS: EMMETT TILL TO BARACK OBAMA AND MY PATH TO AUTHENTIC ISLAM

—⸻—

Zaid Adib Ansari

DISCLAIMER

I have tried to recreate events, places, and conversations from memory. I have attempted to maintain a degree of anonymity in some instances by changing the names of individuals and places. In addition, I may have changed some identifying characteristics and details such as physical descriptions, occupations, and places of residence.

TABLE OF CONTENTS

Acknowledgments

Many hands and hearts assisted this work. I began writing my memoir in Atlanta, Georgia, in 2007. I placed it on a shelf for two years while I lived in the United Arab Emirates from 2007 to 2009. I then resided in Cairo, Egypt, from September 2009 to September 2013 and resumed writing in Cairo in late 2012. I completed this labor of love in Atlanta in 2015. I soaked a few tissues with tears along the way as I shared drafts with family and friends after rewrites and edits. I want to thank Lorrie Hariston for her insightful suggestions and editorial assistance. I am also indebted to Anne Kane for her meticulous technical assistance. Ali Abdullah, an intellectual companion, provided me with valuable feedback about candor. Gerard Ibn Earl Bilal lent me his media-savvy ear and reminded me of an important subject I neglected. I appreciate his review and comments.

My dear brother, Bilal Abdul Kareem, your spiritual input, lively enthusiasm, and practical assistance turned out to be a game changer.

Thanks also go to Sabriyya Abdur Rauf, Jamila El Amin, Danny Bellinger, Darlene Hawkins, and Sumayyah Hill. I am grateful for your reading, editorial advice, and encouragement. Your support helped me endure.

Noura and Rhadiyah, the two wings that give flight to our family, I don't have adequate words to express my gratitude. You both lived the rough times with me every step of the way. Rhadiyah, I thank you for your subtle reminders to not to give up. It did not go unnoticed. Noura, I pray your painstaking reading of early drafts, your suggestions, and your financial support is placed on your scale of good deeds. Thanks go to all of my children for your prayers.

Finally, all praise belongs to Allah (God). O Allah, this memoir is about the life you gave me. I pray readers find it a source of healing and guidance.

INTRODUCTION

Emmett Till's murder occurred in 1955. It frightened me. His murder felt personal. I struggled to understand what it meant as I was just a few days shy of ten years old. Till went to buy candy shortly before he died at the tender age of fourteen. His murder ushered in an era of African American resistance to white terrorism as never before. Nevertheless, his death threatened my existence. His murder continued to shatter safety for all black men.

History lives. The past lives in the present. It produces meaning. With the wind of history at our backs, humans navigate unknowns. I grew up wanting to fathom unknowns. Emmett Till's murder started my quest to unravel things. I journeyed within to confront my deepest fears. His murder also propelled me outward to grab and remove the cloak of fear. Racism hides behind masks. Racism is a noisy and silent fear. It is fear alien to the fragment of human existence that craves light, clarity, and reason.

I wrote *Cracked Mirrors: Emmett Till to Barack Obama and My Path to Authentic Islam* to clarify the visceral meaning of black life in America that began for me over fifty years ago. My memoir, I trust, will assist readers to embrace yesterday's denotations that I experienced then and that I still wrestle with today. Emmett Till and President Barack Obama each occupy a historical and spiritual space and time. I don't like describing black people's struggle against oppression as civil rights, or even human rights. If forced to choose, I'd rather call it human rights. Both terms do injustice to describe what is at stake. From that point on, I navigated Yellow Springs and the other America with a cracked mirror. I chronicle the nuance of race and class; the contours of emotional and spiritual reconciliation; love for myself, my family, and finally love for all people. I describe my voyage across the bumpy terrain of symbol and reality. It records my journey, as I saw it and lived it, from the death of Emmett Till to the presidency of Barack Obama and their unintended brotherhood.

The trans-Atlantic slave trade did not occur because some European businessmen decided all of a sudden to sail over to Africa, capture some people, and then go to America to sell them. The economics of slavery grew to be much more than a venture capital start-up proposition in America. The economic aspects of the slave trade advanced capitalism in America and laid the foundation for the country to become the leading economic power it is today.[1]

The moral problem of the trans-Atlantic slave trade has affected a diverse number of people, nations, and human institutions. As a chronological metaphor, the politics of denial to minimize the harm of slavery and to create an image that slaves and their descendants deserved mistreatment and exploitation have set a dangerous precedent that endures in America.

Slavery defines America more than any other historical event. I own three profound books that demonstrate the veracity of my claim. The first book is Karl Polanyi's *The Great Transformation*.[2] Then comes David Baron Davis's *The Problem of Slavery in the Age of Emancipation*[3] followed by Edward E. Baptist's *The Half Has Never Been Told: Slavery and The Making of American Capitalism*.[4] I also have other works that converge on and support what each of these books presents. The claim of American Exceptionalism hides the most distasteful reality, and it comes to life in history. American slavery manifest this as untrue more than any other event. The often-used political refrain "May God Bless America" encourages delusions. Many African Americans grew up wrestling to reconcile the entitlements of exceptionalism and the claim that "America is exceptional above other nations on the earth." I questioned both pronouncements at a young age.

The names Emmett Till, Trayvon Martin, Michael Brown, and Eric Garner stir up potent evidence that challenge American Exceptionalism and the claim of God's special blessings on America. In my book, I invoke the image of an event, a cracked bicycle mirror, to characterize my sojourn in America to reclaim my humanity. My cracked mirror lives as a spiritual metaphor to denote my efforts to experience life as a contiguous event instead of fractured images. I believe my story raises important questions for anyone who seeks to unravel the physics of history and seeks to understand a universal spiritual yearning. My spiritual yearnings led me to Islam.

My book begs the following questions: Why are Americans violent toward people of color? Why has America been engaged in wars in every century? Why can't America shake off the stupor of racism? Why are so many Americans of all ethnicities in pain? The claim that America is still building a more perfect union fails to convince me that America is a work in progress. I believe that after 230 years of the American Empire, there are large numbers of people in America that still consider African Americans as quasi-citizens of sorts.

In spite of this, I understand that there are some who are committed to fulfilling the vision that America is a work in progress. I believe the jury is still out about whether America is moving toward its claim that it can treat all citizens equally.

I don't claim to have answers to every question. However, I believe my memoir illustrates that my struggle to find answers and your innate desire for answers are similar. I pray that the process I describe of mending my cracked mirror, over decades, will inform and enrich your life.

–Zaid Adib Ansari, June 2015

LIFE ON A BIKE

I learned my first life lesson on a twenty-four-inch red Schwinn bike. It was my first bike without training wheels. Most bikes in the 1950s had alloy metal frames and thick rubber tires. My bike proved to be no different. My bike also had a black cylinder tire pump, the kind you hold with one hand and pump with the other hand. The tire pump air smelled like warmed metal and diluted motor oil. The smell produced a pleasant whiff of owning a bike.

My first lesson in social class peculiarities came from noticing other Yellow Springs bike riders. A few white kids in Yellow Springs, Ohio rode English bikes are known for their light weight and sleek design, and that set them apart from the bikes other white kids rode. Another simple truth was that white kids who rode English bikes did not use greasy hair oil. They did not slick their hair down like Elvis Presley. They did not smoke Lucky Strikes or Camels. They were naturals for English bikes. I knew that most of their parents had a connection to Antioch College, as either graduates or professors.

There were a lot of American bikes and a few English bikes in Yellow Springs in the 1950s. Even if you said you did not notice the bike disparity, you noticed. If you noticed as I did, the bike you rode said something. You noticed it because the Beatles had not made it big yet, and nobody sung "Kumbayah, My Lord" given the fact that the 1950s did not promote open displays of racial tolerance. How ironic the song "Kumbayah" became a symbol of interracial hand-holding to promote understanding and integration in the 1960s. Its origin, according to some research, is an African American Gullah spiritual from the 1930s. The title translates to "Come by Here" written during that time." [5]

Nonetheless, I knew a black kid who rode an English bike.

I could not tell if "acting white" made you ride an English bike or riding an English bike made you act white. Either way this kid and his entire family were standoffish Negroes who rolled their Rs when they talked.

That is what we called them: R-rolling Negroes. These Negroes could not wait to see white folks they knew on a first-name basis. White folk made them happier than a lost puppy that finds its way home.

On the far right, my father William S. Hawkins and I were photographed in the Yellow Springs News, May 1955 for the beginning of the summer baseball league.

Now on this hot September morning, I rode my bike to a small, dusty baseball diamond located on the southwest corner of an elementary school lot in Yellow Springs. I hung my ball glove on the handlebar and tucked my hardball inside the palm space so it would not slip out. I coasted to a stop. There, on top of a slightly raised pitcher's mound, I got off my bike, pushed the kickstand down, and walked over to three black boys and a white kid. I greeted each by name. Then I asked them to show me what they were holding.

I just knew they held a nickel pack of baseball cards and the hard bubble gum that came with it. I suspected they were haggling over Hank Aaron, Willie Mays, Mickey Mantle, or maybe even Minnie Minoso. Having a baseball card of one of these supermen mimicked a sensation like hearing the crack of the bat in Yankee Stadium.

They did not have baseball cards. What one of the boys cradled in his hand was far from something that innocent. He held a copy of *Jet* magazine. It showed black-and-white photos of a murdered black boy, Emmett Till. It showed his mutilated body. It showed his bullet wounds. His face looked like a large gray and bloated sponge. I felt the salty taste of vomit ease up my throat.

"What happened to him?" I asked.

"He whistled at a white woman," the tallest boy said as he read the article to all of us.

The *Jet* article said Emmett went to Mississippi in the summer of 1955 to visit relatives. There, in a small Mississippi hamlet, he tried to flirt with and whistled at a white woman. His behavior constituted a mistake few Mississippi Negroes would make. Emmett Till did not understand. Emmett came from Chicago.

He didn't see his blood leaving his body or fear death after sunset on that fateful day. He did not realize white folks would come to kill him that night over his flirtatious banter with a white female store clerk. He wound up beaten, shot, and drowned. Emmett Till died at fourteen.

In *A Death in the Delta: The Story of Emmett Till*, author Stephen Whitfield explained the ideology of lynching. He connected this ideology to the context of Till as a Chicago boy.[6] Whitfield elaborated on the events that lead up to Till's abduction and his murder. Whitfield wrote that Emmett found himself with his relatives and friends on August 24. Till accompanied them into the village of Money, Mississippi. He asked the white cashier for a date on a dare from his cousins to prove wrong Emmett's claim that he had a white girlfriend in Chicago. The grocery store belonged to Ray and Carolyn Bryant. Ray was traveling out of town the afternoon Emmett visited, and Carolyn was working in the store with Juanita Milam, her sister-in-law.

Carolyn testified that when she gave him change for some bubble gum, Emmett squeezed her hand, asked "How about a date, baby?" and wolf-whistled at her. Carolyn and Juanita decided it would be best not to tell their husbands about Emmett because they knew the deadly outcome that would follow.

Nevertheless, Ray Bryant learned of the incident from one of Emmett's young cousins. A few days later, on August 31, a fisherman found the mutilated body of a human being at the river bottom. A 125-pound cast-iron wheel from a cotton gin held the body down. Gunpowder burns on the right temple showed they shot Emmett Till at close range. Emmett also suffered a wound from an ax blow.

"Many southern race murders end with a dead black victim and life going forward for whites as if nothing happened. Emmett's death turned out no different. Emmett's mother refused the silence of fear and grief, and she began making plans for a public funeral for Emmett in Chicago so the world could 'see what they did to my boy.'[6]

I remember the images of Emmett Till, and I can only guess the expression I wore on my face. I bet it resembled the expression I see on my oldest son's face when he wavers between awe and fear. In front of my eyes, the picture of Emmett Till's grotesquely mutilated body whispered rage. White people killed him for whistling. I knew that African Americans had suffered horrible things in slavery. I knew terrible things still happened to black folk in America. We all knew white women were off limits. "Don't get caught fooling around with white women" functioned as a warning and an unwritten code. The wisdom to avoid white women became a fundamental survival principle black parents gave their sons before sending them out into the world of white folks. Most black men knew white men could become violent about their women.

My young mind struggled to digest the pictures. The images of Emmett's body crept down my throat, settling in the pit of my stomach. I could not understand what had driven these white people to murder a young boy and throw his body into the river. I would come to learn, painfully, that deadly rage directed at black men often occurred in Mississippi and other places in America.

I would also come to learn violence against black men occurred every day around the world. Why do white folks hate us? My mind stumbled for clues. Just clues. Answers cause finger-pointing. Evidence and facts assign blame. They will kill you for blaming them.

No sane black person wants evidence or facts when clues are all that's needed to numb the pain and chase away naked fear even for a few minutes. I could not tolerate much beyond a vague picture that this may have happened before, many times. I hoped it couldn't happen to me. I needed to believe that.

I looked at all of the pictures of Emmett Till and decided I had seen enough. I lifted my bike from the dusty baseball diamond and rode through a small opening between the fence and the backstop. The narrow space caused me to crack my bike's mirror on the corner of the fence. I did not stop. I just kept on riding, away from the pictures of Emmett Till.

As I rode away, most likely back home to safety, I noticed that the top part of my bike mirror reflected a significant image; it magnified the objects in it bigger than they actually were. The bottom half of the mirror, beneath the crack, showed me a smaller image while the upper part appeared blurred and more prominent. The two separate, fractured parts of the mirror showed me two pieces of reality. One part of the mirror showed what remained behind me. The other part of my cracked mirror foretold what I would encounter for years to come. The images stuck in my mind, stretching across my youth and well into my adult years.

Keep in mind, at nine years old I held this cracked mirror as a lens to see my life. I could see sleepy Yellow Springs flanked by American bikes and English bikes as mostly a safe place. I could also see that the rest of America would be a deadly and dangerous place for black boys and black men.

I knew nothing about murder and violence as a child. I did not understand why Emmett Till's flirtation with a white woman unearthed murderous rage. It did not dawn on me until many years later, when I pulled back the veil of Americana, that I understood the rotten, corrupted root of this primal hate and murderous passion. Its threat surpassed prejudice, a timid name for racism in the years before the black consciousness movement.

The so-called Indian tribes understood this rage. Many tribes endured an experience of murder and rage. They suffered rage across the length and breadth of America. African Americans and Native Americans tried to escape the violence and anger white settlers called "manifest destiny." Native Americans understood too well the murderous rampage that ended Emmett Till's young life.

Jet magazine's black-and-white photo of Emmett Till became a barometer for personal consciousness and a structural litmus test of commitment to the civil rights movement. Emmett's murder showed the world that ethnic cleansing started as an American convention long before Kosovo and Rwanda. It unearthed what thousands of so-called Negroes endured, long after the end of institutional slavery. Black people learned how to survive a cracked mirror existence, living on a knife-edge amid the social and political institutions of violence, intimidation, and the deliberate creation of an African American inferiority complex.[7]

Denying black people humanity in America became a best practice methodology for an American exportation of racism to the apartheid government of South Africa. America's racist history proved to be a laboratory for toxic socially constructed images. Indians, Hispanics, and African Americans shared the poisoning that produced a phantom of history and culture. African Americans became "niggers," Indians became "savage redskins," and Hispanics became "wetbacks." As a socially constructed export from America, blacks in South Africa were "Kaffirs." The same racial slur only differs in words, not meaning.

America's socially constructed image of African Americans—born in antebellum cotton fields and institutionalized as a means of denying our humanity—destroyed our self-respect. The images also created a deadly climate of violence against black people in America that continues to endure.

The day I saw Emmett Till in a fifteen-cent *Jet* magazine, black life in America came into sharp focus. I needed to survive the climate that tossed

Emmett's mutilated body in the river. Seeing his picture forced me back on my bike. I rode away, not even stopping to mend a cracked mirror. Blood and terrorism drenched Emmett Till's America. These horrors thrived and evaded justice for three centuries. For most of my life, I lived in fear on both ends of a cracked mirror. I had good reason to be afraid.

A Flicker of Light

Tecumseh, the Native American and Shawnee chief, lived in an area between Chillicothe and Springfield, Ohio. [8]

Historians report that he frequently traveled to the village of Yellow Springs just to drink from an iron-rich natural underground fountain that pours from three large fissures that give the village its name.[9] I followed Tecumseh's footsteps growing up in Yellow Springs and felt the same icy cold water numb my teeth and send a jolt to my forehead. Like him, I experienced the lush green foliage of summer, and I watched the trees in a place called Glen Helen turn brown and become just naked branches against the winter sky. Centuries apart we experienced the silence of the Glen broken only by the rhythmic patter of water across jagged rocks. In a similar fashion, our destinies suffered the same fate with the arrival of white people in the sixteenth century. Native Americans and blacks suffered humiliation from a racist social construction. It set in motion the tyranny of "so-called progress," the runaway train of manifest destiny that trampled African Americans. The same runaway train carved out a barrier that separated Native Americans from their natural surroundings, the rich land of America. For black folks, so-called progress meant slavery. This same so-called progress created an impenetrable barrier of separation from the grassy plains of Senegambia (southwestern Senegal and where the Republic of the Gambia touches the mouth of the Atlantic Ocean). Diane Chiddister reports that "Tecumseh's attempts to solidify a Native American confederacy gained him notoriety among American commanders and he "loomed as a serious menace to further American expansion". In a last attempt to halt American encroachment,

Tecumseh's warriors and the British fought Americans at the Battle of the Thames in Canada in 1813. Tecumseh died on the battlefield. This defiance removed him and his people from the hills and valleys of southwestern Ohio.[10]

Nevertheless, Yellow Springs did not succumb as much to the brutality of aggressive capitalism as other places in America. Robert Owen and his followers founded Yellow Springs in 1825 to create a socialist community where residents owned property collectively and worked together. Also, Yellow Springs became one of the stops on the Underground Railroad. Yellow Springs provided a safe climate that offered stability and safety to former slaves. It also became a haven where former slaves could earn a living.

The town's landscape in the 1950s looked like a snapshot from Norman Rockwell's lens. It was possible to stand in the middle of the main street at 11:00 p.m. and experience the stillness of the night interrupted only by the faint whistle of a distant freight train. The town's woodlands, abundant greenery, unpolluted streams, natural bike paths, and parks gave the village character. I had no idea that Gaunt Park, where I played baseball and learned to swim, began as a gift to the widows of Yellow Springs from Wheeling Gaunt, a former slave. Wheeling Gaunt gained his freedom in the 1860s and became a wealthy landowner. Yellow Springs' public schools never mentioned a word about Wheeling Gaunt's charity or his past as a former slave.

I also didn't know why Yellow Springs became safe for black folk. Moncure Conway, the son of a slaveholder, migrated to Yellow Springs with a colony of freed slaves in 1862. Conway as the pastor of the First Congregational Church of Cincinnati, an abolitionist whom Scott Sanders, the Antioch University archivist, calls a "maverick," was visiting in Yellow Springs- where he had friends- when he learned that the slaves had fled the plantation when the Union Army marched past Falmouth as fighting raged around Fredericksburg. Conway left at once, hoping to bring the slaves back to Yellow Springs.[11]

The small group of courageous white people, like Conway, who walked the talk against injustice always amazed me. I am particularly impressed by those who acted in an era when most white people held black people's suffering in less regard than animal suffering. Some of Yellow Springs' oldest African-American families were among Conway Colony descendants.

Despite its unique history and charm, Yellow Springs could not dodge the forces of a racist, capitalist America entirely. "The Springs," as we liked to call it, functioned as a safe haven for slaves seeking freedom. The town protected slaves from slave catchers. It inspired men of vision and justice like Horace Mann and Wheeling Gaunt to promote the growth of the mind and the heart. Nevertheless, in spite of these good men, Yellow Springs shared in Emmett Till's violent end with my other America. In the end, Owen's dream could not shield me from what I saw on the baseball diamond that sunny morning.

Freed from Pretense

My father's birth took place in Georgia, but he grew up on the west side of Dayton, Ohio. In those days, Dayton maintained foundries, machine shops, and hundreds of metal fabrication plants. It's heavy use of coal made it a drab gray industrial town. Scores of black men migrated from the south on Jim Crow trains to work in the hottest of its backbreaking factories. The promise of employment brought my father's family from Georgia to Ohio.

The two-story family home, where my dad grew up, sat on Germantown Avenue, not far from Roosevelt High School, an all-African American school he attended until tenth grade.

He told us that he left high school to work. This claim only held a dash of truth. His departure from high school resulted from more complicated factors than a sixteen-year-old leaving school to help his mother. My grandmother's depression and her heavy drinking compelled my father, I believe, to retreat into a solitary world. My grandfather, Walter, disappeared before my dad reached his ninth birthday. My dad had not heard a word from him for over forty years when my father's half-brothers and half-sisters, Walter's other children, contacted my dad as Walter lay on his deathbed in Virginia.

I remember the night my father drove our wood-paneled station wagon out of the driveway and traveled southeast from Ohio to Virginia to meet his estranged siblings. In Virginia, Walter had acquired property and other assets. He had done well. When my father arrived, he asked his half-brothers and half-sisters to read Walter's last will.

My dad pondered every line while sitting at the family's kitchen table. The will did not mention him. Granddad Walter left him nothing.

Dad, turned to my mother, and made a gesture to leave. My mother said he did not utter a single word on the long drive back to Ohio.

He never mentioned his father or his siblings again. Walter left my dad speechless and empty. Not recognizing my father in the will hurt him, deep in his soul. This time, the pain was more severe than Walter's disappearance forty years before. Recalling my father's anguish troubles me even now. I am troubled that Granddaddy Walter abandoned my father twice. My father shut off his feelings most of his life. It took me years to fathom his pain.

As I grew up watching my dad cope with his pain, I also learned how to deal with this distant past. When my father did not come to my sporting events or my school outings, I felt let down, as my dad must have felt like as young boy. He was too busy. He worked two jobs. He felt too tired. At times, I feared, he drank too much. I learned to retreat inwardly like him.

My father searched, mostly in the wrong places, for his fractured identity. Granddaddy Walter's silent departure from my father's young life molested all of us. My dad felt overwhelmed and burdened to stake a claim as a man, carrying a broken and warped yardstick of manhood. He tried to achieve happiness as material success in white America. Happiness without white society's ratification made success for him hard to find. He thought as many black folk and white folk do that a happy life is objects. If you don't get them, they will get you.

The game of life had a stacked deck. The card dealer cheated, but black folk played the game. If you didn't play, then go to a grave freshly dug. Go find a bottle. Go drown in anger. Go crazy.

The rules were simple then and, sadly for many young black men, are still unpretentious. I finally grasped the bigger historical picture as the brutality of racism made its mark.

The widespread despair among black folks in my dad's post–Great Depression neighborhood smothered hope. I peeled away layers of family secrets and learned why he withdrew into the world of fear, self-doubt, and unexpressed anger. His last stop ended in the bottle. Despair and poverty in his neighborhood gobbled up young black men. My father did not escape. The pervasive reach of Jim Crow reigned. Jim Crow's grip regulated cultural life and personal life. At the cultural level, colored movie houses were tenacious Jim Crow barricades and havens of enjoyment at the same time. Like many towns in the Midwest, Dayton had formal and informal Jim Crow arrangements that made Black movie houses shrines.

The Regal Theater during the 1950s welcomed a young black man's pompadour. The plateau-looking haircuts peeked over the back of velvet-covered seats while Tarzan outwitted scores of spear-tossing Africans and cowboys chased disorganized Indians across dusty plains. I knew the colored-only Regal and West Dayton did not feel like downtown Dayton. Jim Crow in Dayton stood for everything my parents hated. It created a caricature life that black folks accepted as normal. My parents believed Jim Crow-inspired a cartoon-like existence that stymied the soul with pretense and shame.

A prominent academic and curator of the Jim Crow Museum, David Pilgrim, describes the history of Jim Crow's inglorious past: "These words are from the song, 'Jim Crow,' as it appeared in sheet music written by Thomas Dartmouth 'Daddy' Rice. [12] Rice, a struggling 'actor' (he did short solo skits between play scenes) at the Park Theater in New York, happened upon a black person singing…some accounts make him an old black slave who walked with difficulty, others say it was a ragged black stable boy.

Whether modeled on an old man or a young boy we will never know, but we know that Rice appeared on stage in 1828 as 'Jim Crow'—an exaggerated, highly stereotypical black character."[13]

Jim Crow arrangements evolved as an extension of slavery.[14] Some contemporary scholars, like Michelle Alexander, argue that neo–Jim Crow arrangements still occur as mass incarceration of African-American males.[15] The grip of the neo–Jim Crow arrangements is more harmful to the psychology of black men than slavery.

In my mother's mind, Jim Crow made pretending a deadly pastime, spiritually. She saw things like pompadours as a shallow masquerade that would drown you in self-loathing. For her, the Dayton Regal symbolized the burden of pretense that made wearing the Jim Crow mask intolerable.

Then an incident occurred to my sister and me that helped our family take flight from the Regal, the west side of Dayton, and everything both symbolized. A boy of twelve or thirteen years old taunted me as my older sister and I stood in line to buy tickets to a Saturday matinee. I was six or seven years old, and he walked over and stood on my toes. Darlene, in one quick and decisive move, stepped in front of me and told the street boy to stop or suffer a beatdown. As it was, he stopped. The theater incident, immortalized many times around the dinner table, became a catalyst for our departure to Yellow Springs. I am sure there were other practical concerns my parents considered, but the story of my sister as the hazel-eyed Avenger was the one most often told.

When we arrived in Yellow Springs, my father rented a property on the main street. The large wood-frame building stood in the middle of the block near an apartment building and the only grocery store in town. Our house doubled as Hawk's Shoe Repair, my father's business. Living there, I believed we had everything. One of the first African American families in Yellow Springs to own a black-and-white TV, we could not imagine life being any better. Years after we moved from our first Yellow Springs home, my mother reminded me that 152 Xenia Avenue had been unbearably hot in the summer and freezing in the winter. The house was so breezy, she said, that I caught pneumonia twice during the few years we lived there. Even so, I loved that breezy, old wooden house. I don't think either of my parents was fully aware that they were pioneers. On the one hand, they endured the currents that dragged the conflicted personality of Yellow Springs toward a conventional America of segregated schools, segregated housing, and segregated public services. Yellow Springs on the surface looked integrated without discomfort. Still, there were elements, people, and forces in Yellow Springs that embraced a segregated America. It hid in the shadows. It held onto stubborn racism.

Some of the Yellow Springs residents clung to a bigoted past in spite of the village's long history of free thinkers and Unitarians, like Horace Mann and Wheeling Gaunt. Yellow Springs could not completely confine the menace of racism to a shadowy past.

Nonetheless, the progressive climate in Yellow Springs encouraged my parents to stick it out. For black folks, Yellow Springs excelled above the surrounding towns.

I grew up watching these two personalities compete to define Yellow Springs. This competition gave me a context, a yardstick, to see and understand how my earliest view of the world formed.

My internal mirror, I would come to see, helped me absorb life and culture in this village and across many years. Yellow Springs was a lens to see my other America. My struggle to understand America, full of greed in the name of freedom and progress, at times, acted as a scary evil clown that frightens children intentionally.

Emmett Till's murder showed me an America that scared me. It cast an image of homegrown terror, pure terror. By the end of the fifth grade, the picture of Emmett Till's mutilated body influenced the way I saw white people. I liked and even loved many. Nonetheless, they also scared me. I had better be careful and make sure I did not trip the "rage switch" that got Emmett Till killed. It made existing in America an art of cautious and careful steps. I sensed, as did many black children, we could only peer at Yellow Springs and white America from the outside on our tiptoes. There, on the cuff of America, we often wondered if it was worth the effort to try to gain access.

For a young boy, the largest door to gain entry into America was school. I wrestled with the question of whether I should bother to do well in school. I knew good grades wouldn't save me from the violence that happened to black boys in places like Mississippi and, closer to home, in Fairborn, Ohio. Fairborn was a nearby hillbilly hamlet always on the verge of violence toward black folks. Pre–civil rights America scared black folks. It promised violence. Ralph Ginzburg, the author of the book *100 Years of Lynching*, uses scores of chilling events to illustrate the severity of the violence that occurred against innocent black people.[16] His analysis also shows that the depiction of the black man as a dangerous, predatory public menace is a complicated half-truth.

Blacks were victims of terror for close to four hundred years. The first report in Ginzburg's book is of James Webster Smith, the first African-American cadet at the US Military Academy at West Point in 1880.[17] Other cadets gagged Mr. Webster Smith, bound him with a rope, beat him, and slit his ears. Ginzburg chronicles similar events from newspaper reports from the

1860s through to the end of the twentieth century. Before black men became a menace to society in the early 1970s, white America had mastered creating an image of the Negro as a dandy, a Jasper, and a buffoon. The degrading images justified terror and violence to control black folk. The images in popular culture of a foolish and dangerous man-child helped create a climate of violence against African Americans. Before the 1960s ushered in books and studies such as Ginzburg's, popular thinking in black communities accepted the white narrative that blacks deserved noncitizen and subhuman treatment. We swallowed this story and promoted it, as well. However, as much as we accepted this narrative, we also used humor to lampoon it and reject its assumptions.

These agile flashes of black humor exposed white supremacy at its core. Our logic was straightforward. If whites were superior, why do they assemble violence, segregate communities, contravene laws, and trample justice to oppress and hold back a naturally inferior race of people?

I used to watch my parents waver between disgust, a good laugh, and soul searching whenever we saw a black person dressed in the red wide-brimmed hats, button-strewn coats, and flounced vests. These were clothes Jewish and Italian clothiers made for the haberdasheries on the colored side of the tracks. These clothes represented white society's image of "their Negroes."

"Look at those fools," I can remember my mother saying, shaking her head and holding back a laugh so as not to spoil her teaching moment. "Boy, you and your sister will never wear these clothes." My mother's message came directly. She was not worried about my sister. Her warning was to me: don't even try to sneak and wear these clown outfits.

I could not get away with wearing pretense costumes, tempting as it was, though, just to see my mother's reaction. I knew it was a redline in our house, and I knew why. I had a little more freedom when it came to hats. My mother allowed me to get away with wearing hats that I tilted, pinched, and crinkled for flare, but nothing much beyond that.

African Americans and most whites by the end of the 1960s were shocked to find that some black men abandoned these costumes for Afro-centric fashions. Some black men in the early 1960s wore dandy fashions with pride. These men, now clinging to a better picture of African American history and cultural identity, discarded their old clothes to burn in the streets of Newark, Detroit, and Los Angeles as black rebellions took place. Ironically, some of the men who fashioned the emblems of pretense became foot soldiers and leaders of black pride. Malcolm X, formerly Detroit Red, showed us that once we awake from pretending and imitating white folk, the mask that hid our self-loathing would naturally fall off. We discarded the masks. It made us human. Alex Haley made millions of Americans aware of Malcolm X's transformation.[18]

Masks and costumes died in the streets, atop their concrete graves. Unmasking gave birth to an owned identity, not one drenched in pretense. Black folk, during the peak of the black consciousness movement in the 1960s, also embraced a self-defense identity. It was an affirmation. We had the right to defend ourselves.

Nevertheless, I was not surprised to see America's media and political establishment twist our right to self-defense as violent predators. The dynamics of self-defense became complicated and nuanced. While black pride gave us the courage to defend ourselves, many black men, though not morally justified, used crime to retaliate, as well. In some instances, it was revenge—though stark-naked revenge is futile. It feeds a cycle of violence. No one wins.

Even in light of these contradictions, some of the uprisings in the 1960s and early 1970s offered a splash of tainted justice. Most whites condemned these uprisings as lawless riots while many black folks considered stubborn racism, job discrimination, biased courts, and police misconduct as lawless. I realized that the law became an instrument to establish a racist status quo. During the 1960s urban rebellions, some black folks felt like "we got them on the run." To many, uprisings were not criminal. It was fighting back. I thought that peaceful protest and gradualism got Medgar Evers and Martin Luther King killed.[19] Over three centuries of violence and injustice to black folks made Malcolm X's statement "the chickens had come home to roost" a logical outcome of the urban riots. Malcolm X made this declaration about the climate of violence surrounding the assassination of President Kennedy.

His statement rang true for the overall climate of violence in America. It even resonated with black folks who could not afford to admit it.

GOOD HAIR

I started to pay attention to my hair when I was twelve years old. I wanted "good hair." My approach began with old pantyhose, affectionately called a stocking cap. Stocking caps made waves and waves killed naps. Black folks knew this. Even a few waves removed bad hair dishonor. Bad hair was kinky hair. To have kinky hair meant you were pure Negro. It was too close to Africa.

Medium-sized pantyhose usually made the best stocking caps. I used to measure the fit of the stocking cap by pulling it over my head before going to bed. I'd check out my hair in the bathroom mirror to see if my hair submitted, shining, with small finger waves.

I'd remove the stocking cap, wet a hairbrush with just a drop or two of water, and apply three fingers of Murray's pomade or Royal Crown's pomade to my hair.

I would brush my hair with long, slow strokes for ten to fifteen minutes before double-folding a white handkerchief over it. I did this nightly. All I had to do next was wait for the waves. The next morning, still half asleep and with a full bladder, I would dash to the bathroom mirror to admire the quarter-inch waves that rippled from the front of my head to the back.

I loved the stocking cap. I loved its miraculous results. This small piece of nylon stands out as a symbol of black unconsciousness. It fought bad hair that was inspired by self-loathing. For most black folks, good hair has always been necessary. Famous black entertainers helped spread the myth of good hair to ordinary black people.

I remember when Chuck Berry, the rock 'n' roll and blues singer, caused me to do a double take on good hair. Berry's hair was "conked," or chemically

Senior High Picture of William Hawkins, Jr., Spring 1964

straightened. He showed the world that his straight hair was like white folks' hair. Authorities arrested him for violating the Mann Act in 1959. [20]

Jet magazine reported the arrest occurred in Missouri. The article said he transported a fourteen-year-old white girl across state lines for immoral purposes. Berry's criminal charge of "white slavery" puzzled me.[21] Why was it called white slavery, I wondered? The official legislation is called the "White Slave Trade Act," but was better known as the Mann Act after its author, Representative James R. Mann.

At the time, I did not know the fine points of law. The term "white slavery" stuck in my mind. I guessed a white female would have to be a slave to ride out of state with a conked-headed Negro, who played an electric guitar. Chuck Berry's antics placed my love for good hair, curiosity about white females, and my affection for the stocking cap at a crossroads. I did not abandon my stocking cap right away. However, I did see my hair fetish differently.

On the one hand, I knew some white girls in Yellow Springs did not feel like slaves when they hopped in the backseat of a 1953 Mercury sedan with a so-called colored boy. I knew so-called colored boys who slipped off in the dark down High Street to a spot without streetlights with a white girl crouched low in the rear seat. My thinking about skin color, hair texture, or the sound of a Negro's voice was a bastard offspring of my parent's generation. They believed that the prototype of beauty was white or light skin, straight hair, and sounding white. In the pre–Black Awareness years, from the 1940s all the way through the early 1960s, no mental or spiritual bookmark existed to self-affirm Negro identity. My parents and most adults their age struggled with identity and often turned to sardonic humor and self-critique to lessen the sting of the pain.

Black folk used humor and lampooned noxious depictions of Negro identity as vaudeville. It gave us a firewall to protect the soul from whispers that said, "You are Negro. You are flawed."

I remember when my mother, for example, saw a large, dark-skinned woman and said, "Boy, she could whip a bear with a switch!" While funny on the surface, her description revealed her ambivalent feelings. She didn't know this woman, but my mother's image of her suggested lampoon and anguish.

My mother's humor pointed to a broader psychological struggle we all faced with a "Negro identity." As much as we tried to dignify it, most black folks knew the white definition of "Negro" was an insult.

As I watched Brylcreem commercials on our black-and-white TV and listened to the jingle, "A little dab will do you," it was almost impossible not to feel robbed by white folks' hair culture. I held a picture of white folk hair in my mind. I saw them flipping and tossing long (we called it stringily) hair over a shoulder, swishing it from side to side, breezing down Route 66 to a song by the Beach Boys. This image made white folks' hair a symbol of beauty and style in pre–civil rights America. As I watched TV after school, it was like swimming upstream against the fierce whitewater of Brylcreem commercials and the blond Doublemint twins. Nothing on TV looked like me. On the other hand, I saw Negro caricature shows like Amos 'n' Andy. This imagery continued through the 1950s and stretched well into the sixties. It provided a perfect flashpoint for disillusioned young black men to burn Newark and Cleveland in the middle of the decade of the 1960s. These riots were fueled by job scarcity, substandard housing, and segregated schools, but these woes only stoked part of the flames. The images of a just and fair America dressed in a red, white, and blue flag always sent two messages to most black folk. One message is that America was morally superior, blessed by God, and responsible for the current state of a free world by liberating Europe from Nazism and crushing the yellow menace, Japan. As far as anyone would have you believe, America's white folks had saved the world. So what if Billie Holiday's song "Strange Fruit" shone a light on the lynching of blacks hidden in plain sight? [22] None of this mattered. America produced double-door refrigerators and electric razors with rotating blades. Much of white America did not notice the homegrown terrorism black people experienced.

The persistent claim of American Exceptionalism was designed to demonstrate that America was the birthplace of freedom and democracy. This claim is a hard pill for black folks to swallow. Still today, in many quarters, America's leading financial centers of power are unwilling to share economic prosperity with black folk, Native Americans, and Hispanics. Poor whites are, unfortunately, swept up in this race-class cycle of bias of blocked opportunity. No one locked out of equal opportunity thinks America is exceptional in a good way. America is exceptionally racist, sexist, and is filled with class bias. As a result, many poor whites become storm troopers to keep black folks down, but at the same time their hatred prevents them from realizing they are pawns in a larger economic chess game. The free labor of black people has been used to constrain white wages. Now Hispanic immigrants are used to suppress the value of black and white labor. Everyone is deceived when race is used as a ruse to hide economic manipulation. By 1965–1966 black folks started to debunk racist social constructions and distorted images of black people, as Nell Painter pointed out in her book *The History of White People*.[23]

Our identification with Black Power informed an examination of our past. We examined African history prior to slavery. Our scrutiny helped many younger black folk reject a manufactured version of history. A transformation of a collective self-concept occurred when young black people started reading alternate accounts of our history. As we studied the past, our activities produced black leaders; many of them are only now recognized for their contributions.[24] As a result, young black folk struggled to introduce Black Studies and Sub-Saharan African Studies in higher education. Many black institutions and majority white higher education institutions resisted. The Black Studies movement set the stage for expanded scholarship and intellectual inquiry. The Black Studies movement would reshape how black people saw themselves. Many white people in the 1960s interpreted black people's desire to learn black history as angst toward white people.[25]

Black Studies movements survived several attempts to dismantle its significance. Its appeal declined. I admit that. Nevertheless, Black Studies emerged as an important feature of higher education. It remains as an important benchmark of progressive scholarship in so-called postracial America. In those days, we had a curiosity to discover our identity and history. Today we dye and fry our hair and spend millions on bleaching creams. In addition, nowadays, young black athletes and entertainers who wear dreadlocks or sport Afros know little about the origins or significance of these hairstyles. For many it is only a fad. In the 1960s, we searched everywhere for identity. We held tightly to the symbols and artifacts that affirmed our stolen humanity. With new insights about the myth of good hair and light skin color, the fabled prototype unraveled like a cheap suit. I traded in my stocking cap and waves for an Afro.

HIGH SCHOOL FICTION

My academic performance in high school was dismal. My sister Darlene, on the other hand, was fourth in her class and a member of the National Honor Society. While she was one of the brightest students in high school, I resisted pressure from my parents to study, preferring idle time and playing basketball.

"Whip my butt as much as you want on report card day," I would say to myself. "I'm not going to stress over good grades, period."

I think, at an emotional level, I saw good grades as an admission that unless I imitated white folks, I'd never get my parents' approval. The pressure to make good grades angered me to my core. My resistance to so-called academic performance was not entirely conscious, and it earned me various forms of punishment on the dreaded grade card day.

My father was beside himself to convince me to "buckle down," one of his favorite expressions. It meant to do well in school. His other favorite expression, designed to push my guilt button, was "Boy, be a credit to your race." That pissed me off. Credit "this," I gestured, at least in my mind, to anyone that tried to guilt me out with the "credit to your race" BS.

My parents exhausted all of the "credit to your race" arguments, "improve yourself" pep talks, and "earn a good living" reasoning. Although I didn't realize it at the time, resisting the pressure to get good grades saved me from a get drunk bottomless rabbit hole. My father fell in this hole. My resistance also saved me from the rice paddies of Vietnam where many of my homeboys died.

My stubbornness, most importantly, saved me from the unchartered wilderness in white folks' wonderland where most of my "I want to get ahead" black classmates got lost.

In my junior year in high school, a Central State College student, Mr. Herb Ellis, came to our school to help the track team as a student intern coach. He was a graduating senior, and the internship was a requirement.

Wilberforce College and Central State College, both predominantly black institutions then and today, were only eight miles from Yellow Springs.

Mr. Ellis was medium height, had dark skin, and sported a razor-part cut slightly right of the center of his forehead and just beyond the middle. Sometimes he wore a herringbone sports coat with a maroon tie. I think he often used a splash of Old Spice cologne. He was a picture of poise. One would not know that he was a world-class quarter-mile runner from his appearance.

His quarter-mile time was 47.5 seconds. His athletic persona was invisible. At five foot seven he could dunk a basketball jumping off the wrong foot. He planned to run in the Pan American games the following year, and as I recall, he did.

He invited our quarter-mile team to Central State to watch a regional track meet. In the spring of 1963, three of us went to Central State to watch Mr. Ellis and the Central State track team.

I borrowed my mother's green Mercury Comet. I traveled on the back road from Yellow Springs to Wilberforce, listening to Mary Wells's R&B hit "Two Lovers" on the car radio. The rich woodlands around Wilberforce had started to bloom green. The afternoon air smelled of fragile sapling trees and wet grass.

When we arrived, small groups of students sat in the stadium, scattered between the first and fourth rows of the bleachers on the home team's side. My teammates and I were excited. I do not recall if Mr. Ellis ran well that afternoon. I remember feeling proud. I remember loving being at Central State. Herb Ellis epitomized the best qualities of Central State. His image became a compass. His presence gave me the courage to stop pretending to feel good about myself.

Look, Mom, no mask. Just "me" was fine. I did not consider Central State a second-rate black college. I saw an opportunity to be myself—my best self.

Picture of William Hawkins, Jr 1963 running on
Yellow Springs High Mile Relay Team.

Central State produced black teachers. It was a place where future black doctors could hone skills.

However, in spite of all the right feelings, Wilberforce College and Central State College in the 1960s were paragons of Jim Crow in Ohio. On the surface, neither school had much status. However, if you dug beneath the façade of imitation and pretense, the value, career, and life potential were there.

On the tip of southern Ohio, both schools are historical evidence of the lingering impact of chattel slavery and Jim Crow's reach beyond the southern slave states. Ohio was, after all, a free state.

A storm sewer separated the two schools as the only physical distinction between Wilberforce College, "church side," and Central State, "stateside." The Methodist Church controlled Wilberforce, and the State of Ohio ran Central State.

Until this day, the Jim Crow footprint remains an undisputed history lesson in every corner of America. You do not need to look hard to find it.

On church side there used to be a small brick multipurpose recreation building. The main room was approximately thirty by forty feet. The building earned the affectionate nickname "Funky Butt" from students. The room's walls would sweat from the vibrating sounds of the Temptations, the Four Tops, and Junior Walker and the All-Stars. The place stayed packed with students and became so hot from dancing that the name Funky Butt was deserved. Anyone that experienced dancing a Friday or Saturday night at the Funky Butt never forgot the joyful bumping and sweating. I was proud to be there. There was no such thing as personal space. I learned dances brought from Detroit, Philly, DC, Cleveland, and other places.

Visits to Central State on the weekends became routine. My feelings about studying changed. I no longer dreaded college. It was no longer a jail sentence. The black college enclave in Wilberforce was a safe haven. My attitude at home and my studying habits improved; in turn, it influenced how my parents dealt with me. My parents no longer insisted on making me attend a majority white school. What a relief!

Their concession to Central State saved me from an overdose of cultural boredom and listening to the Beach Boys or Conway Twitty.

As my attitude continued to improve, they reciprocated with less pressure about everything.

I read widely, completely absorbed. I read everything I could. I read the newspapers. I watched the news and struggled to understand the changes I saw taking place. I tried to educate my parents, and anyone that would listen, about the civil rights struggle. Instead of diving into pastime activities like pop-culture music or watching Dick Clark's *American Bandstand*, I discovered Curtis Mayfield's lyrics and listened to Nina Simone. Mayfield's song "Move On Up" was a message. It was spiritual, and it promised victory. Nina Simone wore her hair natural and had an African-looking cloth as a hair wrap. She lived in France and was dark skinned. Her persona and her music were a message to be me.

In our home, there was usually a semi-formal breakfast on Sunday morning. The two local black churches rarely pulled us away. My mother would start with fried apples, followed by more heart-numbing black folks food. Around ten thirty we would turn on the TV and chat over a good, hearty breakfast.

One Sunday morning, as we watched CBS News, a regular program paused with a report of a church bombing in Birmingham, Alabama.[26] Four girls died in the blast. I flinched, as though someone slapped me. All of us flinched.

"Why do they hate us so much? What in the world did these four girls ever do to them?"

First Emmett Till, now these little girls. I knew of nothing that black folks had ever done to justify the violence and hatred we received from whites. It made no sense to me.

As the direct-action tactics of many civil rights groups increased between 1963 and 1964, the spiritual and cultural landscape of Yellow Springs—and, to a lesser extent, the rest of America—transformed. Black folk and white folk entered a space of muted discomfort, much like an annoying toothache that is not enough to put you down, but too annoying to ignore. This bombing was an act of terror to keep us colored, and my deepest core feelings screamed to fight back.

The terrorism early civil rights leaders faced, such as Ida B. Wells, who fought to stop lynching in the 1930s and 1940s, set a standard for resistance. She threatened to petition the World Court and bring charges against America for genocide.

The widespread terror of Ida B. Wells's time only abated twenty years before I was born.[27] In my birthplace of Springfield, Ohio, a so-called colored man suffered the lynch mob in downtown. He hung from a lamppost for three days. The lynching message said, "Stay Jim Crow Colored or hang on this lamppost."

In the fifties and sixties, Fairborn, Ohio—just seven miles down the road from Yellow Springs—had a reputation as a redneck, anti-Negro town. Most black folks were afraid to stop there.

I remember when my little league baseball team played there. The tension on the field muted the cheers from the fans. I feared they would jump us if we beat them badly or if a conflict developed on the ball field.

In the two years between my junior and senior year of high school, I felt the earth shift under the feet of white America. The civil rights movement, however, did little to ease the fear that many black folks harbored when it came to white terrorism. Dr. Martin Luther King, Medgar Evers, [28] Fred Hampton, and Mark Clark[29] all paid dearly in the quest to lay this fear to rest. These men and others died as white terrorism went unabated.[30] They were assassinated along with others not as well known.

A widespread response to the civil rights movement came from America's politicians and business elites. They wanted to create and advance an image that full civil rights would produce a dangerous Negro. It would make a monster. Negroes would threaten law and order. A Negro that would dismantle Jim Crow is a dangerous Negro. This argument urged gradualism and compromise. I hated the rhetorical question, "Is America ready for a black person as such and such?" The question seemed to suggest that white folks needed to take their time to accord me rights that were constitutional—the nerve.

Is it not ironic that the denial of constitutional rights for black folk in these years, in the name of law and order, is similar to a retraction of constitutional rights today, in the name of national security?

Strange as it may seem now, in the pre–civil rights years of the early 1960s black men in America did not evoke fear as a public enemy. We were more likely to be victims of terror and lynched.

The March on Washington, which took place on a sunny August afternoon in 1963 had been the flagship of the movement.

I remember watching it on TV, staring at hundreds of thousands of people who filled the National Mall, challenging American apartheid. On that day, for many blacks and whites, the image of a cowering, frightened black man changed to a man filled with fearless determination. Our floor model TV almost blocked the entire picture window of our prefabricated house. Its monstrous size underscored the growing spending power of many black folks. Small pieces of my memory resurface even today to stir feelings about the events that challenged America on that day. No wonder men like George Wallace, the racist governor of Alabama were beside themselves. The civil rights challenge was like a speeding cargo train, without breaks, carrying heavy loads of dark history, barreling down on the remnants of slavery. It smashed the sacred relics of an invincible white man towering over a trembling Negro. In many ways, the voices of that day still strike fear in despots. The struggle of black folk in America taught the world a methodology of protest and struggle. That day filled America with lessons that some quarters have not yet learned.

My civil rights aspirations had not matured politically. My vision was narrow but meaningful. Across the street from our house there was an orchard, home to about forty sheep. Our house was not in the country. In the Yellow Springs of my youth, a walk of a few yards in any direction put you near a farm. Living across from the Orchard made North Stafford Street unique. I used to stand at the end of our driveway and bat rocks over the orchard fence. Sometimes I would aim at the sheep. My goal, far from a malicious one, targeted sheep as they stood to nibble low-hanging apples. Friends would join me now and then. The seasoned sheep rarely moved from incoming batted rocks. They knew we were lousy shots.

I watched on our TV the large crowd of black and white folks on the National Mall on this historic afternoon. I was just as content, however, to watch the summer sunlight dance its rays across the apple trees.

I watched and listened to the entire "I Have a Dream" speech. My mother got off work at 3:30 p.m. and I usually had chores to finish before she arrived. I cannot recall doing chores that day.

Dr. King's dream speech was historic for many. That day, for me, it meant that I lived on a delightful street with an apple orchard nearby. Dr. King's dream, in simple terms, meant I could live in peace. I could have freedom and dignity. I could enjoy the apple orchard and its sheep. It was just that simple.

I wanted Dr. King's motif of "let freedom ring" to silence the silly discourse about the status race occupied in white America. This was a discourse that expected me to consume without question or protest weak excuses to prevent me from having the full accord of rights. I wanted to see Jim Crow end, and I wanted my life to be as natural as the orchard across the street.

I risked additional mirror cracks from a naive narrative of tainted racial tolerance instead of a story about truth and justice. The narrative said that black folk had to be tolerated. It treated tolerance as a summer cold, something that did not happen out of season.

My struggle to resist the deadly effects of American racism made it clear that, without courage, my view of the orchard would forever be lost. By late fall of my senior year, I was determined to find the courage to look at my cracked mirror afresh. My courage came from my connection to Central State.

In a curious way, Yellow Springs prepared me to make friends at Central State. I was open to understanding people from diverse backgrounds. Black folks became my worldview. My perspective shifted from a narrow, provincial southwest Ohio point of view to places and themes far beyond the green farmlands of Yellow Springs. Central State opened a chapter that illustrated a fresh picture of black America. It was a paradigm shift.

My new male friends and their homegirls helped me expand my worldview of black folk. With free access to my mother's car on weekends, I became the go-to driver for burger runs, and that helped me become an opaque observer.

I studied their voices, their words, and their speech cadence. Each vibrated a different big city. It was like living in a different country. All of it was new and refreshing.

One of my new friends, Alfred, a sophomore from Chicago, was a serious accounting major and determined to graduate and make it big. I admired how he finessed manhood. He did not use mack-daddy scripts with black women as the "Hey, fine thing" approach. He spoke with a calm reserve and a confident smile. He did not wear a pretentious mask.

I admired him and emulated his polished style. Respect felt right, and it usually got results. Young black women took me seriously.

In October 1964, I turned nineteen and could finally buy 3.2-percent beer. Sure enough, soon after my birthday, I found myself on a bar stool at Ye Olde Trail Tavern in downtown Yellow Springs, with my State of Ohio driver's license in hand. A watered-down Miller High Life sat on the table.

I had "arrived" but it felt strange and empty. My discomfort grew as I listened to the Beatles singing "I Want to Hold Your Hand" on the jukebox. My white classmates chatted about how many beers it took to get a buzz.

I found my balance at Central State. It helped me reconcile the cracks in my mirrors of perception of old and new. I felt self-assured.

In my senior year, while I sat in homeroom, the assassination of President Kennedy occurred. I was hurt and angry. I thought to myself, "They killed him because he was trying to help us." I thought JFK's murder happened because he fought for black folks' meager right to vote, eat in public restaurants, and go to school. That Friday night the whole country came to a standstill. The TV played patriotic music, and the networks suspended all of my favorite shows. Kennedy's death, or rather the manner of his death and the Oswald cover-up, convinced me that black folks meant little in the scheme of things.

It stood to reason that if white folks would kill one of their own over the Negroes' desire to vote, we should never again look to a white person, president or otherwise, to save us.

I reasoned Kennedy's death should have sobered black America. The cause of his assassination, I learned later, was not limited to civil rights. Nevertheless, I felt there was no limit to what white folks would use to silence any voice that challenged the race-class hierarchy in America.

America changed and I changed. The ruthless hand of the invisible power brokers snatched away Kennedy's life and dealt a blow to the middle class and working populism. I switched gears as well. Even though my mother encouraged me to apply to Kent State University and Carleton College, neither school could offer a supporting backdrop to be my best self. Neither school gave me what Central State offered. I redefined my thinking about higher education. It had to include my history, an unbiased space for my ethnicity, and eventually, a spirituality that would not betray me.

Resurrection on Monkey Island

A lot of black folks in Yellow Springs, drunk on decades of self-loathing and pretense, referred to the all-black institutions Central State College and Wilberforce College as "Monkey Island." We borrowed this from the movie *Planet of the Apes*. Our poisonous joke for these two colleges was a painful reminder of a self-deprecating humor that underscores deep-seated self-bashing; it stems from a deeply scarred self-contempt that still lingers in the minds and souls of black folks.

Just two weeks after I graduated from Yellow Springs High, I took a remedial English class from Professor Gertrude Engels at Central State. Professor Engels was no more than four feet and eleven inches tall. She wore her blond hair in a neatly fashioned bun. She was tough and fair and spoke with a thick German accent. Her brisk manner and formal demeanor projected affection and humor. She would not hesitate to use it warmly. On the first day of class, she sent us away to buy copies of the Harcourt and Brace grammar manual and E. B. White's *The Elements of Style*. She told us, "Come back as soon as possible but take a long look at the bookstore. You will visit it often."

I found my way around campus, paused at the college bookstore as she said and stopped to pick up my ID card. I was an official CSU student. I smiled with delight.

I was so happy to be on the campus I grew to love. I listened to Professor Engels's lectures with the singular intent of passing her class and enrolling in Freshmen English in the fall. We learned grammar from writing essays. By midterm, I courted a love affair with writing.

Being able to write gave me access to my feelings and thoughts. Writing was a mirror and a map. It was a way station to the adult world brought closer than ever before. It helped me sort out growing up in Yellow Springs. It made education personal.

Writing helped me divorce grades as social currency. It was like a shovel to bury the "be a credit to my race" delusion.

I started to see Yellow Springs as a slice of a big picture. Yellow Springs conjured a combination of envy and guilt. It was an envied village because it had smart white people, a good college, and more than its share of black folks "who did not know their place".

I embraced the liberating power of writing. It became apparent why black folks stayed dead so long. It underscored why whites prevented us from reading and writing during slavery. Expression is raw, primal power. It brings dead things to life. It kills lies and deception.

Broad reading and writing about overcoming the stigma of black folks suffering helped me find answers to troubling questions. It directed me to understand the fears that inspired the murderers of Emmett Till. I understood why the boldness in Emmett Till's gestures toward a white woman threatened a sacred mythology of white inviolability.

Emmett Till's killers saw themselves as defenders of a white female's sacred virtue. His killers were from the poor, marginalized white working class that William Jennings Bryant attempted to unite with ex-slaves during the Reconstruction Era.[31]

From the earliest days of America's existence, white folks created space to nurture the myth of white supremacy. The complexity of how poor whites saw blacks as labor market threats and as existential threats is not trivial. Marxist explanations are not capable of explaining the complexity of how cheap black labor frightened a white working class. In many ways, they feared an efficient economic order where white privilege held no advantage.

If the citadel of white privilege cracked, all would be lost. The façade of white supremacy trembled under the delusion that "niggers will sleep with our women and take our jobs." A fear that hordes of black men would somehow rise up like violent animals and rape white women and deprive white men of jobs is at the heart of white vigilante episodes.

The Ku Klux Klan is made up of cowardly and angry white men in bed sheets. The organization's origins grew from social and economic factors that marginalized and manipulated them. Today the same social and economic forces tap into nativist fears that white people are losing America to nonwhites. These types of fears appeal to the worst kind of racial politics. Complex class and economic factors help shape a rationale to deploy marginalized whites as storm troopers during economic and political crises. The end game is to ease white anxiety as a morsel of psychological comfort food.

Economic downturns usually increase Klan membership. Even now some of the loudest and most hostile opposition to US immigration comes from the Ku Klux Klan and the Republican political party, many of whom are Klansmen in suits and wing-tip shoes.

Writing about race and class dynamics helped me defuse and depersonalize my overly emotional responses to racism. However, it did not happen overnight. I was still tense about injustice. In a pointed personal way, writing helped me unravel my simmering anger. The worst oppression many black people experienced came from not being able to express anger or challenge the humiliation of racism. I saw writing as a weapon to fight back.

Polite expression and politically correct expression, like the integration narrative of the middle class, behaved like a concession, not liberation. It's squeaky voice echoed weakness in a prison of assimilation. It produced self-hatred. Black folks had drowned in a the sea of muted expression for three centuries.

I redirected my anger to writing about the racist lies that were repeated about black folk. I used short stories and poetry to channel my anger.

Professor Engels also gave us a voluntary reading list of classical books, including some so-called "Negro literature," and she encouraged us to read many as books and articles as possible. After class, I used to park my mother's car under a few large maple trees near the college's administration building and read, sometimes for hours on end. It was there, under those trees, I discovered Langston Hughes's poetry and Richard Wright's insightful book *Native Son*. I read *The Catcher in the Rye* in that tranquil shady place.[32]

My thirst for reading and ideas continued to grow. I turned twenty that fall. I was determined to express myself. Other folks' discomfort with what I said and wrote did not worry me. With each returning visit from Central State to Yellow Springs, I could feel eyes searching my face. Black and white friends were not comfortable with me as in the past. Adults whispered that I was a disappointment. I kept my lip trigger cocked with a full magazine of profane adjectives to warn meddling eyes and disapproving frowns.

I sensed things were changing as black people now attended college in numbers as never before. I joined the ranks of a black-baby-boomer college enrollment surge. This trend was bound to take place.

From the late 1940s to the early 1960s, the GI Bill opened an additional educational opportunity for the middle class. The GI Bill supported thousands of armed force veterans returning from World War II and the Korean War to pursue a college education. Parallel state and federal educational support emerged for nonveterans. This development enabled many black youths to enroll in higher education institutions. The change in access to higher education for black people outpaced a willingness in white America to accommodate larger numbers of educated black folk. Something had to give.

The American government and some business establishments embraced the concept of an emerging middle class. Economic mobility became a reality for many whites. While the trend did reach some black folks, its impact declined because of stubborn Jim Crow barriers and entrenched institutionalized racism. Most whites in America gave little thought to how these trends shaped daily life for black families. It was silly to expect equal footing.

The only truthful measure of equality was when black folks had decent jobs, good schools, and adequate housing. The rhetoric of fair play and attempts to appeal to the moral consciences of some white folks was a waste of time.

It made no sense to stress over unrealistic expectations. This picture, as a slight-of-hand called equality, gave me mental and spiritual heartburn. The promises were empty. They created delusions I could not bear. The fake promises, if believed, would compel me to tread, like a lab rat, in a black middle-class maze.

The thought of marrying a light-skinned elementary education major from Newark or Baltimore scared me stiff. I'd be trapped. I would probably buy a house in an "integrated" neighborhood. I'd get drunk every chance I could. I would sneak out of the house from time to time to smoke a joint. I would probably take a run at infidelity if I had the nerve.

When I looked at many of my Central State classmates, this picture came to mind. The path leading to the so-called "professional Negro" promised land was a trick and a cruel one.

A lot of black folks from the big cities longed to be in this picture. I studied how they thought and behaved. I used to admire their big-city flair.

I grew to understand that many of them were as scared and lost as black folks from small towns. All of us tried to make sense out of the rapidly moving social and political landscapes in America. My observations helped me understand how dissimilar and the same black folks were from region to region.

Regionalism has always been significant in black communities and college life only magnified these already strong identities.

I spent a good deal of my freshman year trying to be invisible. Nevertheless, by the end the year, I embraced my roots and could hold my own against classmates from the city. I got along with almost everyone and I had earned a reputation as a decent brother. I took pride in the fact that most students assumed I must be from some big city because I handled myself with a flare of detachment and street smarts.

I had two fights in my freshmen year, whipping both of my east coast opponents easily. After the second fight, people treated me with a newfound respect. I overheard one of them say, "Don't play Hawk close; he fights for keeps and he'll make a point to hurt you."

I did not like to fight, but if you dragged me into a fight, I'd make you think I was crazy. Between 1965 and 1967, my simmering anger came to a head. I remember one of my mother's friends said, "That nice young man, Billy Hawkins, has a mean streak."

I gave myself permission to be edgy. I needed to confront racist behavior, imagined or real. I countered personal insults of any kind or disrespect, perceived or fancied, with the statement, "I dare you." My fist stayed cocked with a sucker punch. Finding peace required changes in me and around me. I needed a change I could feel and touch. I wanted to dial down my anger a notch or two but reducing it would take time.

During the summer break from Central State in 1965, I found a job at General Motors Delco Moraine in Dayton where I worked as a laborer. I worked there for a little over a month before my supervisor—who looked like Elvis with bad skin—fired me.

Most of the whites at Delco had big V-8 Chevys. They came to Dayton from Eastern Kentucky or Eastern Tennessee. Black folks called them hillbillies. I called them hillbillies as well. There was no such thing as political correctness in the 1960s. Some of them seemed like the characters from the 1970s movie *Deliverance*.

I unhooked aluminum insulation liners for refrigerators from an assembly belt and placed the liners on wooden skids. I had worked there for a little over a month when one of the liners fell and cut my arm. My manager fired me on the spot. I should have seen it fall, according to him. He told me, "We don't want no trouble 'cause you went and got yourself killed on the shop floor."

"Right," I mumbled under my breath. "You fired me because blacks were taking jobs from white boys."

Getting fired upset my father. He felt I had lost a good job. As far as he was concerned, all I needed to do was to try harder to get along with white folks.

"Boy," he said, "I used to work with hillbillies like them at Wright-Patterson Air Base. I took their crap because Wright Pat was a good paying job."

I didn't argue with him. He did not understand. I just didn't have it in me to absorb large doses of racism. If I continued to work there, I would end up punching out one of those guys.

With about 160 bucks in my pocket from the previous year's income tax refund, I bought a one-way Greyhound Bus ticket to Boston. I watched Yellow Springs shrink smaller and smaller in the rearview mirror of the bus with delight.

I picked Boston because of the large number of universities. In my mind, Boston was an evolved Yellow Springs. My inspiration came from a family trip when I was fourteen. My memory of the east coast lingered, and Boston seemed close enough to New York to be similar.

Old memories as smells and sounds convinced me Boston was the right decision. Boston meant adventure and independence. The safe surroundings of Yellow Springs and even Central State became too constricting. I felt alive holding on to a stubborn determination. I wanted to prove my father wrong that I did not have to accept racist abuse to have a job.

When I planned my journey to Boston, I encouraged my friend Freddie to join me. Freddie thought Boston was a liberal city. It was a good place to meet and date white girls. That was not at the top of my list. I sought to work and experience living in a large city. I had mixed feelings about white females. Most of all, I would not endure racist abuse by Eastern Kentucky hillbillies for three- fifty an hour.

We looked for a YMCA when we got to Boston. It was an inexpensive place to stay. We were advised to stay at the YMCA in Charlestown and, naive to the ways of Boston, we took the advice. Little did we know that we were headed for a racist neighborhood. When we emerged from the subway at Haymarket Square, most of the white folks on the street looked at us as if to say, "Are you crazy?"

The next morning, Sunday, Freddie and I bought a *Boston Globe* newspaper to job hunt. The thickness of the classified section gave me hope that I would secure a position in some air-conditioned office. I would be respected and earn a decent wage. After all, this was Boston.

We walked the pavement for five days straight without a nibble. On the seventh day, Freddie went to Western Union, picked up some money that his mother sent, and caught the Greyhound back to Yellow Springs. I refused to give up and leave.

By this time, I had about thirty-five dollars to my name and I was scared to eat. I would rather be hungry than have to sleep on the Boston Commons and drag around my brown corrugated cardboard suitcase. It took just another couple of days to find a job at the Somerville Smelting Plant. I mused about the irony of working at the smelting plant instead of General Motors. Independence turned out to be more important than the nature of the job.

I worked the afternoon shift until eleven at night stripping tar from old telephone cable, dragging the stripped bundles of wire into a machine that smashed the wires into a bale, and then loading it into a smelting cooker.

When I blew my nose, the tissue was black and my mouth tasted like I had been licking a wrought iron fence. Nevertheless, by the end of the week,

I had over one hundred dollars—enough to pay for my room at the YMCA while I continued to look for a better job.

When I talked to my mother about life in Beantown, I yeasted up its goodness. I still wanted to show my dad how right I had been.

By the middle of June, I was lonely and did not know a single person. I could not get my hands clean from the soot. Even though the soot depressed me, it also increased my resolve to endure. The following Monday, near the end of the month, I caught an early train and got off at the Huntington Avenue station. I walked up Huntington Avenue with my Sunday *Boston Globe* in hand. Looking around I tried to take in as much detail as possible so I could figure out quickly where to go to find a job. Work started at three, so I was in a hurry. I needed to find a place to put in a job application.

I spotted a middle-aged white lady on the corner of Huntington Avenue and Massachusetts Avenue and approached to ask her for directions to an office building nearby that advertised a job as a mailroom clerk. Before I said a word, she turned to me with a subtle smile and asked, "Young man, are you lost? Are you in college? Are you looking for a job?" I told her yes to everything.

She opened her purse and took out an ink pen. She gestured with her forefinger to hand her the newspaper. She wrote down a name and phone number. She said that I could probably get a job working with kids from Roxbury, a large black neighborhood in West Boston. "Don't wait," she said. "You should go call the number now."

The light changed for the second or third time since I had stopped her. I thanked her in a voice barely louder than a whisper. My eyes filled. My heart pounded.

I walked back down Huntington Avenue to find a phone booth. I stepped into a booth that smelled like urine, but I barely noticed. I turned the wobbly spindle dial. After a couple of rings, a female voice answered, "Roxbury Work and Study Project, how can I help you?"

I said I wanted to apply for a job. She asked me if I was in college and looking for summer work. She explained to me how the Roxbury Work and Study Project operated and asked if I could come to the Northeastern University campus at one o'clock to apply.

I told her that I would love to, but I needed to go back to the YMCA in Charlestown and change clothes. I had to be at work in Somerville by three. She paused. I said, "Hello, are you there?"

She said, "Yes, my name is Mrs. Haygood and my husband and I manage the project. You will either be painting houses in Roxbury and Dorchester for low-income black homeowners or working as a recreation leader on a playground and taking the children on field trips. You will live in a dorm on the Northeastern University campus with free meals and board and earn forty dollars a week. You will be paid an additional $250 scholarship stipend at the end of the summer when you return to school. Are you still interested?"

"Yes," I replied.

She said, "Well, OK then, you're hired." She told me to go back to the YMCA and pick up my belongings and head over to my new home on campus. She and her husband would meet me in their office located in the basement of the residence hall.

I also remembered I didn't have a check coming since it was the first day of the new workweek. I called the smelting plant and told them I found a better job.

My eyes welled with tears as I hung up. I walked to the subway station and caught a train back to the YMCA.

FENWAY SUMMER

The Roxbury Work and Study Project, located on the campus of Northeastern University, was within walking distance to Fenway Park. The program recruited forty interns: eleven black, twenty-nine white. My roommate, Dick, was a preppy white guy and a Harvard undergrad. He wore a sweater around his shoulders and penny loafers with no socks. He was easy to get along with though our conversations rarely got beyond small talk and were just enough to break the ice. Perhaps, because of this, I did not realize how far apart our worlds were until he told me he had lost one thousand dollars in a poker game. While I stood there open-mouthed, he laughed and said that he had won and lost a thousand dollars several times; it was no big deal.

The orientation week for the Work and Study Project was conducted at Boston University. By the end of the week, almost everyone found a romantic interest. Many of the white females were ready to confront the black man and white woman taboo. I had my eye on a tall, black girl from Roxbury. She was a picture of poise and good manners. Both of her parents were professionals, and her sister attended a local college. At first she sounded white because I was not accustomed to her New England accent. I grew to love to hear her speak. She was sweet and down-to-earth.

I spent a good deal of the orientation period fending off the attentions of a petite, very attractive Jewish girl, who shadowed me the entire week like a plainclothes detective. I became so used to seeing her around every corner. I expected to see her hand creeping under the stall with a roll of toilet paper.

After several subtle hints, she invited me to her room. I rejected the invitation, fearing that I'd find myself engaged in some half-drunk sexual encounter motivated by pity. Her eyes revealed pain that neither grass nor sex could remove.

I knew romantic liaisons with white girls could be dangerous. Racism was alive and secret rendezvous with white females could be like sniffing glue. It could produce a short-term high and a nasty crash. The encounter had a price too high to pay. It could lead to a fight with some "townie" over a white girl. I did not want to put myself on the path that got Emmett Till killed. There were still plenty of white folk around who would flip out at the sight of black men and white women together. White folks had constructed a powerful mythology for the sanctity of their women. It was a myth white people and black folk believed. The myth was so pervasive that both races were buried in different cemeteries. Even in death, black people were untouchable. This was just one example of the madness that underscored the extremes of white supremacy. To these types of white people, black folk were "niggers" even dead.

My friend Victor, from the Bronx, thought I was crazy to reject her offer. He lectured me that she was prettier than most young women in the program. With his street reasoning, he called her "ripe fruit."

"Hawk," he said, "she was yours for the picking."

I knew what Victor didn't know. He didn't know two things. One was getting with this girl, however lovely, filled my mind with the sound of ice breaking under my feet. Her face told me I was an outlet for her deep emotional issues that had little to do with me. The weight of old sorrow was heavy and it seemed to weigh her down. To me, her distant sorrow was like thin ice. When you hear the ice crack, it is too late. The other thing he didn't realize was how conflicted I felt about using women. Most young men my age used a Genghis Khan approach to romance: capture, ravish, and depart. I knew that using women and then discarding them was devastating.

Victor didn't know I was torn about how I viewed women (on the one hand that was decent) and how I treated them (on the other hand that was wrong). I also grew up as a "Genghis Khan–Mack Daddy" devotee. I had hurt women before. I had been a player of sorts during my senior year of high school and in the first semester at Central State. I knew it was dead wrong, but I was too concerned about peer opinions to stop. I didn't want them to say that I wasn't a player.

There are many men, from all races and cultures, that want to flee from this evil but are too concerned about "stupid group talk" and "stupid group think" to break away. This is a serious problem for African-American men and other men. Most women will attest to this as fact. Moreover, I was more concerned with learning the job than socializing. I knew there would be plenty of time to have fun in the weeks to come. Also, at the time, I was not able to give myself in a relationship with a white female, regardless of her appearance or personality.

On the job site, interns worked in groups. Some supervised playgrounds while others painted large Victorian houses in Roxbury and North Dorchester. Black families bought many of these houses after a mass exodus of whites in the late 1950s and early 1960s. At intervals, usually no more than a two-week span, the playground group rotated with the painting group. Everyone welcomed the rotation because of the stress of dealing with fifty kids on the playground or from putting up scaffolding and painting.

I actually enjoyed putting up scaffolding and developed a skill for it. My forte was setting up and breaking down the framework quickly. Our crew loved me for this because it meant we could finish early, pile in the bus, and get back to the air-conditioned dorm. While many folks think Boston is cool or cold all of the time, summer in Beantown can get as hot as a day in Georgia.

After running up and down ladders on ninety-degree July afternoons, I thought of nothing after work except a cool shower, cold ginger ale, and a good book. I would lie on my bed, chilling out and trying not to fall asleep, and miss dinner in the cafeteria.

In the evenings, if the program staff had not made plans, I usually tried to find something to get into in Roxbury. Most nights I could find an informal get-together on the Hill, as we called it and hang out there until the last train or bus departed from Roxbury to the Back Bay.

During my days off, at times I felt a strange sense of familiarity settle over me—like I had lived in Boston before. I would venture off on my own, often under the ruse of shopping. I just wanted to meander here and there. I would

Picture of William Hawkins, Jr working Scaffolding at the Roxbury Work and Study Project in Boston, summer 1965.

walk up Blue Hill Avenue, stop at a deli across the street from Kasanofs Bakery to buy raw peanuts, or head off to the cluttered bookstores in Harvard Square and Kendall Square. Other times I'd spend an afternoon wandering around Filene's Basement or walking down Mass Avenue to Spinelli's for some fried crab and clams. It never mattered much. My wandering stirred similar feelings my Stafford Street orchard gave me. I was at peace, free, and solitary.

By mid-August, I felt ambivalent about going back to Central State. I thought about trying to transfer to a school in Boston but realized that it was too late in the year to transfer. Even if it had not been too late, I figured I had better go back to Central and pull my grades up from where they were only hovering a shade over 2.0.

If I was honest with myself, the biggest reason to return to Central State was to sever emotional ties with my Boston girlfriend. I felt she was too serious and too clinging. I had a reality check one evening. We were alone at her house watching footage of the Watts riots on TV when, suddenly, she turned to me and said, "We can have sex! I love you." All summer I had pressured her into sex. Now, all alone at her house, I could not. Her pronouncement of love scared me speechless.

I had heard the words before from girlfriends back in high school and one at Central State. I had even tossed the words around myself. However, the way she said it scared me.

I didn't love her and I was ashamed. I had feelings for her, but not like hers. We did not have sex that night or any other evening. All I thought about was breaking up with her before I returned to Central State.

Before that night, I had promised to write her every week. I knew, in my heart, I would not. Since I did not sleep with her, I figured I would go back to

Central, and she would get over me. My rejection hurt her deeply. I had never hurt anyone like that, that I knew of. When I saw her several years later and said hello, she turned away in disgust. I deserved it.

The final week of the program was emotional. I said my goodbyes and made plans to take a bus to New York. I wanted to hang out with friends for a few days, but by the time I arrived at Port Authority, I yearned to get back to Ohio.

When I finally arrived at the Greyhound station in Springfield, Ohio, my mother sat waiting in her car. Her warm smile eased the transition back into emerald green farmlands around Yellow Springs and Wilberforce. As we rode south on Highway 68 to Yellow Springs, I experienced a mix of security and resignation. Nothing had changed. I was back in Ohio on the doorstep of ho-hum until classes resumed at Central State. Just shy of a month in Yellow Springs, I was almost crazy with boredom.

Church Side

I drove over to Wilberforce to settle in when I knew students would start trickling back. I was happy to rent a room on church side to leave dorm life. It was also cheaper. I noticed that some freshmen had arrived for orientation week. A lot of the upper-class guys used to drift back that week to get first pick of freshmen girls. I remember four or five of us sat on a long lounge sofa in the student union watching the new crop of freshmen females and their parents. I guessed we must have looked like vultures perched on a fence in our Afros and dark sunglasses. We got startled looks from some girls and their parents. We knew how we looked. No Joe College here; hard-core brothers we were. We laughed and slapped hands, "Damn, life is good."

That year I decided to "buckle down," as my father liked to say and work harder. My enthusiasm for the new semester was partly driven because I wanted to delve into an analysis of the intersection of race and class in the American political landscape. In Boston, I had discovered the poetry of LeRoi Jones (aka Amiri Baraka). His poetry inspired me to write. I loved his voice because of its dominant use of rhythm and climax. His skillful manipulation of identity and discovery unsheathed my spirit. His poetic voice rang clear.

I had discovered the relevance and power of the essay. My cherished affection for short stories and poetry was rapidly making room for my fondness of the essay. I was influenced primarily by Amiri Baraka's 1965 essay "The Revolutionary Theater," published in the publication, *Liberator*. It had been rejected by the *New York Times* and *The Village Voice* based on a flimsy claim that the editors didn't understand it.[33] I equally enjoyed Baraka's anthology *Home: Social Essays*.[34]

Picture of William Hawkins, Jr in Boston summer 1966.

I surmised that using the essay as a tool could be a potent weapon against racism and persuade semiconscious students that activism should become a minor discipline to support any academic major.

I decided to double major in English and political science. My political science professor looked like Richard Dreyfuss. He sounded like a Marxist and he focused a good deal of our class work on social class dynamics. He also emphasized the impact William Jennings Bryant had on the populist movement during the Reconstruction Era. My creative writing class, taught by Professor LC Phillips, exposed me to a broad range of writers from Emily Dickinson, Emerson, Richard Wright, William James, and other classical writers like Melville. I read Ginsberg and Kerouac but did not take away any spiritual lessons.

Flicking through the pages of Ginsberg's *Howl and Other Poems*, I realized right away that he wasn't talking to me.[35] He spoke to white folk who were trying to escape the Ozzie and Harriet prison in which they found themselves doing serious time. I had no issues with his choice. I understood how it gave them freedom, the same way LeRoi Jones's writing helped me to break free from an Amos 'n' Andy maximum security joint.[36] Both 1950s TV shows were caricatures of blacks and whites in America.

Professor Phillips was one of the few non-black faculty members at Central State, and I believe he was there because he wanted to be, not because he could not cut it at a white school. He was not trying to save black folks either.

His physical appearance was that of a stereotypical English literature professor in a corduroy jacket, suede elbow patches, and thick black eyeglasses. He looked every bit of a man of letters. He helped us develop voice, and he affirmed our diverse use of the written and spoken word.

My writing class was composed of mostly artist types who shared a similar space within the growing black consciousness movement. In the early 1960s, black fraternity members stood at the top of the ladder of campus social hierarchy, followed by athletes, the career-minded folks, and those determined to make it in white America at any costs. The Afrocentric misfits, artists, activists, or others who joined organizations like the chess club made up the bottom rung. However, by the end of 1965, the artists and activists ascended. As an indication of our growing influence, our writers club invited LeRoi Jones to visit the campus and give a reading of his work. No more than thirty-five students attended. One professor sat quietly in the rear of the auditorium. True to his mastery of the music in verse, Jones had us on our feet several times shouting, "Right on!" As we walked from Galloway Hall to the dorm, I was pleased to recognize my path was not on a black middle-class trajectory that other classmates followed.

After Jones had finished his readings, a few of us got together in Hughes Hall to drink Colt 45 and Ripple. We talked about the significance of Jones's poetry to enhance the development of reading and artistic endeavor. To many of us, Jones was one of the principal voices of the Black Arts Movement. The Black Arts Movement supported and informed important aspects of black culture in hairstyles, clothing, and new trends in black music.

In 1965, seeing blacks wearing Afros was not common. In our small group, everyone who could grow an Afro wore it with pride. Ironically, those with the largest Afros usually had the heaviest endowment of mixed ancestry. I had more forehead than Afro, but I had mastered the "Afro scowl."

We sensed that our divorce from the mainstream look was a vital tool to assemble a new identity. In those days, an Afro was more political than cultural. My nappy head belonged to me. I did not need to press it, burn it, or grease it.

The previous year I had thought briefly about pledging a fraternity but quickly dismissed the idea. By now it was clear to me that black Greek organizations were often tools of white racism and the house Negroes' linkages to silliness in concert with the white power structure. Deliberate or just unconscious about the dynamics of black liberation, black Greek organizations on Central State's campus supported a rejection of Black Studies and African Studies classes. They were complicit with the stooges in the administration building to silence our demands for such classes. They controlled the student newspaper, *The Gold Torch*, and used the paper to dispute our demand for Black Studies and African Studies. We countered with a mimeograph news sheet we published.

From January to June of 1966, I balanced my activities as a writer and an activist with having a good time. I still partied on weekends. A fair number of women on campus noticed me. Even though I had developed a great deal of self-confidence, I also knew a shift in power relations on campus attracted some of these women to me. Students that used to hang out with black fraternities now attended Black Power rallies. For many women, a relationship with one of the "Brothers" was the "in thing."

That spring I wrote several short stories and poems both inside and outside of my creative writing class. Professor Phillips and some of the other students who loved writing, like William Harris, himself a talented writer and long-time resident of Yellow Springs, encouraged me to write. They advised me to write as much as I could. They told me to spend quality time developing my craft. "Hawk, don't just rely on your poetic talent," they said.

I had never actually considered myself poetic, but I could not deny that creativity was more spontaneous and in step with my self-awareness and my comfort with a black identity.

My largest hurdle on the path to serious writing was the lack of discipline. I also wrestled with the idea that all art was useful and good. I did not buy that. Art that didn't support liberation was a distraction and it could become a tool of oppression disguised as art. Furthermore, I only wrote when I felt like it, or when I had a writing assignment.

As the year unfolded, nothing stayed the same very long. It was 1966. Two years passed since I graduated high school. Two years since I freed my mind from a narrow, provincial outlook.

A lot was taking place in America in these two years. A war in Southeast Asia was dividing the country. Moderate civil rights voices were being muted by Black Power; several urban riots shined a light on America that tarnished its claims as the land of equality, prosperity, and freedom. A new type and class of leaders were forged on the streets of America and in rural hamlets throughout the South.[37]

President Obama was five years old in 1966. Emmett Till had been dead for eleven years. History does not wait for us to connect the dots.

A Tipping Point

By May 1966, I made plans to return to the Roxbury Work and Study Project. By the middle of June, I made my way back to Boston with a critical eye on the city's racism. I hadn't focused on Boston's entrenched racism as much the previous year. The Haygoods returned to run the program and only a handful of interns from the previous year returned. My new roommate, Everett, was already a close friend from the previous year. He was a sophomore at Morehouse College in Atlanta. We had stayed in touch, bonding over our shared views on black people and the struggle for civil rights and dignity.

That summer fewer interns were interested in partying. At first I put this subtle change down to a different mix of personalities. As I look back, 1966 was a turning point in the 1960s. A growing sense of isolation and disillusionment occurred among those fifteen to twenty years old from every ethnic background; fear and urgency drove us to identify and connect with movements that took action. Also, 1966 became the year America's blind prosecution of the war in Vietnam moved to the defeat column on the scorecard of winning.

President Johnson's announcement that 205,000 American troops in Vietnam were insufficient only added to the tension. Also, to deepen the alienation among black folks and white people, 1966 was the year that Huey Newton and Bobby Seale formed the Black Panthers. Stokely Carmichael and Charles Hamilton wrote the book *Black Power*, coining the term that catalyzed a paradigm shift in black America.[38] Instead of inclusion and integration, Black Power advocated breaking America's grip on black and brown communities.

Most black men of my generation could not return to the Negro ethos of the 1950s, re-embracing a numbing trance that accepted an equation of white equaled good and black equaled bad. There was nothing magical about 1966. It was a tipping point.

NEVER CURSE TIME

I could hardly believe what had happened in the two years since high school. At times, I was hesitant to own up to my Yellow Springs roots. But after two years, I grew to appreciate how life in the Springs helped me navigate the complexity of race and social conflict. My Yellow Springs upbringing gave me an advantage my friends from New York, Philadelphia, Detroit, and Boston did not have.

Yellow Springs gave me access to white folks with their guard down. I sat in a front row seat and watched them drown in their white supremacy myth. Watching white folks act on the myth they were special and America is blessed tortured me growing up. I believed it then. Now I did not. It became funny of sorts.

Even today when I hear a politician end a speech saying, "God bless America," I wonder to myself whether he or she should ask God to guide America to practice what it preaches. It seems, though, most of the media and political narrative in America uses the word "God" laced with cynicism and theater. Some of the most violent racists use an American-flavored "God talk" to promote an agenda of nativism and racism. It sickens me.

I looked with suspicion at young black men my age that sided with leaders who wanted political and social integration but were too timid to articulate what black communities needed. The word "power" was poison in their mouths. I was furious with Central State's refusal to offer African History and African American History classes. I refused to accept the dominance of a white value system. It did not matter in the circles of power that a body of scholarship existed on African Americans' struggle for fundamental freedoms and human rights.

Central's administration and board of trustees dismissed our demands as unimportant. Their hubris backfired.

I was determined to learn my history by any means necessary. I was committed to challenging the norm of begging for accommodations. I demanded the self-reliance and resulting power I could get from learning my culture and history.

A small but growing number of black students on campus felt white folks at the state level controlled the administration. State-level whites led the effort to prevent having African History and Black Studies classes.

In September 1966, we formed a campus-chartered organization called Unity for Unity. Our purpose was to bring Black Studies and African Studies to campus and to eliminate compulsory *Army ROTC*. We also wanted to foster black cultural activities on campus.

In November, Unity for Unity organized a rally against the war in Vietnam and invited George Ware from the Student Non-Violent Coordinating Committee (SNCC), known as "Snick," as the keynote speaker. He was well known for his ability to catalyze protests and other activities on black campuses.

George was about thirty years old at the time, and far more mature than most of us. He had developed a reputation for his fieldwork as a SNCC organizer. He also completed a bachelor's degree in chemistry at Fisk University and was a persuasive advocate of Black Power. I admired his quick wit and his knowledge about black folks' struggle in America. His presence, knowledge, charm and candor became effective tools to promote Unity for Unity.

As he closed his speech, he argued that black soldiers in Vietnam were nothing but "cannon fodder" and mercenary slaves. He drew on examples from racist events in American history, such as the Brownsville Affair, to support his points. The Brownsville Affair earned its infamous name because of what happened in the town, Brownsville, Texas[39] at the peak of white vigilante impunity in 1906. A fight occurred between a number of black men and a bartender. The bartender died in the fight and a police officer suffered gunshot wounds. At the end of the melee, the white townspeople attacked members of the Twenty-Fifth Regiment, an all-black US Army unit stationed at nearby Fort Brown. The regiment's commanders testified the soldiers were in their barracks all night. Nevertheless, with evidence planted against them, the entire regiment faced hearings prompting their discharged. This travesty of fairness and justice cost them their pensions. They did not receive compensation from the US government until many years after the incident.[40]

George concluded his talk with an analogy that compared President Johnson's ambivalence to black people's struggle for civil rights with Central State's President Harry Groves's opposition to offer African Studies and Black Studies classes. The entire student body rose to their feet. George's talk was an important turning point that helped Unity for Unity break the hold black Greek organizations had over student life.

After George's speech several Unity for Unity members met to plan our next move. Our interest went beyond demanding African History and Black Studies classes. We expanded our requirements to include the administration take a public stance against the war in Vietnam and abandon compulsory ROTC training for students.

We neglected, however, to articulate how the details for realistic campus reforms could occur, due to our immaturity. We were also distracted from practical aspects of university reform by our overused rhetoric about Uncle Toms and the white man.

Our novice fixations on labeling and blaming, along with the generous amounts of weed we smoked prevented us from reaching large segments of students.

Unity for Unity attracted loyalty more akin to that of groupies. With the exception of a few core members, our belief that higher education should embrace our racial and cultural history did not appeal to a majority of students. Several mainstream students rejected our rationale. Nevertheless, our social status on campus increased. Our Afros, manner of dress, and other artifacts of black cultural nationalism drew many young men to identify with us. We also attracted young black women—without question if you had an Afro and maintained some ties with Unity for Unity, it increased your chances that you would become popular with young women.

Inasmuch as we became a novelty, many of our political positions had merit. We were against the war in Vietnam for good reason. Many of us knew classmates that lost a draft exemption and were compelled to fight in Vietnam. Many died or returned half-crazy from what they experienced in the rice paddies. However, in all fairness, I must say that some came back intact.

SNCC, which was gaining popularity as a student protest movement, emerged in 1960 from efforts by the legendary activist Ella Baker to organize black college students from Shaw University and North Carolina A&T University.[41] These students refused to move from a whites-only lunch counter at a Woolworth store. Within two months other students joined them and coordinated sit-ins throughout the South to demand access to public accommodations. Over the course of the next decade, civil rights activism moved beyond lunch counter sit-ins as SNCC evolved. When the influence of integrationists like John Lewis and Julian Bond waned, SNCC's new leadership, led by Stokely Carmichael, articulated a new message.

The new voice of SNCC reflected black folk from cities in the North and Midwest. It was a message of homegrown power, not integration. The new SNCC message urged black folk to draw from our own resources to become self-reliant. It advocated the natural acquisition of power instead of assimilation. The new SNCC message affirmed what I believed, that integration was ineffective and insulting.

In December, we asked two members from SNCC to return to campus on a permanent basis to help us organize. SNCC's philosophy advocated the removal of social class and other artificial divisions among black folks. The way to do this, according to SNCC, was organizing the black community. The civil rights movement had already produced several establishment leaders who lacked historical and political vision. SNCC attempted to counter this trend by living in the community, winning the confidence of local residents, and organizing at the grassroots level. Unlike mainstream single-issue civil rights organizations, SNCC was not just interested in voting and eliminating segregation from public accommodations. SNCC advocated that the black community should govern itself.

SNCC believed that the self-appointed leaders wanted entry through any door white America was willing to open, no matter how tight the squeeze.

When the narrow access did open, most of us realized the tight squeeze induced complacency and compromise. We also felt that self-appointed leaders failed to challenge America's political and social elites to accommodate the needs and aspirations of the black working class.

SNCC struggled to overcome the illusion of progress symbolized by a few black mayors, congressional representatives, and other low-level officials that emerged from obscurity into political life.

SNCC fought hard to stop the masses of working-class black folk from dozing off to sleep because some black man wore a dashiki over his three-piece suit.

SNCC's model also meant that the organization's coordinators would not ask regular folks to do anything that its organizers would not do. SNCC's leveling of the Negro middle class's elitism and deemphasized access to white centers of power and influence appealed to me.

Between 1966 and 1967, student appetite to work in and with black Greek organizations on Central State's campus faded. Some of the student disinterest occurred because of the popularity black consciousness issues had on a growing number of students who refused to accept an integrationist rationale. In many parts of America, black people remained economically and politically invisible. This issue was epitomized by the limp zeal and the watered-down aspirations of black Greek organizations that didn't go beyond a "house nigga" elitist agenda. The compromises self-appointed leaders promoted became hot buttons that sent my emotional mercury into the red. The last thing I wanted to hear was a historically and politically unconscious Negro, with scotch whiskey on his breath, pontificating about so-called Negro progress.

The message of accommodation, in my view, was nothing more than quota showcasing that allowed white corporations to proclaim they hired a few black folk. This tactic was a trifling, pitiful attempt to appear progressive. The establishment leaders' begging strategy would not advance meaningful jobs. I believed, and most of the Unity for Unity hard-core members also believed, the jobs that begging produced were nothing better than "yes, massa" jobs. It didn't matter if the begging produced a job that required a necktie or did not require a necktie.

Oddly enough a good shaking of the politically correct bushes and trees, even today will show where the advocates of accommodation are hiding. They are entrenched in America's political life, as athlete elites and icons in the entertainment industry. They patiently wait to launch a beggar's comeback.

Another incarnation of an ahistorical black leader is one who endorsed a right-wing, even fascist, antiblack agenda under the disguise that a postracial America trumps racism. They argue that racism is dormant and black folk are to blame for their problems. I certainly admit that there is too much emphasis in black folks' culture of playing "poor little me" and the victim. Nonetheless, it is hard to deny that there are significant numbers of white establishment actors that promote patterns of stubborn racism. It is also tough to ignore that there exist several handpicked black Uncle Toms and too many self-selected black Uncle Toms who endorse neoconservative racism, like the ones on a popular cable TV network. These impulses by Uncle Toms to endorse racism existed in the late 1960s among sellout leaders. However, they did not attempt to pander to white interest openly, as many do today because this type of betrayal would have earned them strong condemnation from black nationalists leaders.

In turn, the racist neoconservatives boast joyfully about the magical spell they hold oversleeping black folk who support their racist agenda.

SNCC helped us sharpen and expand a paradigm to deconstruct the brutality of slavery. It helped us debunk blatant racism. It supported our rejection that everything is peachy by an examination of objective historical facts.

When I read C. Eric Williams's book *Capitalism and Slavery*[42] and listened to Malcolm X's post–Nation of Islam speeches,[43] I made an intellectual and visceral connection with Africa. For the first time, I came to grips with the realization that "I am an African."

The self-defeating quest to be judged by the content of my character and to be a credit to my race were slogans smartly disguised, which I now rejected with facts. I was fine with blackness and with being African.

I accepted my African reality. I advocated it. It became a weapon to resist white hegemony. Emmett Till's murder was an existential assault. His death made it clear that blackness constituted more than a reactive ideology. It meant survival.

My work with SNCC showed me that the lofty slogan that all Americans share, as equal partners in the American dream, was not a dream. It was a nightmare. As I woke up, I was determined to take my stand on an African identity. It was a position worthy of sacrificing everything, even life itself.

Reading helped me to understand the history of slavery and the domination of so-called "third world societies" by America and Europe. Profound and broad reading helped clarify the processes of social and economic racism.

I acknowledged that American culture bruised my self-esteem and caused self-loathing. My waking experience was not unique. Most black folks had experienced some form of self-loathing before they awoke angry.

One of the most deadly concoctions of American-styled racism was a belief that God made black folk inferior. Few black people in the 1950s did not long for "good hair," as straight hair, light skin, or preferably both. These physical features opened a door to social mobility and even dating and marriage.

To be an "ugly black nigger" was the mother of insults. Homicidal words. Nevertheless, when these assumptions were swallowed, black folk and white folk as well, could shrug their shoulders and secretly blame God.

The books I read during these years, like Basil Davidson's *The African Slave Trade*, documented the violence many nations engaged in to enslave Africans. [44]

I read a lot about colonialism and racism, but I couldn't find any literature that adequately explained the reasons for the intensity of the violence toward Africans in America or in other countries of the African diaspora.

Basil Davidson, Chiekh Anta Diop,[45] and even Lerone Bennett in his book *Before the Mayflower* [46]—none of them unraveled reasons for the visceral hatred and brutal violence directed at Africans in America. It troubled me. Other countries in the West, home to enslaved Africans, did not exhibit the violence toward slaves like slaves in America experienced.

The problems of economics and xenophobia only scratched the surface of more profound issues. I wanted answers. I speculated the root of racism was spiritual. I was sure most whites had no clue about their visceral hatred toward people of African descent.

I came to grips with a pivotal reality when I turned twenty-one. Eleven years before, the picture of a murdered Emmett Till affirmed my humanity. Looking back at myself as a nine-year-old, the tragedy of Till's murder was my first trusted teacher outside of my home. It taught me that the American construction of being a Negro was a deceptive concoction that suggested, at one extreme, that I was a happy-go-lucky man-child. On the other extreme, it depicted me as a dangerous menace. The latter extreme sanctioned my murder and the murder of countless black men without remorse. The image of Till's bloated body taught me the value and sanctity of my existence. It taught me what my color meant to some whites. It scared me that some white Americans were capable of killing me without guilt. That they could kill me without hesitation showed me I couldn't afford to doze off for even a second. It was not because I committed crimes against them. The reason was my mere existence.

Nothing explains persistent racist violence against black people. To me, it was an outright refusal that black people shared a common humanity. Some corners of the American clergy justified slavery with the Bible. Other Christians were staunch abolitionists. They denounced slavery with the Bible. Both camps exposed Christianity's vulnerability to economics and politics. For me, Christianity was empty and divorced from God.

God would not guide a nation that was built on cruelty and injustice. The hypocrites who advocated this type of religion represent voices without substance.

It angered me that many black folks remain blind. We blame ourselves for not living up to standards white folks block in the first place. Even today there is a narrative in some of America's social and political centers of power claiming that America exports justice and democracy around the world. A claim of this nature is filled with sound but no substance.

America's promotion of democracy is conditional. The conditions rest on accepting or rejecting American political and economic hegemony. Resisting American hegemony can land a nation and their leaders on a terrorist list nowadays similar to the widely used FBI "black agitators" list in the 1960s. The words "black agitators list" still amuses me. Sign me up.

UNDER NAT'S SHADOW

Unity for Unity developed strong ties to SNCC's George Ware and Ernest "Trap" Stevens. Both men became our visiting professors for activism, black history, and the freedom struggle. They mentored us in revolutionary rhetoric and activism. They stayed near our campus for months at a time in a black-owned motel. We went there for meetings; we took our girlfriends there; we partied there; we got high there.

The motel's décor accented a countryside motif. Rooms were forty dollars a week and the thickly embroidered yellow drapes blocked sunlight and guaranteed privacy. The motel's owner kept the grass cut like a golf course and the area around the rooms were dotted with tall trees near a natural waterfall that refracted a prism of light from an autumn sun.

When George and Ernest were in town, we visited them and listened to harrowing stories about organizing black voters in Mississippi and adventures with revolutionaries in Cuba.

I received most of my revolutionary coaching from George, who told me, "Hawk, read the books that will shift your parochial, country-ass view from civil rights to Black Revolution." I believed I was already there. George did not think I had gone far enough.

He told me, "Hawk, the same white folks that stop black folks from voting in Mississippi make napalm bombs for Vietnam. These same racists run the death squads in Bolivia and they killed our leaders, like Lumumba in Africa. They kill brown folks in rice paddies. I ain't never seen a yellow person and that's just some more racist stuff the white man invented. They'll pull you over in Mississippi and kill your black ass just as quick. If we aren't ready to fight them by any means necessary, we might as well just line up with the Uncle Toms, and kiss butt right along with them."

Then George said, "Hawk, you aren't bout that and me either, so we better get our act together and organize this campus."

After George's frank talk, Mike Warren and I urged Unity for Unity members to pull back on partying and getting high. We got serious about challenging the "Toms" in Bundy Hall to accept our demands for African Studies, Black Studies, and to drop compulsory ROTC.

President Harry Groves and Dean Charles Flowers knew we were trying to take power from them. They knew student support for Unity for Unity would increase. They understood we could make the campus ungovernable. We frightened them.

On a Monday night in October of 1967, around nine o'clock, several Unity for Unity members went to the President's residence at the edge of campus. We stood on his porch and chanted as one voice for him to come out and meet our demands. He didn't come out. After about twenty minutes, someone threw a brick through his front window. A lump rose in my throat as big as a goiter.

The administration accused Mike Warren, the face of Unity for Unity, of throwing the brick. Mike did not toss the brick as I recall. He was on the porch to deliver a signed petition for African Studies and Black Studies classes and to relax compulsory ROTC classes. Mike was our spokesperson.

The following morning, the administration expelled Mike in an attempt to get tough and thin Unity's membership. They miscalculated our resolve and our response. We prepared to fight with everything we could muster.

Word spread across campus that the Uncle Toms in Bundy Hall expelled Mike Warren. Groups of us huddled in the student union to plan a response. We sat and talked about our next steps.

Another Unity for Unity leader, Ed Hunter, also known as Little Jazz turned to us and said, "If we punk out now, we're finished."

Ishan Abdul Aziz, known then as Butterball because of his robust frame, pulled me to one side and said, "Hawk, we need to bum-rush these Tom's… you ready?"

"Damn skippy," I said to Butterball. "Let's take Bundy Hall and hold the Tom's hostage."

Butterball and I deputized about ten brothers to block the exit doors. We gave instructions to let students leave but to keep the employees in the building until the administration reinstated Mike. We insisted that they also agree to start Black History classes and drop mandatory ROTC. Meanwhile, the Dean of students walked up and told us to be good and mind our own business.

Butterball said, "Dean Flowers, Negro, please, you will hear from us soon." [47]

I asked two brothers from Youngstown, Ohio, to watch the main entrance door. "Don't hurt anyone," I said. "But let them know we're not playing." These two young men most students considered crazy though not mentally ill. They seemed willing to push the limits for what they believed. Choosing them to watch the doors was a good decision.

When Butterball and I reentered Bundy Hall for a second time, Dean Flowers stopped us in the hall outside the registrar's office and gave us the "don't throw your life away" speech.

"Dean Flowers," Butterball said. "We aren't playing. We just chained the doors, so tell everybody that they're staying here until President Groves meets our demands."

As Butterball was speaking, one of the women from the registrar's office walked up and began scolding us. She told Butterball and me that we should be ashamed. Without knowing that she crossed my red-alert line, she went on to say, "And you are not a credit to your race." I bit my lip and just looked at her. Out of respect, I held back what was on the tip of my tongue.

I turned to Dean Flowers and told him if he did not do exactly what I asked, I would rip off the cord from the floor lamp and hog-tie him with it. I said firmly, "Go call Groves and tell him we want to meet." He stared at me in disbelief.

The situation had grown to be tense and much more than I predicted, but it was too late to walk away. The chief of the campus police, Captain Bell, ordered the four or five campus officers over to Bundy Hall to deal with the situation. When they arrived, they found a couple hundred students sporting

Afros protecting the chained doors outside Bundy Hall. The irony was both sides knew and liked the other. I scanned the faces of the campus police, and I could tell some admired the courage we showed.

We misunderstood completely what was at stake from the confrontation before us. We believed after shaking our fists and shouting "Black Power" for a few hours, Central State's administration would cave in. We underestimated the high stakes the school faced.

I could not speak for everyone that day, but one of my biggest dilemmas was the fact I couldn't stay mad at Dean Flowers. I would never have thought of hurting him. He was a product of a generation of black college graduates that wanted to advance educational opportunities for black folk.[48]

Dean Flowers, born in 1929, graduated from three different universities, served in the Korean War, and pursued an academic career, holding several positions. Given what he had achieved and overcame in his lifetime, a confrontation was inevitable.

I had remembered a year or so before he had lent Mike Warren a couple hundred dollars to pay the rent. Even if the loan were not paid back, Dean Flowers would not trip out. Deep down we all recognized that he cared for the students; he just could not support our commitment to a black ideology. He had spent his entire career as a well-behaved Negro and a credit to his race. He did not understand us. And we didn't understand why he would not support a Black Power agenda.

Dean Flowers invested his life to prove that black folks could better their lot quietly without upsetting the order of things. I remember the confused look on his round and aging face as he wondered why we would throw away our future this way. For our part, we did not understand why his generation wasn't jumping for joy that young black folks had the courage to confront deeply embedded racism.

By midday, the press came to campus to cover the events. The brothers from Antioch College in Yellow Springs heard what had jumped off and they came to join us. Antioch had admitted large numbers of students from the so-called ghettos of America in a bid to improve its "diversity." The crew from Antioch didn't know Dean Flowers and the keystones (campus police), as we called them, because of their semi-professional demeanor. I worried things could have gotten really ugly. They were ready to throw down on some Uncle Tom's.

Nearly half of us were packing in those days. If we had been scared enough or pushed too far, some of us would have come out shooting.

I remember thinking one of the two sides was going to give in before things got out of hand. Neither side budged.

The shaky truce that had endured for a year or so between Unity for Unity and the administration was about to come to a loud and decisive end.

Unity for Unity's siege of Bundy Hall and Wesley Hall was the tipping point for the board of trustees. I suspected the governor of Ohio was happy to give President Groves the green light to call in the Ohio State Patrol. By mid afternoon on the second day, several hundred state troopers converged on campus in battle formation. We fought them, mostly with sticks and rocks, but also hand to hand. Then around sunset, the state patrol withdrew.

A lot of us were chanting a victory prematurely. I could sense something else, far worse, was coming. I stood in the shadow of Nat Turner's revolt. [49]

I knew it would be just a matter of time until my fears of far worse arrived.

By 10:00 p.m. the same day, we decided to let the employees go home and abandon Bundy Hall. We retreated and focused our occupation on Wesley Hall. Over the course of the day, we heard rumors that President Groves got the green light from the governor to call in the Ohio National Guard. The threat of armed soldiers with overwhelming forces thinned our numbers.

We made our stand at the entranceway to Wesley Hall and piled chairs in front of the entrance about eight feet high as a thousand National Guard troops arrived, armed with M16s.

They parked their green camouflaged jeeps, hundreds of them, on both sides of the highway that ran north and south adjacent to the campus. For years Unity for Unity's rhetoric proclaimed our struggle was with white America. It was no longer rhetoric. White folks, with guns, came to test our resolve.

Our takeover to demand change to include African History classes and Black Studies classes threatened to shatter the mundane arrangement that white folks and most so-called Negroes cherished. The social order we had questioned and challenged for years counterpunched.

The National Guard arrested over five hundred students. They packed us in buses and off we went to the county jail in Xenia, Ohio. Around ten thirty we walked toward the jail's entrance, still shouting "Black Power" and shaking our fists. The National Guard surrounded us on every side.

Almost inside the jail, I heard someone shout, "Hey, Hawk, your mom's here!"

Sure enough, there was my mother, walking toward us briskly. When she reached the armed troops, she yelled at them to get out of her way.

"Don't you touch me," I heard her say to four or five visibly intimidated young white boys with M16s.

So there I was, a big-time Unity for Unity revolutionary, being rescued by my five-foot-three mother. She drove from Yellow Springs to Xenia in a raincoat, a pair of house shoes, and hair rollers. "Mom, go home!" I barked at her.

The look on her face told me she realized the bad spot she had me in. "I am OK, Mom," I said. "Just go home." She was embarrassing the hell out of me!

There was so much commotion going on that only a few noticed my mother. As I watched her retreat to the car, I shook my head. "Damn," I whispered to myself. "Mom's got more heart than most of us."

Toward Gray Winter Skies

With just two days before the annual Thanksgiving Day recess, the Governor of Ohio ordered Central State closed until January 1968. The school closing did not come as a surprise. It sealed shut a door on an important period at Central State. It also singled out a key milestone in my mirror-mending process and for my personal development.

I needed to review the events that lead to the takeover of the Administration building at Central State. I wanted to examine how events unfolded and impacted my life. My senior year of high school was the starting point. Hanging out at Central State helped me change. It facilitated a deeper understanding of myself and it assisted me to embrace my ethnic identity.

Before the last year of high school, my thoughts about black people were shaped by the philosophy of nonviolence. They rested on the core principles of the civil rights movement developed in the fifties and early sixties.

At Central State and living in Boston two summers, I developed an Afrocentric (African-centered) worldview. Over the two years, I read a lot of diverse books. I wrote short stories, vignettes, and poems and I embraced life fully.

The Unity for Unity rebellion at Central State was a culminating event. By the end of the rebellion, and even before, I viewed the goal of assimilation and integration as a ridiculous insult to my humanity and dignity. I did not need proximity to white people to be human. It seemed to me that a notion of nonviolent protest depended on assimilation into white culture. The logic was it would solve our problems. The philosophy advanced a premise that proximity to whites in employment, education, and other spheres of life would save black folks from themselves. While neatly gift wrapped in the language of rights and equality, the argument for assimilation and integration made me sick.

Even the very essence of America's philosophy of rugged individualism and self-reliance did not support the pathetic integrationist rationale. Black folk in America, since the end of slavery, only wanted a chance to live in safety and participate in public life like others. We wanted to educate our children, open businesses and work without the constant threat of unfair treatment.

Black folks' aspirations for freedom and dignity would not be achieved through integration or assimilation. We needed unfettered opportunity without contrived racist roadblocks. We did not need assimilation. Dr. King is reported to have said, we could be brothers in humanity, but not brother-in-laws.[50]

His statement eluded many whites. Many whites interpreted that having equality with them and competing on a level playing field gave black folks opportunity without merit. Our three hundred years of slavery counted for nothing.

I pondered the irony of the American experiment. Whites came to America to find opportunity on a level playing field. They wanted to overcome tyranny and oppression in Europe. But the manner in which they pursued freedom was to commit genocide on the native inhabitants and enslave millions of Africans. The hypocrisy astounds me.

I was astounded by the hypocritical narrative of America's claim for justice and freedom, underscored my experience with George Ware and SNCC after whites left SNCC leadership positions. This development also reinforced my rejection of American double-talk. In the new SNCC whites were welcomed to help but not lead.

Stokely Carmichael resigned from SNCC in the spring of 1967 and nominated H. Rap Brown as chairman. My experience with SNCC and Unity for Unity gave me a frame of reference to understand the emerging philosophy of black liberation. Activism became more important to me than graduating college. I attempted to remain committed even as SNCC infighting increased, and Unity for Unity dissolved when members graduated or left school.

The conflicts between SNCC and the Black Panthers intensified and clashes between the Black Panthers and Ron Karenga's Organization US took a deadly toll. Some claim that Robert Williams and Malcolm X vied over credit for keeping the revolution alive. These claims are not entirely supported by facts. Many observers report SNCC and the Black Panthers had no problems until Eldridge Cleaver stepped in between Stokely and Huey.[51]

Moreover, I sensed some of the romance had seeped out of the black liberation movement. The movement was unable to offer practical and realistic alternatives to counter mainstream integration.

The force of passion from the black revolutionary movement declined. I saw it when John Coltrane died. Of course, he had nothing to do with the diminishing intensity of the black liberation movement, but his death placed a watermark in my mind. I was hanging out with a friend listening to a Sonny Rollins LP when I heard Coltrane died. The velvet mesh covering my friend's Harman Kardon speakers pulsated like a healthy heart. We were smoking marijuana. A good deal of smoke filled the room. There was so much smoke it was difficult to see objects in the room. There was a knock at the door. We paused and looked at each other. Junior Newsome, a neighbor, and a Yellow Springs police officer, stood there.

No amount of fanning could hide the smoke. My friend cracked the door open. I could feel a lump in his throat next to the one in mine. "Tell Hawk to turn his car around," Junior said. "It's parked in the wrong direction." He then left. We exhaled relief and disbelief. He did not haul us off to jail.

I could not speak to my friend's inner thoughts, but I doubt they were any different from mine. I needed to change. There were just too many narrow escapes with dangerous, stupid stuff. I was doing a lot of things that could erase my future or my life.

Larger forces were shaping events more than I realized. On the same day Coltrane died, Stokely was in London to give a talk on the dialectics of black liberation.[52] He explained why the black liberation struggle now embraced Marxism. Black leaders, like Stokely, no longer focused on overt racism. Some of the leading voices of black liberation were now talking about global dialectics and oppressed workers.

Most of the rank and file in the black liberation movement did not have a clue why this shift occurred. A few predicted it would happen. I feared to express how the change felt. It sure felt like a convenient sellout. The punch was so hard the movement needed to take a standing eight count. We were dazed.

In the vacuum, we got high and waited for someone to point out a direction. Clouded by uncertainty we struggled to define who we were and what we should do.

During this time, Unity for Unity's mentor, George Ware, and Stokely Carmichael traveled to Cuba to attend a meeting of the Organization of Latin American Solidarity (OLAS).[53]

Internationalizing the black liberation movement in America did not advance Black Power. In fact, it decreased its practicality. The image of Che Guevara holding an assault rifle diverted our attention. It helped weaken our resolve to build schools, foster economic development, and establish safe communities.

Rubbing elbows with delegates from Algeria, Guinea, and Nasser's Egypt shifted Stokely's view from fighting racism into an international class struggle under a Marxist ideology. I believed Stokely Carmichael's international framework with iconic figures like Fidel Castro made him a less effective leader for a Black Nationalist agenda. Stokely's shift in ideology influenced George Ware as well.

Thelwell wrote in his book about Stokely, *Ready for Revolution* that after the OLAS conference Stokely and George left Cuba for North Vietnam.[54] However, before the plane could reach its stopover point in Madrid, it turned around and returned to Havana. Cuban intelligence received reports that members of the CIA were waiting in Madrid to seize Stokely and George when the plane landed. The unintended impact of SNCC's involvement in international revolutionary politics affected us as well. George and Ernest "Trap" Stevens[55] came to Central State as organizers. The FBI and other intelligence gathering organizations watched George and Ernest regularly. Our association with them put us under scrutiny as well.

The FBI spent millions of dollars to discredit and destroy black organizations. The federal government's claim of upholding constitutional guarantees of free speech was duplicitous at best. The murders of Malcolm X, the Black Panther Party leader, Fred Hampton, and Dr. Martin Luther King all showed evidence of federal involvement. When direct federal involvement did not occur, prior knowledge of plots to kill many black leaders was not disrupted.

Even though black liberation was an imprecise concept with vague pragmatic goals, the federal government did not hesitate to disrupt and discredit these organizations. Each of these developments caused me to ponder and rethink my position.

I also reconsidered the impact of the 1961 affirmative action legislation. In the minds of many black folks, this legislation weakened a need for black activism. Also, I needed to reconsider why black leaders did not prepare adequately for the white backlash to affirmative action. We knew it was coming. Challenge after challenge filled the courts. When Richard Nixon was elected president in 1970, some affirmative action gains in employment and housing were halted or slowed.

Many whites were saying to governing bodies, "Don't you dare water down my white privilege. I have no problem with black disadvantage."

Even in light of challenges during the Nixon presidency, affirmative action was opening doors and scaring whites. On the other end of the racial landscape, the advocates for integration mounted a comeback.

Unity for Unity's targets for change, African History, and Black Studies no longer were relevant to most students. Our quest for self-discovery required cultural identity and our starting point was Black Studies. I had to face the question of what was next in the black liberation movement.

I also had to ask, why did SNCC or Unity for Unity exist only in name? Why were members of the Black Panthers either in exile, in prison, or dead? Why, after Dr. King's assassination, was our only means of protest to burn down black neighborhoods? I could not answer these questions. I did my best to camouflage my fears.

To compound the confusion, some of us were conflicted about college graduation and landing on our feet in the world of the black middle class. It was hard to reject our upbringing. Some Unity for Unity members went back to Central State to complete a degree. Only a handful remained committed to the movement.

I was determined to stay faithful to a black ideology even if it meant dropping out of college. My attitude was immature, I admit. Nevertheless, it was consistent with my stubborn nature to hold out.

With the campus closed, we decided to retreat and regroup.

We spoke to George and Ernest, and they suggested that we spend time at a cabin that belonged to Ernest's family, just outside Detroit. We loaded into Butterball's Plymouth and a rental car and drove north toward a gray winter sky.

We spent time at the cabin preaching to one another about the decadence of almost everything. Our deliberations acted as a sugar pill to calm our anxiety. The retreat did the opposite. It forced us to face our contradictions. We preached to each other about the white man, but we had no answers to address the issues confronting the black man. We were confident that our pronouncements, filled with cutting historical analysis, possessed profound wisdom. Our rants were not praxis.

We left the cabin with nothing gained. Our paper-thin justifications shielded us from facing a coarse reality: The movement was dead. Nevertheless, we still searched for a resurgence.

We returned to Ohio and visited Antioch College often even though Central State did not ban us from the campus. We went to Central State, but it was not as before. Central State's students had returned to a pre-1960s mentality. It was a job factory for colored people. Many students were content being "colored" again. On the other hand, Antioch students rejected overt racism, and there was a climate of activism. Black Greeks were once again popular and visible on Central State's campus. Several students focused their attention on medical school, law school, graduate school, and well-paying jobs. Our years of diligent work left a faint footprint. Our vision of a black consciousness revival could not overcome the gravity of the black middle class promised land.

The years we spent fighting for the establishment of African History and African American Studies disappeared with the arrival of the Ohio National Guard. I was desperate to find a context for meaningful activism.

I decided to spend more time and energy at Antioch College. It was logical. It was a comfortable and safe place to raise money from affluent white hippies. People there were sympathetic to civil rights or at least they felt guilty about the history of slavery and the oppression of black people.

The right combination of guilt and desire to see change always produced a couple of hundred dollars, if not thousands of dollars, at every fund-raising visit. George and Ernest were Master's in combining both elements. I admired George particularly, as he gave reason after reason why white liberals should empty their pockets. He urged them to call their wealthy fathers somewhere in suburban Connecticut for money to support the movement.

If they did not do this, they were no better than Bull Connor or George Wallace. I learned fund-raising from watching George. I had the hang of it by February 1968. Butterball and I visited Antioch's cafeteria and raised enough money to leave Ohio for South Carolina.

SWEETLY FRIGHTENED

George and Ernest asked Butterball and me to help support community organizing activities at Benedict College in Columbia, South Carolina. They asked us to work with some of the black students. Our experience at Central State should help students avoid mistakes and stay focused.

The SNCC tactic of "organizing" took me a while to grasp. Unlike other civil rights groups, SNCC developed a broad view of the community, unrestricted to a single objective like voting.[56]

SNCC concentrated on strengthening the black community's ability to govern itself in local politics, selecting teachers, shaping school curriculum, and building a healthy cultural life. SNCC also worked to support family life. It sought to help black men remain in the home.

My first morning in South Carolina, I ate fish, grits, peas, and rice on top of fluffy brown pancakes. I snuck a glance at the breakfast table to see if anyone noticed my surprise at eating dinner food for breakfast. No one noticed. This cultural shift in eating intrigued me and it felt delightful. I fancied to myself the breakfast food came from a Caribbean or African influence.

I remember turning on the local black radio station with delight. My ear for music changed. I traded in my Motown affection for Stax, the Memphis sound.[57] Otis Redding was a revolutionary poet and Sam & Dave's song "Hold On" was more poignant than "We Shall Overcome." Memphis was soulful. Memphis was blacker. It did not court crossover. So what if white folks did not understand the lyrics. In my view, the Memphis sound did not need mass appeal.

There were several women activists already working at Benedict College. One of them caught my eye immediately. I met Leah after a couple of weeks in Columbia. She was twenty years old, had flawlessly smooth dark-brown skin and kept her hair in a short Afro. She was thin but proportionately attractive. We connected immediately. I was determined not to repeat my "charm and then run from intimacy" routine like I did in Boston.

Leah dropped by the house from time to time with three or four other young sisters to arrange meetings and print flyers on a steno machine. She and the other sisters had escaped the cycle that plagued too many men in Black Nationalists organizations. They were activities-focused and didn't waste time by getting high. It sure seemed like they did not need an elaborate philosophy to take action.

It is worthwhile repeating again that many black radical groups failed to find meaningful, concrete goals in the late sixties. Groups uncertain about their relevance and roles turned to smoking grass and eventually using coke and heroin. These deadly diversions supported widespread drug epidemics throughout black communities in America during the waning years of the black nationalism movement.

The early days of black nationalism were best captured in the statement "I am black and I am proud," which made ethnic pride a reality on the street. It also helped lower black-on-black crime and hard-core drug use as well as it promoted other behaviors that made many black communities better places to live.

Cultural black nationalism was consumer friendly because it did not demand a political stand, unlike political black nationalism. Changes in attire, like wearing African clothing, having natural hair and the like, and some changes in individual behavior, like not using hard drugs, were sufficient. Drug use in pop culture and in black nationalists movements were not liberating; it only impaired our ability to implement concrete activities.

By the end of 1968, drugs and alcohol use destroyed many black radical groups and the activists who founded them. Even if the destruction was not immediate, the damage was far-reaching. Huey P. Newton, for example, co-founder and leader of the Black Panthers, died by the hand of a drug dealer in

1989 when a drug deal soured. Huey's substance use consumed him for many years. In the end, it killed him.

Looking around the landscape of black activism, it did not take long to identify the successful black radical groups that moved forward. It was because the black women in these groups were sober and they worked without distraction.

Most of these sisters were intellectually and emotionally a step or two ahead of us. One time Leah and I were passing out flyers in the "Black Bottoms," a phrase I heard my father used to describe the tin and cardboard shantytowns in southwest Dayton. Black Bottoms had existed long before the word "ghetto" was used widely. Most black communities of any size had Black Bottoms. In Columbia, the Black Bottom shanty dwellings of tin and scraps of wood stood side by side. Suddenly, from the corner of my eye, I saw her burst into tears. I knew exactly why. Even when poverty and oppression were less noticeable, her oval chestnut eyes would fill with tears. Her discipline kept them from brimming over. Instead of crying, it made her determined to help. She was only twenty years old and her commitment shamed me to look inward.

When I gathered some money together to buy weed, Leah's typical protest was silence. She disapproved strongly of my wasting time and money to get high. My usual stupid response was to say it expanded my consciousness.

Politely but firmly she would say, "Baby, don't let that stuff mess you up." Her coaxing me to stop only fueled my guilt. I felt vulnerable and then I would pout. She would sway me away from self-punishment.

"I love you," she would whisper. "I just don't want you to get hurt," and she would call me Billy. To her, I wasn't Hawk, the revolutionary. I was just Billy.

Smoking marijuana, drinking, and listening to Coltrane, the Ayler Brothers, or Otis Redding evolved from pastimes into painkillers. I knew many men in black nationalist organizations were depressed and broken by the end of 1968. Getting high and listening to music filled a void.

I was enamored with the idea of being in love with Leah, but anything beyond the realm of an idea frightened me to no end. When I pressed the idea against the mirror of reality, as a daily commitment, of holding down a job, and perhaps marriage and even children, I stepped back. The requirements demanded deep commitment. I just wasn't ready.

At twenty-two years old, I saw being in love as a single act play. The cast of characters tried their best to make it look real, but it was just acting. No one dared to fidget in the scratchy costumes or grimace behind the masks. I feared my parents were right. I should stop this Black Power playing around and get a job and a wife.

Starting a family was a facade of stability. It was a comforting lie that some blacks repeated because we were supposed to believe it was good. To me, a mortgage was as threatening to the revolution as a token job.

Leah never crowded me with the middle-class Negro love mythology and this scared me even more. I knew sooner or later the mythology, shrouded in her ability to frighten me sweetly, would eventually land me in a black church where I would say, "I do." Leah was the real deal, "a keeper." I knew that. I talked manhood, but I was still terrified to make a commitment. I feared that my resolve to resist being in love would fade. It was time to run.

I convinced her I needed to handle some revolutionary issues in Boston. My words were nothing more than a ruse to halt our relationship. I vanished. I feared that a commitment to love her would creep up on me. I scraped some money together and caught a flight to Boston. I never spoke to her again. It took several years to forgive myself.

Running from the Bitter Dog

I faced a quandary after a month in Boston. It was now clear to me that the revolution was not in books or slogans. The authentic revolution was in the daily lives of ordinary black folk. Black Boston's streets were alive with proud-looking black people. I began to see Black Power as black businesses. Not just black people who happened to have a business. These were conscious black men and women who opened businesses to achieve self-reliance and self-respect.

I noticed that the Nation of Islam had several stores on Blue Hill Avenue. They presented a side of Black Power I had not seen in Ohio or down South. They wore suits and a tie; they were polite; they did not swear, and they abstained from drugs and alcohol. Even so, I thought they were not militant enough to lead other black folks. Nonetheless, their pragmatic approach to owning and operating black businesses appealed to me. I thought about my father's strong work ethic when I patronized them in Roxbury. Sadly my view of black consciousness was more romantic than practical.

With my mind on blending into Roxbury, I traded in my colorful dashikis for knitted casual shirts. My shortened Afro now rested under a black Kangol hat tipped to the side. I sported black wing tips and a full-length black leather coat. I thought this style was a fitting blend between the revolutionary look of the Black Panthers and a hustler's appearance, accented by the Kangol hat, casual knit shirt, and the wing-tip shoes. I did not neglect to spit-shine my wing tips. The spit-shined shoes were more of a testimonial to my upbringing. My work in Dad's shoe repair business trained me to respect shoe care.

I was back on Blue Hill Avenue in the mix, as they say, without a job. I wanted something I couldn't put my finger on. It included making money but not just chasing a dollar. I could find some dignified work or, as a last resort, I could launch a victimless hustle.

I tried to sell nickel bags of grass here and there without much success. Street hustling wasn't glamorous. It required a mindset dedicated to "grind" above all else. To make money, it had to be all about money. But most of all, it represented everything I had denounced for years.

I was just getting by, but I was better off than when I was merely day-dreaming that the revolution would not be televised.

I watched the summer turn into a chilly fall. That October my dearest friend Butterball joined me in Boston. We rented a second-floor apartment on Blue Hill Avenue right across the street from a well-known Jewish bakery. It was a decent place for $125 a month. As the weather changed, our small gas-powered heater did little to beat back the Boston cold. In spite of all of these problems, our new apartment, and a fresh start in Boston, gave us hope that better days were ahead. On top of all this, I was gaining weight and eating better.

I ate kosher cold cuts and salads from a Nation of Islam Deli and a bean pie every now and then from the Nation of Islam bakery. I drank guava juice from a swirling dispenser that sat on the counter next to the cash register. Its placement made it hard not to order another glass.

However, from time to time, I smoked hashish and chased down the harshness with a gulp or two of the "Bitter Dog." The Bitter Dog was a combination of white port wine and concentrated lemon juice. The Bitter Dog was a Black Panther favorite. Any self-respecting Black Panther had undoubtedly taken the Bitter Dog for a walk. The Bitter Dog was a rite of passage. [58]

I drank with caution, though. I feared the Bitter Dog would plunge me into the same deep, scary hole my father and his cut buddies had dug for themselves. The name Bitter Dog rang true. It was bitter going down and the hangover made you feel like a dog. In the end, I fled from the Bitter Dog.

I also looked for a crap game now and then in an alley near Blue Hill Avenue. When I managed to find a game, I knew it could end badly. Many young brothers in Roxbury were still tipsy on self-loathing and they would not hesitate to kill you. You could die over a twenty-nine dollar pot. Beneath my revolutionary rhetoric and my professed love for black people was a reality of what it took to survive in Roxbury, hiding behind a shadow of danger.

I knew a crap game could become a potential flashpoint. I witnessed games where a winner was forced to keep playing until others won their money back. Based on what I had seen in that Blue Hill Avenue alley, I imagined a scenario where I'd insist on leaving while resting my fingers on the pistol in my coat pocket. I'd firmly tell the loser that I was leaving, in spite of his protests. "Don't make me take my hand out of my coat pocket," I would declare with a steely expression.

In a few days or a week at the most, the crap game loser and his boys would be looking for Butter and me. They would be ready to settle scores. I didn't need that crazy cycle.

I'm sure deadly encounters between young black men nowadays doesn't differ too much from conflict in the past. Beef between young black men then and now is a formula to kill or be killed in the street or some dimly lit hallway. This period in black Boston was filled with disease and cure. The twisted strands of tribalism that turn a black man against another over a crap game or the color of a handkerchief share similar pathological roots. We failed to overcome the effects of slavery physically and mentally. We nurtured a culture that glorified violence and conflict in the name of being real men.

Our secret cultural reality is filled with fear and anxiety that we aren't close to any legitimate definition of manhood. Thus, we pretend being hard is manly.

On the other hand, there were symbols of hope and promise. I remember walking down Blue Hill Avenue one day, and I heard James Brown's "I'm Black and I'm Proud" spilling out from a speaker.

The Godfather of Soul's refrain of "Say it loud!" met by a chorus of kids shouting "I'm Black and I'm Proud!" was not just music. It was a shift in how we felt about ourselves after a long journey from hating blackness to a children's chorus singing, "I am Black and I am Proud."

I realized that my father had been singing a version of this song, along with thousands of other black men from his generation. Their rendition smothered under Jim Crow. It was drowned by what killed Emmett Till. They sang it nevertheless. They lived it with resilience and grit.

During this time in Boston, everything in my life was pushing me to reevaluate a coexistence in white society.

I had reached a point in my life where I wanted to work and function without the risk of destroying a chance to have a normal existence. I feared, most of all, ruining my soul. I knew that a dead soul is smothered under layers of disease from that old enemy Pretense. I wanted to feel genuine without selling out.

I asked myself, "Don't you need to at least try to hum the 'I am Black and I am Proud' lyrics at a job?"

My upbringing, one that valued hard work above most else, tormented me. I longed to have a job. This longing pestered me. It languished under my stubborn zeal to change the world of white folks.

True to my roots, I craved hard muscle-twitching work that would cause me to taste trickles of salty sweat flowing from my brow across my lips. Nevertheless, I feared that dormant Negro middle-class aspirations would emerge. It laid powerful restraining hands on me.

I did not possess my parents' grit. I had replaced one fear for another. They feared not being able to make a place for themselves in white society. I feared I would make a meaningless place.

Their fear helped them endure unspeakable humiliations while my fear helped me throw hard but inaccurate punches at white supremacy. Black folks in their generation did what conditions demanded. I used to complain about their passive accommodation of brutal racism. However, I came to appreciate their grit. It paved the way for my generation to fight back.

We terrified our parents and men like Dean Flowers. We threatened to destroy their expectations of the life they wanted for us. They feared we would spoil the sacrifices they had made.

My parents, I must admit, had the patience to let me find my own way. They did not interfere with life's test. They were confident I would find a way to overcome my rage.

I started to see during that chilly fall in Roxbury that there was enough room for me to be true to what I learned on the dusty pitcher's mound in

Yellow Springs. I could embrace what the Roxbury Work and Study Project had taught me about love and heartbreak. I'd be true to what George Ware and Unity for Unity taught me about living with principle and conviction. In the end, I could be true to what my parents taught me about being a man and a decent person.

I realized I could be true to falling down and true to redemption. I embraced, finally, that there had to be a way to express deserved anger and forgiveness. I was committed to make things right. Most of my life, I sensed that there was a path that would allow me to reconcile both aspirations.

I did not need to choose one over the other. I loved the fact that I could scrutinize my anger at injustice and racism in white America without drowning in it.

I could forgive without losing my zeal to fight racism and injustice. What I did not realize then was that forgiveness and true love is spiritual.

Rip and Run Tired

In early fall of 1969, I read William Grier and Price Cobbs's book *Black Rage*[59] on an American Airlines flight from Boston to Dayton. My anger had abated. I could contemplate racism and injustice without slipping into a rage. It amused me I could read *Black Rage* rage free!

Over the past few years, I had experienced an endless stream of angry thoughts and feelings that paralyzed me before this long-awaited change occurred. It had left me gritting my teeth. I couldn't concentrate. Now, with my anger over American racism tamed, it no longer placed me off balance as before.

Rage's sly cousin, fear, was also in retreat. I also came to grips that I ruined relationships by sprinting away. When I owned up to my fear of commitment and closeness, guilt and remorse declined.

When the flight landed, I made my way back to Yellow Springs to live in my mother's apartment until I found a job. Going back to finish my degree wasn't on my radar. My concerns ran to smaller things. The pieces of my cracked mirror were coming together. The broken slivers showed me the distance I was from things that gave life meaning—the things that ground us in who we are.

I wanted a pair of sneakers. I bought a pair of high-top Converse, two pairs of thick white socks, and sweatpants. I looked ill at five foot eleven and only weighing 150 pounds. Eating better became a top priority. I played basketball three to four times a week in Antioch's gym. I was delighted that I was still quick. I could still dunk. I could take one step, one dribble, and slam with both hands.

I experienced a sense of feeling whole and alive that I hadn't felt since I was eighteen. I had just turned twenty-three. I was finally in touch with a part of me that had been lost in a cave of racial conflict, despair, and anger.

The sounds of squeaking gym shoes and the ball going through the net riveted me with renewal.

Running up and down the court was better than being high. I enjoyed fatigue. Rolling up a joint was gone. I wasn't alone shifting the pace of my life. Several of us, weary from years of deep anguish and impotent rage, looked for a shady spot to pause and rebuild. The basketball court was perfect for me, but it was only a start. I could not bring back a past life in a worry-free Yellow Springs. Nothing could bring back a pre–civil rights era slumber. I wanted to move forward with security rather than go back in time. I wanted a job. I wanted to find an apartment. I longed for a balanced life, but I was still committed to the struggle for justice. I set my aim on both.

STAFFORD STREET

The deep rust color of my parents' house had faded. Most of the gravel was missing from the driveway and the white trim around the roof had started to peel like the bark of a birch tree.

We had new neighbors. There were more whites living on the formerly all-black Stafford Street. A few mixed families lived at both ends of the block. The spacious apple orchard of my childhood, where sheep once grazed, was now home to a six-unit apartment building. The middle school, across from the orchard, had become the Yellow Springs Municipal Building.

My parents had been on the brink of divorce for a number of years. My father's slide into alcoholism accelerated in his fifties. His body and mind had suffered from years of hard work and hard drinking. Shortly after I returned from Boston, he became ill and required hospitalization. I went to visit him in a Springfield hospital. My heart sank when I sat by his bedside. I feared he had lung cancer from years of chain smoking.

I realized he had suffered from an alcohol binge, and the subsequent detoxification process made him delusional. I felt a wave of relief after sitting at his bedside for a few minutes.

For ten minutes, my father lay there, talking to himself. He did not recognize me. Then, suddenly, he looked at me.

"Do you still smoke?" he asked slowly. "Got cigarettes on you?"

"I quit smoking," I answered. I kept the visit short. I felt numb and at a loss for words. I left and almost ran to the car that my mother insisted I borrow from her to visit him. I had dreaded the visit even though it was the right thing to do. My emotions were twisted and shaken, but I survived nonetheless.

I sat in the car and thought back on the times when he drank less. My father was a resourceful, ambitious, self-taught sheet metal technician. He embodied a solid work ethic and he was a master at working with leather. Our shoe repair shop was a Yellow Springs landmark. He was helpful to strangers and to people he knew.

It was hard not to recognize the good in him. An illustration of this quality presented itself when one of my sister's classmates was paralyzed in an auto accident. The young man had little mobility. My father made an extension for his hands from metal prongs and leather straps. He used my father's invention to hold books to read, use a typewriter, and other daily tasks. The injured man reminded my sister of my father's help at a fifty-year high school reunion.

My dad was also a benefactor to a number of young men who wanted to work. Our shoe repair shop was like a job-training program for struggling young men, black and white.

The forces that accelerated my father's drinking, along with thousands of black men, into the bottom of a bottle of whiskey, came from a mixture of toxic historical events and wicked double standards. Black men dealt with these forces daily. The mixture shaped how they coped with the harsh, dirty, marginal jobs they worked. The typical job paid barely enough to feed and care for their families. I watched my father drag his weary body through our door late at night. The next morning he would push his worn-out body back through the door to a second job before we stirred from sleep. He clocked twelve to fifteen hours daily. He worked like this for nearly four decades.

Daily humiliation spared no black person. It only varied in the degree of pain one was willing to recognize or resist. Black men were probably the most aware but were also the least willing and able to fight back. The stakes of losing were too high. Losing, among other things, meant being homeless before homelessness was a social type.

Many a Friday night, I watched my father and his cut buddies crack open a new deck of cards, gamble for chump change and knock off a couple of fifths of Scotch. When it was warm enough, I used to sit on the front porch and listen to them go back and forth with each other. Before midnight, they were usually drunk and their conversation echoed pauses of laughter and remorse.

They complained about their jobs, the way things were, and their deep anguish for feeling like Negroes instead of Americans. I laughed though I felt guilty for laughing, at their best effort to talk with each other. It seemed like nonsense to me. They used these gatherings to heal wounds. They found kinship in my father's living room. They poured alcohol on the wounds that came from the hard, dirty jobs they worked in the foundry, the railroad yard, or the slaughterhouse. Scotch whiskey and card games numbed the pain when they were younger. Later in life, as they aged, like my father, the combination killed them.

Each of them coped as best they could. Coping, I suppose, took shape from one's tolerance for pain. It sprung from how much one could endure. Coping also revolved around "fight or flight" survival instincts. Most black folks in America developed an array of complex psychological tools to combat a wicked and persistent spiritual pain that grew in the bowels of a racist America.

I believe there is little difference between the pathology of alcohol addiction in my father's time and the use of drugs in my own. Alcohol and drugs aided our escape. His was the fantasy of inclusion into mainstream American society. Mine was winning the fight against racism. Sadly, using chemicals to mask the pain made our temporary relief delusional.

My father's generation drank because it was legal. It was legal and easy to kill the pain of not feeling like men in control of their lives. My generation used drugs because it was illegal. Illegal usage meant defining control even if this meant prison or self-destruction.

In the end, it didn't matter if it was legal or illegal. For me, escaping the spiritual blindness of alcohol and drugs should embolden black men to challenge and overcome the residue of slavery and Jim Crow. For centuries, the sucker punch of alcoholism and drug addiction had landed on the jaws of black folks and Native Americans. It was finally evident that the best counterpunch was getting sober. I knew these were dark times for black men, and it scared me. As a small boy, I realized I would need to deal with this mess one day.

I remember reading somewhere that the members of the multiracial American band WAR were inspired to write the song "Slippin' into Darkness." They gained inspiration from the song "Get Up, Stand Up" by Bob Marley and Peter Tosh.[60] In many ways, the lyrics in those two songs typified the generations to which my father and I belonged.

The social events of my parents' world and my world collided as the decade of the 1960s ended, and the lyrics of "Slippin' into Darkness" spelled that out:

> "Slippin' into Darkness
> When I heard my mother, say
> I was slippin' into darkness
> When I heard my mother, say
> (Hey, what'd she say, what'd she say)
> 'you been slippin' into darkness, oh, oh, oh
> Pretty soon you're gonna pay."

The black liberation movement had not moved beyond angry symbolic protests. The movement did not critically examine itself, or its leaders; instead, it slipped into darkness. Initially, the aim of the black liberation movement was to reclaim our humanity, snatched away by slavery and Jim Crow racism.

Faithful to the lyrics of "Slippin' into Darkness," the time to pay had come, and pay we did. Even now, over a decade of the new millennium, we still are paying. The darkness that engulfed black folks also covers the soul of America. The American Empire is crumbling under a dark moral degeneracy that is nearly irreversible.

My pops and his cut buddies knew all too well what was in that pit of darkness. They are excused. My generation fell in this pit because we did not evolve spiritually. We have no excuse.

The way I see it, we attempted to create a philosophy of redemption based solely on race. Our philosophy was not connected to removing all forms of injustice. The racism we denounced stifled our relevance because we allowed the racist to trap us within the construct of race. We also did not connect our redemption to God's guidance.

I labored for years to understand why my father's pain smothered hope.

I understood as I aged. However, I was too afraid to face what he saw in that dark chasm. I saw the dark red eyes of our lesser self as I marshaled the courage to look. The dark blinded eyes came from rejecting spiritual answers.

Those hideous eyes of a lesser self stared me down. I should have told my father, "I love you, Dad. I understand your pain and I got your back."

WHITE FOLKS & A NAPPY-HEAD POET

In a cold swimming pool, white folks swim anyway.
Shivering, they climb out and dive back in over and over again.
Very white, and sometimes red from a belly flop
But no nappy head lay hidden in a dry towel
Just sun tan lotion and giggles…proud artifacts of white attire that
smelled like success
And rubbed on like a shield
No Negro could steal.

Our souls have layers. Each wrinkled layer has an imprint of small victories or significant defeats that stays with us and urges us on to navigate our way from dark impasses to light passages and open space. This is the fabric of memories.

There were a couple of black-owned taverns in Yellow Springs, but one sticks out. A street near one tavern was inhabited by a couple of extended families with branches of cousins, aunts, and uncles. They would appear suddenly from behind torn screen doors that gave free passage to the smell of collard greens and other odors from black people's stoves. These smells exist in small black enclaves throughout America.

There was a mean old dog called Rufus or Raymond that would bark and cough as it roamed the adjacent alley. It bellowed with a mucus-filled growl as if to say, "I'll bite one of you young fools, so back up. This is my alley."

It peered out through a dingy, yellowish white, cloudy eye. It moved with a lumbering gait. This dog, a bully of sorts, has a fond place in my recollections.

Important pieces of my cracked mirror were mended by these memories.

Everyone liked the tavern owners. They drove nice cars and kept the juke-box filled with the latest R&B and blues records.

I visited this tavern when I returned to Yellow Springs in October 1969. I wanted to reconnect with people from Yellow Springs to show them that I wasn't angry as before, regardless of the stories they heard. I was proud that I didn't drink, smoke, or get high on drugs. I walked over to a table of folks I knew. They were anxious, so I sat down quietly and ordered a Coke. I bordered on tears watching my childhood friends drink. I knew thin slices of circumstance separated us. I wondered if they realized, as I did, that a wider world was busy shaping our lives on every level. Some of the shaping was driven by a myth of unconditional interracial friendship. This social vaude-ville was widespread until "Black History" started a new narrative. It was a narrative that made my former friends uncomfortable with me.

After years of masking and doubt, I realized that my anger at white people was natural. I became an image and a poster child of the angry black man. Many from Yellow Springs heard that I was an out of control public enemy. I was an Afro-wearing menace. I had lived this image, true enough. However, now I had matured beyond it. I wanted my old friends, black and white, to hear me out.

I realized most of them did not see the historical context of slavery and Jim Crow as I did. My awakening was dizzying and frightening to others.

When I embraced my anger, it was startling. I saw America without fiction.

I came to grips with the cruelty black folk and Native Americans endured.

When I peeled back the events of history, it is clear that black people have faced terrible circumstances. It always puzzled me why some white folks was shocked that I was filled with anger and rage.

It also troubled me that black people took a slow wandering path to re-claiming our dignity. Most black folks, in my view, spent far too much time trying to allay white fears. It seemed that black people were happy to model Roy Wilkins and Dr. King. If we expressed the indignation of Denmark Vesey or the resistance of Nat Turner, black people and white folks would tremble. White people's fear and trepidation were to be expected. Most white people figured, sooner or later, they would face black rage and anger.

I alienated almost everyone by my sudden and violent departure from the American dream, or the American nightmare as Malcolm X once called it.

By rejecting a rationale of slow compromise and accommodation, the dream claimed that blacks and whites should live together in an integrated society as long as power remained in the hands of white folks.

The politics and economics of white domination created an invisible and untouchable space in America. The same immutable power structure remains fundamentally unchanged today despite the fact that a distant spiritual cousin of Emmett Till, President Barack Obama, lives in the White House. Emmett Till and Barack Obama are viscerally connected.

In profound ways, Till and Obama have thrown American racism into a tailspin. Emmett Till's murder was a tipping point. It signaled the establishment of a redline black folk drew in the social and political sand of America. Till's murder took place at a time of deep racial tension to create a perfect storm to rouse black folks to fight back. President Obama's election as a two-term US president stirred up latent white supremacist fears that people of color could politically dominate America.

One of the most disturbing ironies that connect President Obama and Emmett Till is a white woman. President Obama's mother was no Carolyn Bryant. However, both men's existence probes an uneasy discussion about black men and white women. This fact is undeniable.

Since the end of the Civil War, America's social and political institutions created a class of poor white folk deployed as storm troopers and vigilantes to murder black men. Many white men feared that black men would cohabit with white women.

It seems to me President Obama's father, a black man from East Africa, was aware of some of the historical risks associated with romantic involvement, and eventual marriage, with a white woman.

Perhaps some of the visceral public outbursts against President Obama are not just because he is black. Some of it may also be because he is mixed. For sure President, Obama's father crossed the invisible barrier that had separated access of black men to white women.

Is it not a paradox that the murderers of Emmett Till may have helped give license to numerous marriages and unions between black men and white women? The answer in my view is yes, without a doubt.

When I think about how America once treated the possibility of intimate relationships between black men and white women, I imagined potbellied white men wearing straw hats, like those found in a Mark Twain novel. Their ruddy faces reveal half-shaven razor stubble. A handkerchief is tied around their necks to absorb the sweat from the Memphis sun. They would sit around a card table in a smoke-filled room littered with half-empty bottles of cheap bourbon, making plans to keep black men and white women forever apart.

Any serious deconstruction of these images and the history that brings them to mind cannot ignore the narrative that links the murder of Emmett Till to the election of President Barack Obama. I am not sure President Obama would agree. He has had little to say about black suffering in America.

In fact, I don't believe he would agree with me at all. Nonetheless, I make this claim from the evidence. In the speech "A More Perfect Union," President Obama crafted a picture of balanced racial culpability by citing white racism alongside so-called black irresponsibility.[61] He seemed to be saying, "I will not make white folks uncomfortable by bringing up vivid accounts of injustice and racism unless I also point out how black people have failed to cope with overwhelming odds."

Obama's speech painted a picture that Americans should look for a race-neutral narrative without outing whites with culpability. Perhaps his advisors felt there was a political danger for him to focus on black suffering. A message touching on black suffering would require an assessment of politics and policies. This type of a review may point to a meaningful redress for slavery and Jim Crow. The implications are scary because of the word "reparations." I am convinced President Obama would not allow that word to roll over his lips. The concept is pregnant with social mathematics because the equation of black suffering demands balancing.

President Obama indicated recently that two notable detractors and other finger-pointing black folks are not welcomed at the White House. These critics insist that President Obama should use the bully pulpit to establish a Progressive agenda and stop protecting Wall Street interests.

I am also sure that America's political institutions and financial influencers do not fear an economic impact resulting from African American reparations. These institutions, however, tremble at the prospect of a national debate that examines the nation's moral culpability for slavery.

This type of discussion would require contrition and responsibility. Never admit culpability, tangible or remote, is an American political posture irrespective of political party.

Objective history does not endorse an acquittal of America's racist past. On the contrary, America's behavior left many whites with a god complex— and left many black folks with a self-loathing complex.

Black self-loathing created signaling. Signaling refers to situational adjustment to disguise ethnic or racial attributes in an effort to blend in. Signaling makes black folks sound white. It also makes white hip-hop performers sound black. It is clear to me that black popular culture has a strong impact on behavior, language, dress, and entertainment in America.

This type of signaling produced black coping to deal with the residue of slavery and Jim Crow. This brand of signaling makes black suffering fashionable in popular culture. It gives me the willies when I see any culture make sport of or capitalize on how black people cope with suffering.

Signaling is also connected to bleaching creams to lighten dark skin. It creates a financial opportunity for companies to profit from black suffering. In addition to bleaching creams, black women spend millions of dollars on hair extensions, weaves, and wigs. All of this is related to signaling.

White society reinforces this type of signaling by preferring to hire black women with fake hair. Some companies will not employ black women unless they mutilate their hair. Many black parents are vigilant to protect their daughters from the tyranny of this Barbie doll syndrome.

I used to believe that only a decisive military defeat of America, by a nation of color, could reverse this god complex that was at the root of black suffering and the black coping mechanism, signaling. Thus, the war in Vietnam actually humanized white America. America was less willing to invade other countries or extend American interest in the years following Vietnam. The war in Vietnam became a litmus test to resist superpower domination. The Russian retreat from Afghanistan in the 1980s turned out to be their Vietnam.

The Western press and many pundits in the Western political establishment saw Russian military failure in Afghanistan as a Vietnam-like defeat. Even today, when Western military power suffers defeat by countries or groups with inferior military assets, the analogy for the defeat is Vietnam.

Rudyard Kipling infamous poem "The White Man's Burden" was a metaphor for the cost of white imperialist rule. His poem exposes the reality of nineteenth-century imperialism and racism most vividly in the verse where he refers to nonwhites as half devil and half child.[62]

Most Black Nationalists and other politically conscious black folk jumped for joy that white America got chastised by little brown folks in Vietnam. "Serves them right," we said. "History and justice would not find its voice in any other way."

But, it was high time to move forward. I had spent too much time trying to change American racism and shame the white man.

I also realized that Afrocentric cultural symbolism was impractical. Black nationalism failed the implementation test. Both felt good, but they did not bring about meaningful change or sustainability. Getting fitted for a black middle-class straightjacket was out of the question. My only choice was "Nation Time."

NATION TIME

On a chilly evening in November 1969, about twenty-five former Unity for Unity members and some black students from Antioch College went to Wesley Hall on Central State's campus to listen to Minister David X Bradley. Minister David X from the Nation of Islam Mosque No. 5 in Cincinnati delivered a "Reclaim Your Own" talk. In the minds of many former Black Nationalists, the Nation of Islam had emerged as the best alternative to deal with the issues blacks in America faced. The Nation of Islam (NOI) opposed integration and participating in politics but advocated economic self-reliance. The NOI seemed like the epitome of black pride and did not condone or tolerate alcohol and drug use in any form, large or small.

The minister delivered the "Reclaim Your Own" lecture as prominently featured in the Nation's weekly newspaper, *Muhammad Speaks*. The lecture was an explanation of point number four of "What the Muslims Want":

"We want our people in America whose parents or grandparents were descendants from slaves to be allowed to establish a separate state or territory of their own—either on this continent or elsewhere. We believe that our former slave masters are obligated to provide such land and that the area must be fertile and mineral rich."[63]

Minister David spoke like Malcolm X, with a heart-compelling logic and dramatic style made popular in black religious and political circles. Bradley's voice rose and fell like a musical score in a great mystery movie. His words were not just heard by the ear. The words also penetrated the heart of people whose parents or grandparents were descendants from slaves, to be allowed to establish a separate state or territory of their own. Heads nodded.

"Teach, brother minister!" one of his aides cried out. "Wake 'em up, brother minister!"

I turned to see who was making these seemingly spontaneous comments. I saw a man wearing a blue uniform and a small, brimless hat. I then recalled there was a military-like branch of the Nation of Islam, the "Fruit of Islam." I figured he must be one of them, judging by the odd-looking uniform.

Then Minister David, who was also a practicing attorney, dropped a deal maker on us:

"We believe that our former slave masters are obligated to maintain and supply our needs in this separate territory for the next twenty to twenty-five years, until we are able to produce enough to supply our own needs.

"Since we cannot get along with them in peace and equality, after giving them four hundred years of our sweat and blood and receiving in return some of the worst treatment human beings have ever experienced, we believe our contributions to this land and the suffering forced upon us by white America, justifies our demand for complete separation in a state or territory of our own."

We listened, laughed, and at times nodded in approval. At other times, we hung our heads in shame. The process of joining the Nation was too easy. "Do you believe what you heard tonight be the truth? Stand up, brothers, if you believe this." Most of us rose from our seats.

"Are you ready to act on the truth you heard tonight?"

We were.

"Then come up and shake my hand and reclaim your own."

I looked around and about twelve of us were in line to approach the podium to shake Minister Bradley's hand. Oh well, I thought, I do agree with what he said tonight about self-respect, cleaning up your mind and body from alcohol and drugs and respecting your women.

All of this made perfect sense, especially the collectivist economics of self-reliance. Still, something concerned me. While I did agree that the white man acted like a devil, this devil stuff did not just mean a description of the evil behavior of white folk.

For the Nation of Islam, the white man as the devil was doctrine.[64] He was Satan mentioned in the scriptures. Elijah Muhammad meant the devil referred to in the Bible. He meant the devil that scared children. He meant the same devil black Baptist church ministers and deacons blamed for making them seduce lonely women in the choir.

In the past to have believed Elijah Muhammad's theology of the white man, I would have to be in a room filled with reefer smoke. To believe my high school Algebra teacher, a white man, was the devil, I would have to be high. He probably thought I was a devil given my antics in his class.

However, by the end of 1969, my criteria for what was believable took on the shape of a mundane yardstick. This yardstick needed to prevent black folk from being Negroes, joining the military, and agreeing with traditional white mythologies about black folk.[65]

Did the yardstick advocate embracing self-reliant economics? Did it reject the limp narrative of freedom and equality with whites on their terms? Did it promote a disciplined sober lifestyle?

If it met these conditions with an affirmative response, even if it was pregnant with mysticism, I was ready to make the sacrifice and endure a bizarre theology.

I wanted a spiritual framework, no doubt, but the most important element in an organization or movement in 1968–1969 was practical social and economic self-reliance. Elijah Muhammad's Nation of Islam fit the bill.

I decided to check things out and bail if the NOI got too unbelievable or weird. Therefore, on November 18, 1969, I joined the Nation of Islam. By April 1970, I received my X. I was proud to be a bald-headed, bowtie-wearing, Fruit of Islam foot soldier. The rationale for obtaining an X to replace one's surname made sense. The NOI taught that black folks' surnames came from former slave masters. The NOI did not claim every members' name is directly attributed to a specific owner. However, the fact that the ancestors of slaves did not come to America with European names is believed widely.

Generations of my father's forbearers passed down these slave names. The NOI asserted that names should have meanings that described one's essence. Since most black folks were a work in progress, the NOI replaced the slave master's name with the X. If there were two or more people in the same mosque with the same first name, as in my case, a number preceded the X. I became William 2X. Another William, a friend from Antioch College, received his X prior to me. This name alteration was the first step in discarding a presumed slave name. I believed, sooner or later, I would discard the surname "Hawkins" for an Arabic name.

A desire to "accept one's own" was increasing in popularity among young African American men and women. The movement to accept "self" propelled a significant number of young African American men to embrace the concept "it's Nation Time."

I wavered between apprehension and excitement that a new identity would help me discard old mental costumes, including the ineffective costume of black nationalism that was all talk but no action.

The Nation of Islam demanded its members lose all vestiges of all pre-NOI "dead world" thinking. The NOI's dead world imagery was best characterized as "Lazarus and the Rich Man" in the Bible.

The story tells of a beggar at the gate of a wealthy man, lying in the dust in body sores, feeding on the scraps from the rich man's table. When both men die, angels carry Lazarus away while the rich man awakens in Hell. Nation of Islam ministers used this image to describe the African American Christian culture of dependency on whites. The Lazarus prototype made divorcing the so-called dead world exhilarating, mysterious, and exhausting. I felt loathing and guilt, and at other times it seemed like I wore a shield that protected me from the dead world's arrows. What I found previously amusing or normal in African American music or dance, I now saw as only dead world artifacts of buffoonery and voluntary slavery. My bowtie was a constant reminder that I was William 2X and a dead world lifestyle that once delighted me were shackles of mental slavery.

My Central State friend Kenneth X, we called him Jabo, which was a nickname from the street he wore proudly. He accepted the Black Muslim theology quickly and thoroughly. I was amazed. I secretly wanted to believe in the same promise he saw. Instead, I saw a grainy movie on a flickering screen. I was constantly leaning forward in this new theater, squinting my eyes, to understand the film. It seemed to me, at times, the NOI theology was just plain fiction. The NOI preached the black man was God. Yes, God himself.[66]

I wondered, "Even me a God?" When my life was filled with things that shamed me? I thought about these claims during NOI lectures. I would read

William 2X Hawkins is seen in the with Nation of Islam members early in 1970.

an article in *Muhammad Speaks* and ask myself, "What prevents you from believing in a NOI theology as Brother Kenneth X and others do?" I feared someone would find me out. I attended Saviours' Day February 1970. It was the annual NOI convention to commemorate the birthday of WD Fard. NOI doctrine portrayed WD Fard as God Incarnate.

I wanted to believe in the doctrine like the other men in the Fruit of Islam. I wanted a NOI conviction beyond the "do for self" teachings of "Nation Time." I wanted to believe in the theology as well.

However, the theology was so mysterious, there was no way to refute or mount a rational argument against it. The theology depended on desperation born from the aftermath of slavery and rampant racism. The theology departed from the authentic teachings of Islam that I did not understand completely, but I remembered that Malcolm X rejected it before his death. The mere numbers of people who seemed to believe it, without question became a proxy proof. This, too, caused me to second-guess my instinct that it was pure fiction. There must be something to this, I thought. I questioned who could make up a doctrine like this.

Moreover, a number of life's aspects blossomed under the NOI's organizational structure. The NOI provided members with a down-to-earth daily protocol. Popular culture in black communities functioned in a similar manner, but it was not like the NOI down-to-earth routine. The NOI produced these outcomes under a banner of self-reliance, not reliance on white society.

It created a subculture based upon practical, self-reliant economics. The NOI owned farms, a trucking fleet, a clothing factory, schools, apartment buildings, and houses. It bought a private jet and trained pilots.

The NOI maintained an alcohol-free and a drug-free environment. The NOI also demanded its members refrain from swearing, abusive behavior, and womanizing.

I did not crave or touch alcohol or any type of drug or tobacco. I was eager to work hard. I no longer feared intimacy and marriage. I longed to marry and take care of a family. I was thrilled with the prospect of having children.

I wanted to find a "queen," as we called NOI sisters. I wanted the normal family life that I noticed while selling the *Muhammad Speaks* newspaper.

I remember a home in Springfield, Ohio, vividly. I knocked on a door to sell a newspaper; a woman in her late twenties answered and welcomed me in. As she went to look for change to buy the paper, her two daughters, a couple of years apart in age, smiled warmly as they sat at the kitchen table doing homework. I longed to have a family like this family.

My inner voice said, "Just get a family like the one you saw in Springfield even if she is not in the NOI." This impulse was just that: an impulse. I had seen non-NOI women married to members. The marriages were not happy.

I realized quite early as a new NOI member that I would need to balance the practical aspects that the NOI made possible with a theology that felt like a cult. The NOI's teachings on family life unsettled me as well.

Women were discouraged from working outside the home. Some male members of the NOI, known as the Fruit of Islam (FOI) were suspicious of strong-willed women and smart women. I remember hearing brothers say, "Man, I just want a baby maker. I don't want to lock horns with some sister after a hard day of work."

Nevertheless, even with these derivatives, I was determined to cope with the NOI theology as much as possible.

I felt reassured when the NOI promoted the practical aspects. The aspiration for land, independent schools, and businesses could solve the puzzle of a nation within a nation.

In spite of the strange doctrine, the NOI experienced significant growth between 1968 and 1972. The *Muhammad Speaks* newspaper listed the occurrence of new mosques, and each mosque was given a sequential number. I watched the numbers increase. It became my litmus test that more black Americans were joining the NOI.

The mosque numbering system gave me hope that the NOI's economic development was responsible for the growth. I hoped that the increase in the number of mosques underscored new members joining because of practical concerns. I hoped that NOI growth did not occur because black folk believed the bizarre theology and doomsday predictions. The NOI's theology predicted that America would suffer dreadful events from the man-god WD Fard and his scientist aboard the mother ship. Most new members only learned this theology after joining.

I was discouraged each time Elijah's predictions failed. WD Fard did not lash America with calamities for her evil treatment of black folk. When Elijah's predictions failed, it made selling the *Muhammad Speaks* newspaper harder.

It also increased my doubts about the NOI's longevity. The failed predictions, in addition, gave ammunition to a growing number of NOI opponents.

I lamented secretly that if Elijah's theology had just stuck to well-known explanations predicting the rise and fall of nations, there would be plenty of evidence to support the demise of white America.

There was no need for wild claims of calamities of punishments from WD Fard and squadrons of mother ships dive-bombing America with weapons of mass destruction.

Most new members initially believed the NOI's apocalyptic predictions. Nearly three hundred years of slavery made it easier to swallow. After years of failed predictions, many of us just hung on because "Nation Time" offered practical answers to old problems.

Slavery's legacy was ample ammunition to advance esoteric claims.

Failed predictions, notwithstanding, I was sick of seeing the desperation in black people's eyes, yearning for a meaningful life, free from getting high or falling drunk, like my father and his friends. I believed a meaningful life in America started and ended with a strong economic and moral foundation. The NOI came closer to providing economic and moral stability than other black organizations.

The NOI's foundation was built on self-reliance and a moral code devoid of alcohol, drugs, gambling, and promiscuity. NOI culture of not toying around with women as sex objects or as pastime fun was one of the most redemptive aspects of the NOI culture.

The NOI's clean environment sensitized me to hate the sour smell of tobacco and alcohol that settled on clothes. These repugnant smells reminded me of the deep pain I felt watching my father and his friends commit chemical suicide. It also reminded me of the anguish I experienced during the traumatic years I experimented with marijuana. Reflecting on these painful memories helped me to endure the bizarre NOI theology.

THE QUOTA

The *Muhammad Speaks* newspaper was a powerful driver of the Nation of Islam's revenue engine and the voice of Elijah Muhammad. The captains, lieutenants, and squad leaders in every mosque would organize the Fruit of Islam (FOI) to sell the newspaper. The financial incentive for FOI individuals was only a token, but it was significant for the local mosque. The message from mosque leaders was clear. The FOI belonged on the streets selling the paper. The reputation and careers of the big-shot mosque leaders, particularly in the large cities, rose and fell on paper sale quotas. Mosques that ordered and sold more than five thousand papers a week received notoriety and respect. The pressure to reach the quota affected everyone. Revenue from newspaper sales, leveraged wisely, bought NOI farmland in the South. It also kept the NOI's top ministers and captains living the NOI mantra, "Money, Good Homes, and Friendships in all walks of life."[67]

In Cincinnati, Minister David X and his wife, Sister Aldena X, were both lawyers. They inspired loyalty from practically every member of Mosque No. 5. Minister David was a man of extraordinary intellect and personal ambition. He struggled, however, with the strong demons of gluttony, shiny cars, and shapely women.

His law practice in the early 1970s commanded respect, even in conservative and racially divided Cincinnati. His clients, mostly black, ran the gambit from commercial to criminal.

At six foot four inches tall, he had a leader's stature. His brisk gait through the halls of the main courthouse, usually followed by at least two or three of us keeping pace a few respectful steps behind, caused onlookers to stop and stare.

Minister David used to mount the podium at the NOI mosque with the confidence of a captain of a battleship, bringing the FOI on security duty to attention. "Salaam Alaykum, brothers and sisters," he said smiling with assurance, and the chorus of the faithful replying "Wa Alaykum Salaam" was earnest and personal. In those early days of his ministerial reign, 1968 to about the middle of 1971, he inspired love more than fear. His tone usually signaled if the lecture was going to be esoteric or down-to-earth. He was no howling preacher. He read widely and could lace up a potent argument even if the subject were the mother ship. He could, just as easily, unravel and trample the compromised logic of a so-called responsible black leader and send him plummeting from a tightrope he walked when he argued for integration in white America. We were happy to share his awe and his power.

Here we were, seven of us, now calling our spiritual home a small converted clothing store at 101 East University Avenue in Cincinnati, our Mosque No. 5. The angular gray brick building sat on the corner of the street in a predominantly black neighborhood two blocks from the midtown Clifton Area Business District and the main campus of the University of Cincinnati. Six of us from our group of seven had dropped out of Central State and Antioch College to join the NOI.

The *Muhammad Speaks* newspaper was not limited to making money. The paper promoted a strategy. Some sections featured a biting critique of the war in Vietnam. Other sections lampooned black establishment leaders and integration. The newspaper painted a picture of NOI economic self-reliance and also featured testimonials from individuals. These accounts chronicled how NOI's teachings woke up black people from a racist-induced slumber. It lauded how the NOI assisted black folks to reject a degrading Stepin Fetchit image of a lazy Negro.

The paper's depiction of a prodigious NOI work ethic lay to rest images of a shiftless and lazy black man.

The paper critiqued the FBI's reaction to Black Power. The paper exposed FBI claims that black agitation for justice constituted threats to national security. The US government and the majority of America's white press typically demonized black ideology as violent extremism. Even today the ripple effect of the Black Power movement's social protest language informs mass-movement resistance tactics across the globe. I believe that during the so-called Arab Spring, calls for a Million Man March was indisputable as a reference to Minister Farrakhan's Million Man March of 1995.

Muhammad Speaks also gave credit, sparingly, to how civil rights tactics and Black Power demands helped to dismantle some of the most persistent and vicious remnants of slavery and Jim Crow in America. Articles explained why American hegemony was failing across the world. The paper also pointed out how America tried to disrupt African liberation movements.

The nationwide circulation of *Muhammad Speaks* pressured civil rights organizations. The articles described how demands by black establishment leaders for assimilation into "a burning house" had deep-seated cultural and emotional roots in white supremacy. NOI ministers often made an analogy of this psychology. The minister would say black folk saw the world through the eyes of white folks. The dependency was so bad that if the slave master sneezed the slave would ask, "Massa, is we sick?"

The paper consistently pointed out how racism stopped blacks from making advances beyond socially and politically prescribed boundaries.

A rejection that the FBI dealt violently with black organizations belies facts. The paper ran articles in the late 1960s that suggested it was the FBI's manipulation of the Black Panthers and Ron Karenga's group US that led to deadly violence.[68]

The intergroup violence of the Black Panthers and US was a mere dress rehearsal for what took place in the late 1980s. During the 1980s black communities were drowning in gang violence fueled by a crack-cocaine epidemic—even though much of it could have been prevented if there were a political will to do so. As early as 1972, *Muhammad Speaks* predicted gang violence and attempts to dilute nationwide black unity were contrived. The NOI and other black groups warned that genocidal campaigns would emerge to keep black folk mentally and culturally enslaved. These stories appeared in *Muhammad Speaks* long before the Crips and Bloods made national news headlines in the late 1980s.

Muhammad Speaks writers lamented that the destruction of black communities was not a priority for black establishment leaders.

The problems that plagued the black community, from drugs to gangs, were well known. Establishment black politicians and the black church were unable or unwilling to reverse these trends.

On the other hand, the NOI kept the message simple: "Stop fighting with white folks over their world and separate from them." Make your own. Be a nation. This philosophy set the NOI apart from other black organizations. NOI language defined a framework that announced we know who we are and, thus, we rely on ourselves.

Elijah Muhammad knew that a particular language could control narrative and behavior. His logic shaped everything from "do for self" to watching the skies for mother planes.

The NOI's process of developing a mental narrative (the internal self-talk) started when one joined. As any toddler knows, imitation supports survival.

Imitation was standard in NOI language construction. Adherence to the dictates of the NOI language secured belonging.

It was important to embrace the NOI language, verbatim if possible. Learning the language meant learning the culture, which in turn secured NOI members. However, the language also prevented critical thinking about the organization's absurd doctrine of mother ships and ancient black scientists who created the white race. Yes, you heard me right. A rebellious but brilliant, ancient black scientist, Yacub, created the white race, according to Elijah Muhammad. This theory is presented in a lessons-based publication called "The Supreme Wisdom."[69]

Many NOI believers would spend hours searching the sky, looking for the mother ship carrying the Holy Scientist that Elijah Muhammad said ruled the universe. I never disputed these bizarre myths publically. I also looked at the sky, on occasion, just in case.

I knew, as did many of my FOI brothers, that the NOI's esoteric mythology was manufactured for the organization's membership in the 1940s and 1950s. The Yacub narrative held sway from the late 1940s until the death of Elijah Muhammad in 1974. Only a few felt comfortable enough to question or dispute claims that Mr. Yacub, a rebellious black outcast scientist, made white folks.

The Yacub story claimed that he had an enormously large head. He created Caucasians on a remote Greek Island six thousand years ago. We were told he used large pins to prick the heads of his laboratory subjects to create a faded race. Somehow he made permutations of the original black man into brown, and then so-called yellow (Asian), and finally to an exhausted colorless entity, the white race.

The Yacub story was so bizarre it was easy to say, "Come on now, this has to have some truth in it. Who could make up stuff like this anyway?"

The NOI appeal rested on the enormous pain of slavery. Only devils could have created something as horrifying as the slave trade. White civilization perpetrated unspeakable crimes like Native American genocide, the rape of black women, and the creation of house niggers and field niggers. The NOI used these facts as circumstantial evidence to support the "White Man as Devil" theology. It was a simplistic argument laced with reductionist reasoning.

Nevertheless this, too, eventually taught me to honor my instincts and never abandon critical thinking in the face of peer pressure, regardless of past evils.

I wore a NOI uniform, learned NOI military drills, and marched in the Fruit of Islam gatherings even as I wrestled with the mythology.

As a result of his demand for complete robot-like loyalty, Minister David X demanded absolute obedience from sunrise to sunset. Mosque No. 5 digressed into a cult. The climate was paranoid, and spying on friends and relatives occurred often. It reminded me of Mao's Cultural Revolution. Almost everyone was on alert to catch hypocrites and sellouts. Minister David X encouraged informing on suspect behavior as a loyalty litmus test. It measured how well we conformed. It worked. Purges occurred at least once a year.

One time, a few of us ate at KFC without his permission. Yes, you heard me, Kentucky Fried Chicken.

I laugh now, but it wasn't so funny then when something as trivial as eating outside of the straightjacket menu was prohibited.

After we had got back to the mosque, we tried to conceal our fried-chicken breath. We were exposed. Minister David made us take the chicken back to KFC.

We walked into KFC wearing our Fruit of Islam uniforms and I shouted, "Hey, there is a white woman's hair in this chicken. I want my money back!" The server dropped the broom she held and ran to the rear of the store to tell the manager. She returned pale-faced. Her hand trembled as she returned my money. Kenneth X nearly spoiled the ruse by laughing loudly. We all laughed afterward. Nevertheless, when we returned to the mosque, Minister David X gave us a tongue-lashing.

Many NOI members from other mosques called us robots. They were right. We were cultish and we would not hesitate to threaten: "Brother, I am about to report you to Brother Captain or the Lieutenants." In some cases the threat was to Minister David X. Some of the infractions were ridiculous.

We understood that when Minister David X shaved off his hair, we should cut our hair. Minister David's leadership also isolated us from a mainstream NOI lifestyle with the exception of selling *Muhammad Speaks*. Many NOI programs were discouraged. If you tried to open a business, Minister David X's loyalists suspected rebellion. "Did Brother Minister approve this business?" was the first questioned asked. If Minister David thought a business became financially well off, he suspected disloyalty.

Minister David X Bradley became David Pasha in late 1970. Elijah Muhammad gave names to his best and most loyal ministers. After the name change, he started to imitate big-city ministers from places like Philadelphia, New York, and Los Angeles. Before the name change, he drove a Volkswagen Beetle proudly. Soon after the name change, he bought several Mercedes-Benz cars. He had two houses. He ate excessively. As Minister David's appetites grew, we spent longer hours on the streets selling back issues of *Muhammad Speaks*. We contributed several thousand dollars weekly.

It was not long before he weighed close to three hundred pounds. The rumor spread he impregnated two of his secretaries. Both women were married to men loyal to him. His alleged promiscuity turned loyalty into disgust for many of his most ardent supporters. His cultish leadership made Mosque No. 5 a pariah compared to other NOI mosques. Other mosques followed the norm of supporting NOI businesses and giving financial support to Elijah Muhammad's national initiatives. Many of us wanted a more traditional NOI Mosque secretly.

This status would have eased my on-going impulse to depart. Nevertheless, the NOI's accomplishments in economics and social reform were enough to compete with other black organizations and keep many of us in the Nation. To me, this should have been sufficient to attract new members. I believe it did bring in new members, those attracted to the promise of nation building.

However, the NOI membership was not as homogenous as it appeared. Many believed entirely in the NOI's doomsday predictions,[70] the Yacub creation story, and a mother ship. They constituted the first type of an NOI old guard membership. Others joined the NOI, in the late 1960s and early 1970s, because it projected a suit-and-tie version of black nationalism. Many believed that the NOI was a disciplined and deliberate organization that could build a black nation.

The first wave of membership type leveled off in the early 1960s. Then membership increased from 1968 to 1973. I reached this conclusion after looking at archived editions of *Muhammad Speaks*. Disillusioned ex-revolutionaries joined the NOI in the hundreds if not thousands. The NOI's response to the change in membership type was subtle. However, there was also resistance to change and any type of challenge to the lack of NOI transparency.

Malcolm X's death was proof of fierce NOI resistance to change. Malcolm X exposed Elijah Muhammad's double standards of private immorality in sharp contrast to the public morality he preached.

Elijah Muhammad preached against sexual contact outside of marriage, but he fathered several children with women who worked for him or served him.[71] Minister Louis Farrakhan has attempted to revise history to justify Elijah Muhammad's children from several other women by claiming Elijah Muhammad married these women. Nothing could be farther from the truth. In authentic Islam, a marriage contract must satisfy conditions: the eligibility of the bride and groom, bride's permission, bride sponsorship, a dowry, and witnesses. [72] Elijah Muhammad's relationship with several of the women he fathered children by did not meet these criteria.

Nonetheless, the NOI's growing popularity filled a void. Black churches and mainstream civil rights organizations failed to address economics. Voting and political accomplishment were insufficient to fix black unemployment, dysfunctional schools, and inadequate housing.

BEAN PIE VOGUE

A few notable black middle-class personalities joined the NOI in the late sixties and early seventies. In 1972 *Times* magazine published a piece about Elijah Muhammad and praised his work. The article focused on how he reformed ex-drug users, dealers, pimps, robbers, thieves, and the hopeless underclass. The article noted how Elijah Muhammad's NOI transformed them into stable, law-abiding, productive, and hard-working black folks.[73]

Times's "discovery" was nothing new to members. Hanging out after mosque meetings or after FOI training drills, we used to trade stories about drug use and promiscuous lifestyles before the Nation cleaned us up. The NOI welcomed the improved image as black middle-class numbers increased. As men and women from the black middle class joined, some NOI norms gained acceptance in African American culture. The bean pie, known before as a strange "Moozlim dish," became an acceptable dessert. The Bean Pie Vogue came of age.

Some of the ministers recognized that the NOI's before and after contrast of a fallen black man or black woman held less appeal to the black middle class. Instead of using the redemption theme, some NOI ministers used the "how black are you" theme to encourage black middle-class visitors to join.

Kenneth X "Jabo" Robertson, who died of cancer in his early forties, argued that white America's family values were more prevalent in the NOI than elsewhere in black America. To Kenneth, a morally upright black man posed more of a threat to white folks than a thug with a pistol. I remember hearing an NOI minister say that the most dangerous black man on the streets was one with a valid library card.

The NOI narrative claimed that a disciplined, morally upright, and conscious black man or woman challenged the white man's tricknology. Tricknology was a NOI term for all types of white folks' deception.

NOI values were essentially the same as Ronald Reagan's family values. Kenneth believed white America was troubled with how the NOI derived these values. The NOI rejected integration and assimilation. Kenneth X said NOI members were sober, hard-working, industrious black folk and modeled responsible citizenship. White America, Kenneth claimed, wanted black people to embrace these values as long as the intent was imitating white people.

He argued that the NOI values were based on a black separatist ideology. Family values from this perspective scared white folks. He asserted white people viewed black family values of this type as militant and dangerous.

Kenneth was a glib, quick-witted, and critical thinker even though he believed in NOI theology completely. His arguments stung opponents like a skilled boxer's stiff jab. I am sure he could have excelled in math or law.

Sometimes when we were out on the corners selling papers, Kenneth would bait an NOI critic into an argument. His eyes would sparkle with delight when a Christian minister or pompous black professional got in his crosshairs. He would feign vulnerability while encouraging opponents to speak their minds. When they did, he would shoot from both barrels of his logic shotgun. The result was a chilling verbal beatdown. His whippings were intense. I loved to watch the expression on his victims' faces when it dawned on them they were outmatched. Most of them would fidget and look to escape. Some just stood there, head still and eyes fixed on a spot on the sidewalk.

Often I would see him whipping someone and I would say, "Come on, Brother Kenneth, let this Lazarus go, and let's get back to selling." He would usually smile and agree.

His love for shapely women was legendary. His prolonged expressive stare at a "thick sister" was like a hypnotic spell.

We would tease him about it. "Brother Kenneth," I'd say, "stop looking at these dead world women like they were a piece of fried chicken." He would then move his head, shaking it from side to side as if he was waking up from a trance. We both would laugh.

Woman-gazing became an inappropriate and pathetic diversion. Looking back, I believed it may have saved some of us from immoral excesses far worse.

We mastered sizing up women as potential converts. Each of us carried a small notebook to record the names of "fish," a potential convert. This term, based on the Biblical idea of fishing for the souls of men, gave us an excuse to proselytize females.

Most of the time, they were not interested in why the white man was the devil or details about the mother ship. Whenever we did manage to bring a female to the mosque, we would daydream about her conversion.

STANDING POST

At Mosque No. 5, selling papers was the first and only priority. Minister David X promised to get us off the corners and give us jobs running one of the businesses he was always on the verge of starting. However at Mosque #5, the great promise of nation building and doing-for-self lapsed into indentured servitude. Minister David X's message to us was, "Get out there and crack!" In other words, sell more copies of *Muhammad Speaks*.

I remember how Greg X, my homeboy from Yellow Springs, kept all of us sane by satirizing our penniless and nearly hopeless desperation. In a loud voice, he would repeat, "No test, no blessings." By then we were all at least smiling if not laughing. He would stare at the sky and cry out, "Test me! Test me! Test me!" All of us would laugh. It calmed us. He gave us hope to hold on.

We were required to sell between three hundred and one thousand copies of *Muhammad Speaks* per week and turn in all the money. The cash made its way to Minister David's house promptly.

By 1971 paper revenue from Mosque No. 5 was several thousand per month. The discounted cost of back issues of *Muhammad Speaks* was 80 percent. Minister David purchased several thousand copies of back issue papers. It was a no-brainer from a business perspective. Labor cost was near zero and expenses were minimal. After of few months of daily selling in downtown Cincinnati, we started to sell in other cities. A paper squad could travel a couple hundred miles to sell. Our customer market was 90 percent white. We used a sales pitch focused on building a NOI hospital or a NOI school. Many whites were sympathetic to our plea. Many donated an amount above the retail price of the paper. The few that did read the paper were typically upset with the content.

The mosque would purchase a few bundles of the current edition for the brothers who sold thirty to fifty papers per week. Most of these brothers were jobholders. Minister David X and his hard-core FOI held them in a lower soldier status. Usually these brothers had wives and children. If there had been a life satisfaction survey for us, perhaps, eight out of ten of the job holders would have scored higher than the full-time paper sellers.

Kenneth X was a lieutenant in Mosque No. 5 in the early 1970s. He was expected to inspire his paper squad to reach the paper quota. Many times, especially in cold weather, we looked for excuses to remain indoors. He gave us pep talks. The talks came every time we were depressed or close to passive rebellion. He would often say, "Brother Minister is about to open some businesses and make all of his main soldiers managers. Brothers, when that happens, we can get those queens and have those babies for the Nation."

I used to try to ignore the pep talks, thinking, "Yeah, right, I'd mumble to myself. That's a bunch of bull." Sometimes I would nod in approval, or at least look like I agreed. My mental disdain grew louder. I feared others would see it.

"Kenneth," my inner voice said. "Brother Minister David is only interested in keeping the money to buy another Benz."

As for us, we slept on the tables in the mosque or on the floor in an apartment. Over two years we moved, usually from an eviction, at least four times between Cincinnati, Dayton, and Louisville.

Paper selling was perpetual servitude. The typical NOI existence that was present in other mosques, as well as common events in the dead world, disappeared. I was unaware of Vietnam War details. I was asleep to the FBI's COINTELPRO assaults on black organizations. I had no clue about changes in black music and black hairstyles. We did not watch the NBA, NFL, or even boxing unless Muhammad Ali was fighting.

Elijah Muhammad's book *How To Eat To Live* dictated meals.[74] Sunflower seeds replaced peanuts as snacks and NOI navy bean soup was a main dish. The NOI custard-styled bean pie was like a holiday treat. Food became a big deal.

The first time Minister David gained weight, he started eating one meal every three days. We followed suit.

I did not look healthy weighing only 148 pounds at nearly six feet tall. I did not sleep well at times because I was hungry.

In my first year at Central State, I used to experience similar late-night hunger, but for good reason. The campus was located in a rural area without late night food outlets. The NOI hunger was shameful and unnecessary. For the first time in my life, I experienced hunger like people in many developing nations.

NOI members were promised "money, good homes, and friendships in all walks of life" if they remained faithful to the teachings. The theological teachings held little motivation for me. Often I was too hungry to care. I was tired of the hype and I wanted to escape. I also resented the fact that the older NOI members were not forced to sell as many papers.

I also felt that old school NOI members were too ahistorical and too apolitical. They were not on the streets twelve hours a day, seven days a week, selling papers. For my taste, in addition, most of them were too pedestrian to understand big-picture nation-building.

A good part of my negative evaluation came from stereotypes. Some of them wore stingy brim Stetson hats and Stacy Adam wing tips. This image was too hustler-like for me. At times, I admit, I was dead wrong about some individuals. I also thought many of the early followers were unaware of the damage caused by the Hollywood movie industry that created black exploitation movies, like the movie *Super Fly*.

I was convinced this movie helped kick-start the exodus from black activism to street hustling. The film glorified "getting one over on whitey" as selling drugs to black folks.

Curtis Mayfield's musical score in the movie *Freddie is Dead* was a potent lyrical exposure. The song depicted the descent from black liberation to street hustling as death and humiliation. The movie portrayed the destructive trend of black hustling that replaced black liberation as a rational choice for young black men.

I pondered the issues of nonstop paper selling and my resentment for some old timers because it underscored a reality that the NOI was becoming another dead-end movement.

The reason Minister David did not force older members of Mosque No. 5 to sell as many papers was political. Minister David knew that the old timers would complain to NOI National Headquarters. Rumors had reached NOI National Headquarters in Chicago that Minister David was hard and harsh with Elijah Muhammad's followers. We were not Minister David X's followers. We joined the NOI to follow Elijah Muhammad.

NOI converts from the fifties and early sixties were the foundation of Mosque No. 5. Many of them were reformed street hustlers, stick-up men, and short con men. They were firm financial supporters. Some of them had belonged formerly to Marcus Garvey's United Negro Improvement Association (UNIA). They held little hope or stock in integration or having jobs in white companies. They believed in doing for self. They were the forerunners and the creators of the sidewalk businesses now common in most cities with sizable African American populations. Some of the early converts, like Captain Willard from Indianapolis, built up significant businesses in cosmetic jewelry and clothing.

Captain Willard was an earring king. He sold earrings and made portable earring cases from fastened-together plywood. A screen door handle fastened the top of the case with a hook latch to hold the doors shut. He used two or three pieces of velvet to cover the inside of the case.

Captain Willard ordered wholesale merchandise from Chicago's Old Town jewelry warehouses or from New York's Seventh Avenue merchants. He was in his mid-fifties in 1975 when Elijah Muhammad died. He often wore a black or brown knit sports suit atop spit-shined Stacy Adam tie-ups. He also donned an oversized bow tie on a white dress shirt.

Captain Willard mastered one of the martial arts and was fit and agile for his age. Quick-witted but inarticulate, he strung together stories and anecdote's on the fly to make a point. The combination of these opposite qualities may seem contradictory on the surface. Nonetheless, many unlettered men from his time were brilliant thinkers and formidable action-takers, and yet they lacked formal training in speaking and writing. He was a natural story-teller and a funny one. None of us was ever hurt when he directed his humor our way. Seasoned for years in FOI culture, he understood not to come off as mean or hurtful. He belonged to the era of messianic followers before Black Nationalists joined the NOI. His focus, and that of many like him, was on black economic progress.

You did not find these pioneers wasting time decrying the evils of the white man, and they were not interested in the armed struggle to liberate the masses. I secretly envied the old timers for the security they found in a rigid and absolute belief in NOI doctrine. Many of them were psychologically secure as devoted followers.

I remember watching the awestruck expression on their faces. I'd ask myself, "How do I get there?" It puzzled me.

However, a few old school members half-heartedly believed in the NOI's theology, and like me they were more interested in nation building.

Nonetheless, many of them from this era watched the skies for the mother ship.

Brother Brozier, another Mosque No. 5 FOI captain, thought he saw the mother ship during a drive from Cincinnati to Chicago to pick up *Muhammad Speaks* newspapers. I conceded that Brother Brozier believed he saw it, although it was hard for me to visualize the ship's existence.

Brozier wore a black stingy brim hat and a thin black tie that fitted tightly around his neck. He fidgeted with his necktie when he addressed the FOI. He wore patent leather shoes and his black trench coat reached just below his thighs. The quarter length coat exposed his slacks made shiny from too much dry cleaning. He sweated heavily, even in cold weather. He would wipe the sweat away briskly as he put fresh cloves in his mouth because he was self-conscious about bad breath.

Brother Brozier was a straight talker and a literal believer in the fall of America. He believed Elijah Muhammad's true followers would escape divine wrath.

The NOI's inexplicable theology of divine protection by mother ships did not stop FBI wiretaps or infiltration by spies and informants. Mainstream media depicted the NOI as a dangerous public enemy. For many it was an organization on the verge of violence or a race war.

The NOI's existence underscores the fact that a substantial number of black folk felt hobbled by the economic and social conditions in America. The pain and frustration penetrated so deeply that even a strange esoteric theology would not prevent black folk from joining the NOI.

The NOI also challenged the strategy that nonviolent sacrifices could change the moral conscience of white America. The NOI's approach was separation instead of trying to amend the hearts of white people.

The existence of the NOI, even now, is a challenge for both black folks and white folks in so-called postracial America.

President Obama represents an achievement of postracial progress for many liberals and a few conservatives. President Obama should be proof of postracial color blindness. Sadly, he is not.

However, for others, Louis Farrakhan's appeal for a separate nation of black people is popular. They both share space in so-called postracial America.

The fact that many blacks believe the NOI is necessary to combat racism in spite of the fact that the president of the United States is an African American underscores a weakness of the postracial claim.

The NOI staged a Million Man March in October 1995. It was a wake-up call for the black middle-class establishment and for mainstream America. The march proclaimed boldly that black men were not just seen on the evening news in handcuffs. The march announced that the NOI was still a force in black communities. It implied that one million black men were willing to listen to Louis Farrakhan.

It is worth noting that a good number of black politicians attended the Million Man March, including Senator Barack Obama. Some offered a disclaimer that "I don't always agree with Minister Farrakhan, but the One Million Man March is right for America." Farrakhan's renewed NOI articulated an agenda to combat gangs and HIV and to strengthen the black family resonated with many.

It was impossible to imagine Farrakhan's Million Man March as I warmed my cold fingers and numb toes while selling *Muhammad Speaks* in the early 1970s. I heard the words on the radio, "Elijah Muhammad died today," and I knew that change was near. His death occurred one day before the NOI's annual Saviours' Day Convention. It was February 25, 1975.

Like many messianic figures before him, Elijah Muhammad's time came and went. I was not distraught over Elijah Muhammad's death. I searched my feelings about the era that had come to an end. I respected Elijah Muhammad a great deal but to move forward, I wanted to wait and see what lay ahead for the NOI. Some of the NOI's leaders seemed shaken. Some felt off balanced because of losing a man they loved. Others, I suspect, were unnerved because they were afraid to lose power and income. Mosque No. 5 members drove to Cleveland to watch the Saviours' Day celebration on a video feed from Chicago. I could hear the chant "Long Live Muhammad" before I entered the hall. The next edition of *Muhammad Speaks* read "HE Lives." The headline mirrored a belief that Elijah Muhammad would never die.

The NOI's street corner "scientists" started to promulgate myths that Elijah was not dead. They said one of his doubles died instead. Elijah's whereabouts, the scientists claimed, could not be revealed.

The NOI's prominent national ministers were among some of the chief scientists. Some wore smug, confident smiles as insiders of the secret. Minister Farrakhan wept at Elijah's death. WD Muhammad, Elijah Muhammad's son and a new leader of the NOI, publically and directly chided Minister Farrakhan for crying. Most of us did not understand why WD publically admonished Minister Farrakhan until years later. I assume WD critiqued Minister Farrakhan because lamenting death shows discontentment with Allah's (God's) decree.

Minister Farrakhan did not understand he was violating a core principle of the creed of Islam. None of us did.

In those years, most Americans saw Islam as a religion for underclass blacks and a few well-behaved immigrants. In the past, many immigrant Muslims distanced themselves from the black Muslim movement. I suspect some did so because they were racist while others knew the NOI did not represent authentic Islam. Before Malcolm X's departure from the NOI, he tried to fit the NOI within a context of a broader Islamic world community.

Black American Islam did gain some acceptance when Malcolm X left the NOI. Moreover, Malcolm X applied authentic Islam the best he could given the context and circumstances of his life.

Nevertheless, it has to be pointed out that the NOI's impact on America is relevant. I do not endorse Elijah Muhammad's distortions of Islam, as do many Muslims in America and abroad.

As Taylor Branch points out, the NOI's iconic figures like Malcolm X and Muhammad Ali were able to build potentially game-changing alliances with Dr. King.[75] The alliances were fragile, but they also frightened the FBI. The FBI's Chicago office cautioned FBI Director Hoover from trying to embarrass Dr. King's association with Muhammad Ali. The Chicago office was concerned "it might backfire because Muhammad Ali was considered widely 'a black folk hero.'"[76]

I thought that some of the so-called middle-class celebrities like Dr. Naim Akbar, Sonia Sanchez, and Joe Tex would help the NOI build a broader base of support among middle-class blacks. I was quick to mention these names in a bid to raise the NOI's status. I had this in mind one evening, shivering from the cold with a runny nose. I was selling *Muhammad Speaks* on a street corner in Dayton, Ohio when I noticed a light-brown-skinned woman. Something about her appearance stunned me. I wanted to tell her that the NOI had well-known black professionals.

She was probably in her late twenties to mid-thirties. She saw me looking at her and she walked directly toward me, opened her purse, and handed me a tissue. "Wipe your nose, brother," she said. "I don't care to read the paper."

Then she paused with a warm half-smile and said softly, with a deliberate kindness in her voice, "Have a nice evening."

She disappeared into the crowd. I tried to picture her light-brown face and how her walnut-colored hair peeped out from under her gray knit hat. Her hazel eyes haunted me for years. Meeting her was no mystical event. It was a lesson I would be happy to learn. My encounter with her helped me forget cold weather for the remainder of the evening. With the death of Elijah Muhammad and the ascendancy of WD Muhammad, many NOI members sensed the organization stood at the threshold of a new day.

MAN MEANS MIND

I thought about my encounter with this affable woman as I walked home one night from the University. Ten years had passed since I saw her. My walk home that night coincided with the date my father died one year earlier. His death still lingered over my feelings.

When my grandmother did not hear from him for a couple of days, she went to his house, the house where I grew up. She could not bring herself to use her key to enter. She returned home and called the chief of police, a family friend. He picked up the key, went to the house, and discovered my father's body. He had been dead for several days. He suffered massive heart failure at sixty-nine years old. For years, I believed that my father resented me for joining the NOI. I knew he was initially uncomfortable with my membership.

At the funeral Eddy, a longtime resident of Yellow Springs and was like a son to my father, said to me, "Well, Hawk, at least you and him will eventually be together." Dad had hired Eddy as a shoe repair helper in his teens and Eddy had been close to my father for years.

I turned to him and said, "What do you mean? Why do you say that?"

He said, "Hawk, all your father talked about was Islam. He regularly talked that Muslim stuff." He said he was Muslim, like his son. Eddy said my dad was pleased that I left the NOI and had adopted authentic Islam.

I have not been able to verify Eddy's claim that my father was Muslim, but I pray Allah (God) accepts my father's declaration.

I lived in Indianapolis when my father died. I moved to Indianapolis late in 1977 to work for a property management company. I left the company after a year when it defaulted. I decided to stay in Indianapolis and found a job as a technician at an Indianapolis steel mill.

The job was hot, dirty, and dangerous. To say I hated working there is an understatement. However, working at this job for almost a year and a half inspired me to rethink my life. I knew being stuck in a job that I hated stifled my potential. The job was an open invitation to live the blues, maybe even drink the blues. I knew that dark place too well.

I decided to leave Indianapolis and return to Cincinnati after my father's death. These memories felt like scenery as I thought about the woman with the light-brown hair and hazel eyes. The dull twenty-minute walk passed quickly. I recalled how her quiet beauty hid behind a librarian persona. I also reflected on how she reached into her purse for a tissue and said, "Wipe your nose, brother. I don't care to read the paper. Have a nice evening." Then she was gone.

The memory endured for ten years. Events had come full circle.

It was clear what my encounter meant as I walked home that night. Her presence foretold of hope that better days lie ahead. She was more than an attractive woman. She inspired optimism. My NOI straightjacket would not remain on forever. All I needed to do was to wipe away the painful memories, like wiping a runny nose. I took her advice. I found the courage to examine old NOI-day fears as WD Muhammad led the former NOI on a new course. The new direction took me away from the mythological voyage of a separatist nation.

WD Muhammad wanted to plot a course and build a Muslim community, not an organization or movement. WD used the weekly newspaper to communicate his vision. He renamed the *Muhammad Speaks* newspaper *Bilalian News*. The name Bilalian comes from Bilal Ibn Rabah, one of the companions of Prophet Muhammad (prayers and salutations upon him). Bilal was an Ethiopian living in Mecca, Arabia, before the advent of Islam. He was a slave and was abused by his owner. When Bilal reverted to Islam, he became the one who made the call to prayer.

Revenue from the *Bilalian News* was less significant to WD Muhammad than *Muhammad Speaks* revenue was to his father. WD's leadership put an end to the long days and nights of paper selling. Imam Warith Deen Muhammad ended paper selling slavery. Members were free to pursue any path. Many started college or returned to finish a degree. Choosing a pathway was challenging. Many still held onto the shadows of NOI myth and intrigue. We did not know or understand authentic Islam. We now had to make personal choices in every aspect of our life, both large and small. It scared many.

Slowly, practically every mosque—now called "masjids"—struggled to build rules for how much of the world to allow in. Masjids also struggled with how much authentic Islam would take root. WD Muhammad faced the possibility of losing the entire community to a larger "Orthodox Islam" that now held appeal to many. Another possibility WD faced was members would not relinquish the past. However, WD Muhammad planned the changes incrementally.

He encouraged his followers to attend biannual collective prayers after Ramadan. Several hundred made the hajj (the pilgrimage to Mecca) with other groups of Muslims in 1976. We replaced white shirts and bowties with ankle-length shirts called "thobes." We covered bald heads with hair at any length we wanted. Everything changed. My realities were better but still challenging. I struggled to make a personal and religious transition. It felt like an uphill run to deal with semi-arranged NOI marriage of five years now in a new environment. By 1977, I had a daughter and faced navigating the new terrain as a husband and father. I loved my wife and daughter yet the challenges that loomed head frightened me.

Reform and Resistance:
Here We Go Again

By 1977–78 many masjids in WD's communities were suffering from moral and ideological issues. WD displayed the American flag prominently alongside the World Community of Al Islam's flag.

The new flag of WD's community was an image of an open Quran superimposed on a map of the world. Imam WD Muhammad had been a leader of the defunct NOI community for three years in 1978. I believe that he understood the scope and the type of issues that supported reform and resisted reform. One of his challenges was to hold the community together and, at the same time, dismantle un-Islamic aspects carried over from the NOI's misguided past.

Some of WD Muhammad's controversial reform initiatives came from a couple of conspicuous positions. One position advanced a view that some aspects of the American Constitution agreed with fundamental Islamic principles. Hard line revisionists saw this as a pure sellout.

The other position advanced a vision that the former NOI community should take on an international presence as a new community, as the new flag symbolized. Other critics viewed the later position as abandoning the American black community.

I believe that WD Muhammad tried to end the NOI cold war waged against the world of whites, various segments of the black middle class, and the American government. Many of these moves were good attempts to institute reforms that could build community capacity. However, some of his attempted reforms played into the hands of those who held on to old NOI thinking and sentiments as he tried to reconcile his followers with America's popular culture.

I believe WD Muhammad realized that if he removed the old NOI cultural norms too quickly his fragile new community would fracture. He needed to dismantle NOI mythology and, at the same time, craft a new messianic language of his own that would guarantee loyalty to his "brand" and his vision.

Brand is to know without thinking. Brand is what every marketing expert drools over. It is what every political hack lobbies for. Most of the time brand creation is invisible. In the end, brand connects us to something we feel.

I believe WD Muhammad employed leadership lessons of organizational control from his father; WD Muhammad understood that language shapes the spiritual and mental framework in African American religious communities. Language directs behavior. Language informs branding.

The statement "Man Means Mind" shaped WD Muhammad's direction to crafting his brand and religious-based ideology. His branding message underscored his belief in the status of the intellect. I watched WD Muhammad's brand of "Man Means Mind" initially increase. Within a couple of years, however, it declined sharply.

I dared myself to connect the dots. I believed WD's statement of "Man Means Mind" placed the intellect on the same footing with the Quran and authentic hadith. [77]

His language resembled nineteenth-century rationalism and neohumanism's rejection of Bible dogma. It struck me that his declaration mimicked the ideas of Descartes and Rousseau. In the so-called Period of Enlightenment in Europe, rationalism flourished and replaced religious fundamentalism.[78]

WD's rationalism advocated that the intellect should take precedence over practically every facet of the new community, including matters of the creed in mainstream Islam. WD's rationalism erected spiritual roadblocks.

I feel this language discouraged some followers from seeking to understand authentic Islam. I also believe he did not set these forces in motion to build a cult. I think his intention was to serve Islam, but from a distinctly African American vantage point. His new language caused some of his followers to question their loyalty.

They had to choose the community or the religion. His narrative advanced the intellect as the pinnacle of achievement in community life.

In many ways, he was correct. However, the role of the intellect in Islam does not compete with or replace the fundamentals of creed or methodology. The intellect is creation, not Creator. Allah (God) gave humans a mind as a tool to study, evaluate, and problem solve the challenges that humans face. Perhaps, at the end of the day, this was what WD Muhammad wanted to establish. Nevertheless, previous trends in African American religious institutions and African American culture handicapped his message. Keep in mind, as well, that he was trying as best as he could to prevent mass defections to the old NOI and Allah (God) knows what else.

In Islam, the intellect is not given reign to change core principles of behavior, morality, or even mundane aspects of the religion. In the same way, culture also does not have free reign to change Islam. Some leaders in WD Muhammad's community justified shaping aspects of the Islamic creed and methodology to fit African American culture. Some African American Muslims also reacted to how Arab or South Asian cultural practices had distorted Islam. Both approaches are incorrect.

Some in WD Muhammad's community felt free to reinterpret the Quran and the teachings of Prophet Muhammad (prayers and salutations upon him). They took license from culture and intellect. One of his imams gave an interpretation of a verse in the Quran and he said, "You will not hear this interpretation from Arabs, Indians, or Pakistanis. My understanding comes from the teaching of Imam Warith Deen Muhammad." I shuddered. He was right about not hearing his rendition from classical exegetical rules. Because of his statement, however, one cannot heap all of the blame on Imam Warith Deen Muhammad.

Nevertheless, at the end of the day, WD Muhammad shares blame in the climate that advanced these notions.

By 1980, many of WD's imams said WD had developed a new school of thought (Islamic jurisprudence). His followers did not need to study scholars of century's past. I struggled with dismay, nausea, and anger. "Here we go again," I said. "Just drink it (WD's Kool-Aid) and don't complain."

The statements that WD Muhammad created a new Islamic school of thought reminded me of NOI claims in the past. Some of the history that advanced these claims is linked to esotericism in African American religious traditions. In the case of WD Muhammad's community, the concept of human excellence was paraded boldly. It was consumed widely. The way the concept was presented, I knew there was likely to be a massive exodus from WD's community. One exit led to the old NOI. Many longed for the security of a vertically controlled organization. The other exit led to authentic Islam. I chose the latter.

I did not know authentic Islam, nor did I know how to implement it in my life. I believed then, as I do now, authentic Islam gave me the tools to understand American culture and interact, upon balance and moderation, with life in America and elsewhere.

WD and his imams claimed that his understanding of Islam would produce a "new age man." It would produce a "New Africa." African American Muslims from his community would lead a renaissance.

I believe that this language placed most of WD's followers in a straightjacket similar to the kind Elijah Muhammad fashioned. The difference between the Elijah's straightjacket and WD's branding, I believe, was the intention.

I don't think Imam WD Muhammad wanted blind followers. I think he wanted to dismantle blind following. However, he unintentionally created a new ethos of blind following. His attempts to decentralize and diffuse the old NOI structure produced a path that many adopted as blind followers of rationalism in Islam.

His emphasis on the intellect prevented his community from establishing an authentic Islamic ethos.

The tenet needed, however, should reject the myth of a special imam and special followers. It seemed that the myth of an anointed leader was alive in WD's community.

WD's teaching also departed from some important fundamentals of Islamic community life. I was not happy to see many women in his community compromise Islamic dress requirements that mimicked Western styles. Some women did so by claiming an unprecedented definition of modesty for women in Islam accented by lavish Western dress.

Dancing and mixed social gatherings were encouraged in some of WD Muhammad's communities. I am sure his departure from the Quran and the authentic Sunnah had no malicious intent. Nevertheless, the distinctly African American Muslim emphasis, produced a dangerous license to promote un-Islamic behavior underneath the phrase "the Imam said." I think, as do others, that WD Muhammad believed in authentic Islam. Nonetheless, an African American religious and cultural tradition to claim an anointed spiritual leader and exceptional group identity advanced a form of blind following that is inconsistent with authentic Islam. Because of these developments, a significant number of people left WD Muhammad's community.

The NOI myth of a unique people is as dangerous to people of African descent as is a white supremacy fixation to white people.

Both identities reject that Allah (God) evolved and established the races of man to recognize the oneness of Allah (God). In both instances, a social construction of race remained intact by advancing the myth of either a special people or a supreme people.

Here I was, once again, face to face with religious fiction.

With these notions in place in WD Muhammad's community, important pillars from the authentic Islamic creed had minimal impact on many of WD's followers. Much of this religious fiction lay at the feet of WD's imams. Looking back I appreciate what WD Muhammad did to move his followers away from more than fifty years of esoteric blindness and polytheism.

If WD Muhammad were unable to establish authentic Islam, many of his imams should share the blame. WD Muhammad's role in the reformation of Islam in America demands respect and his effort should not be trivialized.

In his struggle to navigate the transition, he gave many of his prominent imams Arabic names. WD Muhammad also had to deal with the resurgence of Louis Farrakhan. WD changed names, I gather from observation, became an attempt to cement two objectives. One objective aimed to help people like Louis Farrakhan to develop a new identity. WD gave Louis Farrakhan the name to Abdul Halim Farrakhan, "Servant of the Forebearing" and it is one of Allah's attributes. The other objective moved the community toward a cultural identity that left the use of the 'X' as a suffix to the slave name.

Both objectives were well intended to support WD's reforms. Both objectives earned rejection by NOI revisionists. Farrakhan left the Harlem Masjid (Mosque No. 7, established by Malcolm X) for the Chicago Masjid. Several enemies awaited to put him in his place. His detractors felt he should serve WD Muhammad without question, as he served his father.

In Chicago Farrakhan was unable to rock the podium as a rapper. Farrakhan no longer traveled the globe as a dignitary. Many saw WD's transfer of Louis Farrakhan as deliberate humiliation.

Other imams moved as well. Minister Ibrahim Pasha left Chicago for Atlanta. Imam Bashir left Brooklyn for Cincinnati. The change occurred rapidly.

I mentioned these moves to a few others. They also believed that WD Muhammad's community stood at a crossroads. As these changes occurred some revisionist elements pushed back.

Imam Muhammad was candid about opposition from some imams. Several were sacked. A good deal of dissatisfaction grew from WD's promotion of the US Constitution and his pro-American declarations.

WD's display of the American flag in the Chicago Masjid offended many. WD went as far as to hint that the US Constitution's architects were divinely inspired. This assertion also stirred opposition. Many of the pre-1960s NOI members rejected WD's sweeping changes and denounced the reforms as pro-American. Even from our Central State group that joined in the late 1960s, some left WD's community for Minister Farrakhan's renewed NOI.

Some old timers, like Silas Muhammad, and others in the habit of watching the skies for the return of the mothership believed WD was the NOI Antichrist. They believed WD Muhammad was prophesized to destroy Elijah's Nation. They argued that his heretical reforms would set the stage for a true NOI redeemer to return. The new redeemer would rebuild Elijah's NOI. Fard's ideology and mystical theology would be gospel once again. Louis Farrakhan, Silas Muhammad, and others claimed they would set things straight.

Departures continued from WD Muhammad's community. Some who left claimed Imam Muhammad was promoting moral laxity. Some argued that WD advocated immorality in the absence of the old vertical power structure of NOI's Restrictive Laws.

Violation of the NOI's Restrictive Laws placed the offending member in one of two restricted classes. For a misdemeanor like offense, the offending members landed in Class C for thirty to ninety days. For more severe offenses, banishment was imposed. These members were placed in Class F on an indeterminate basis.

Many of WD's followers were no longer just whispering that he was destroying the community. Some insisted he was an interloper. At times these claims produced angry verbal confrontations and, in some instances, these encounters became physical.

Opposition groups believed WD Muhammad was a sellout from the true teachings of Elijah Muhammad. Some believed that WD's reforms promoted fornication, adultery, drug abuse, and marital discord. I also witnessed problems increase as the fear of the NOI's Restrictive Laws declined. The fear of banishment from the community no longer shaped obedience. The tendency toward moral laxity was not because WD promoted moral decay.

WD's removal of NOI's Restrictive Laws exposed a hidden underbelly beneath the facade of a morally upright community. WD Muhammad did not foster corruption. On the contrary, corruption existed in the NOI long before WD Muhammad's reforms.

WD, without question, attempted to embrace authentic Islam as he understood it. However, his struggle during the transition from the NOI to develop his community was challenging. His attempt to navigate a transition from the past created formidable barriers to establishing a new community.

The entrenched culture of the NOI fashioned members to choose community over religion, blind following, and vertical authority. It was a badge of fidelity. Some of the cultural nuances from the NOI carried over to WD Muhammad's community and prevented a lasting impact from some reforms.

WD encouraged individual morality as a choice, not as a stick to whip followers into conformity. He removed threats of the NOI's Restrictive Laws of banishment or beatings. This didn't silence the revisionists. Some of them wanted to return to handing out beatings for Restrictive Law infringement and banishing wayward members. WD's transition to authentic Islam was also resisted because many of his followers experienced racism from Muslims in immigrant communities. Today, many African-American Muslims claim that some immigrant Muslims are racist.

I experienced, as a WD community member and ex-member, blatant and subtle racism from Arabs and South Asians (Indians and Pakistanis).

I remember incidents when Arabs and South Asians spurned us at social gatherings and even at times of worship on purely racial grounds.

These racial and class fractures still persist in many American Muslim communities.

After 9/11 and the rise of Islamophobia, many Arabs, and South Asian Muslim leaders expressed empathy with African American Muslims. They experienced from white people in America what African Americans and African American Muslims had experienced for decades—vicious racism!

Some conceded that their attitudes and behavior before 9/11 toward African American Muslims was unjust, if not racist. Some immigrant Muslims came to this realization when white people openly referred to them as "sand niggers." The aftermath of 9/11 woke them up to a reality of America that many immigrant Muslims denied previously.

The most significant obstacle, however, in reforming the community was Louis Farrakhan. The departure of Louis Farrakhan and his open defiance of WD's authority open a door to the past. The door remains open.

Farrakhan walked away from WD's community in 1977. By 1979, he financed *The Final Call* newspaper. *The Final Call* was a new and improved *Muhammad Speaks*. By 1981, Farrakhan had enough support to reestablish a Saviours' Day meeting in Chicago.

Farrakhan's departure was no mere hiccup, as some critics suggest. Farrakhan's exit from Imam Muhammad became a turning point. His departure caused grave instability in WD's community. His retreat to the old NOI instigated defections to several destinations.

Some members left to join the Naqshabani Sufi movement while others found refuge in organizations like the Islamic Circle of North America (ICNA). Others drifted with no particular affiliation while many others identified with the Quran and Sunnah Society of North America.

These events occurred, in part, to WD's response when Farrakhan revived the old NOI. WD's lack of a strategic response to counter a significant number of defections accelerated the community's decline and exposed its lack of relevance among Muslims in America.

In response, I believe, WD attempted to revive a NOI-styled language with more emphasis on race. However, his rational humanism and Islamic pluralism narratives, under a canopy of interfaith activities, also caused defections. I also believe that WD's discourse about the intellect and reason, along with his language of racial solidarity, caused problems for some of his followers. Also, his decision to pay a surprise visit to Saviours' Day with Farrakhan in 1986 prompted many of his followers to doubt WD's wisdom.

Minister Farrakhan named the theme of the Saviours' Day celebration "A Tribute to the Honorable Elijah Muhammad." The event took place at the University of Illinois at Chicago.

Many believed that the Saviours' Day celebrations held since 1981 demonstrated Farrakhan's rise and his day in the sun. It proved that the NOI was on the rebound while the relevance of WD's community faded. In addition, tensions reappeared when WD Muhammad decentralized the organization's power in Chicago. Some of his family members and other NOI old-timers realized his reforms robbed them of a lifestyle of privilege and money.

Farrakhan's departure also promised to revive the old NOI culture of a royal family. It sought to reestablish a hierarchy of privilege and money for a selected few. Farrakhan's ascendancy brought back garish fashions, flashy jewelry, and high-end luxury cars. The NOI's tendency toward flash and splash always struck me as a pernicious form of decay. Some of its top leadership dressed and behaved as brazen mack-daddy pimps. In many ways, the NOI reflected some of the street slick styles often seen in black churches. The black church cultivates garish-dressing ministers. My father called them pulpit pimps.

I believe that all of these stirrings caused WD's credibility to declined. Many of his followers projected him as a messianic icon like Elijah Muhammad. Some embellished his importance in the broader Muslim community while others inflated his knowledge of Islam. For many of his followers, WD was more than a "mujjadid" (a reviver). Some followers claimed he was the prophesied Mahdi.[79]

The trend in African American freedom movements to look for or create a messianic leader was still present in WD Muhammad's community. His followers' promotion of Imam Muhammad above his status underscored an old pattern in black American religious communities. The trend was to manufacture an anointed leader and a chosen people. WD Muhammad did not start this trend. Nevertheless, he did not do enough to avert it either. I believe that history will show, however, that Imam Muhammad was a not cultist. Neither was WD Muhammad a garish showoff. He had to struggle with his family's love for the old days, and he had to fight with some old guard imams against the gravitational appeal of the NOI. In the end, he had to combat the messianic sentiments of his father's era, but he was unable to overcome some of these elements.

Moreover, he removed NOI polytheism. His followers are believers in Allah (God) and they follow Prophet Muhammad as the final Prophet (prayers and salutations upon him).

I believe WD Muhammad did establish several innovative practices, but his errors should be viewed within a broader context of what he tried to accomplish. The great scholar of Hadith Shaykh Nasir Deen Al Albaanee is reported to have said, "Just because some people fall into innovations, does not mean innovations fall into them."[80]

These shortcomings should not avert positive outcomes in the future. I believe WD Muhammad's community will continue to support and advance authentic Islam in America and elsewhere, Insha'Allah (God willing).

"Education is a passport to the future." Malcolm X

The NOI years gave me mental flash cards that did not affirm or support the fundamentals of authentic Islam. The NOI statement often cited, "My people perish for the lack of knowledge," rang true to describe the injunction "the Imam said." Opinion does not have a sacred precedent over the Book of Allah, the Quran, and authentic statements of Prophet Muhammad (prayers and salutations upon him). I rejected the mantra in WD's community "the Imam said." In some instances, this intonation opposed the creed of Islam and authentic traditions of Prophet Muhammad (prayers and salutation upon him).

I needed to pursue two types of knowledge. I needed knowledge of authentic Islam, and I needed to complete a college degree. I tackled studying authentic Islam on my own as best as I could. I undertook the second knowledge endeavor with determination as well.

I enrolled at the University of Cincinnati (UC). I had earned enough credit hours from my days at Central State to transfer into UC as a sophomore. I paid for tuition and books with a combination of government grants and money I made from selling body oils, earrings, and silver jewelry.

I made good grades. I read broadly. My thirst to learn went beyond required courses. I lived in the library. I sat in the book stacks, reading, studying, or taking notes. I avoided the library's common study areas to side step distractions.

I had lost too much time on street corners selling *Muhammad Speaks* and standing post at night to guard an empty mosque to waste time exploring college life. I had been there and done that. I also realized that college social life was dangerous morally.

After years of living under the NOI Restrictive Laws, I was not confident about my resolve to avoid temptation. I received attention from younger female students. It was flattering, unnerving, and scary.

Most of my classmates were more than ten years younger. I was nearly thirty-three years old. Many students thought I was smart, hardworking, and no-nonsense. I kept my focus on school. I pondered what I'd experienced during the NOI years. I recalled the tough, painful days. These memories strengthened my determination to graduate. I took eighteen to twenty-two credit hours on a quarter system because I didn't want to spend two years as an undergraduate.

When scheduling conflicts arose, I'd take the two required courses at the same time. I would attend the first class for one hour and ease out at the break to attend the second class. The registrar's office did not catch the conflict.

Taking course overloads and enrolling in two classes simultaneously put me ahead by two-quarters.

Some members in WD's Cincinnati Masjid said, "Zaid thinks college is greater than the community. He no longer follows the Imam." They were right. I didn't. I had a mission.

I caught the attention of the head of the Criminal Justice Department when I applied for graduation spring quarter of the first year.

"Zaid," he said. "How did you manage this? We knew you were bright and motivated, but how did you manage to graduate in one academic year?" I told him a half-truth about hard work. I neglected to mention overscheduled class enrollment and taking two classes at the same time.

He encouraged me to apply to the graduate program. He told me that I would likely get a full scholarship and a living stipend.

At that point, I was a few hours shy of graduating. I enrolled in summer school for two honors courses. Both classes would give me enough credits to graduate.

A professor from Ghana supervised my first honors paper. He chaired the African Studies Department and encouraged me to research and write about the eighteenth-century West African jihad movement of Uthman dan Fodio.[81] I poured myself into reading, cross-referencing, and learning as much as possible about the subject. I earned an A grade.

He mentioned, in a note at the bottom of the paper, that research should be objective and unbiased. Some of my conclusions were not objective. Some conclusions reached were filled with a lot of zeal but lacked scientific rigor.

Writing the paper, moreover, informed my love for research. I enjoyed the challenge of interlacing data and narrative. I was delighted to discover and reconcile disparate findings. I realized research possessed the potential to secure answers regarding things and events not known or misunderstood.

Historical research demonstrated the power of bringing distant events to life. I pushed forward with one paper down and one to go.

I tackled my second honors paper, "The Balfour Declaration of 1917."[82] A Palestinian-American scholar and tenured history professor supervised that paper. In spite of my limited academic research skills, I was confident that my dispassion from a climate dominated by "the Imam said" would serve me well. My new path dictated that I would not need to adjust my thinking and conform to expectations from WD's community.

I wasn't interested in imitating Farrakhan by castigating America or emulating WD's position of a non-threatening Americanized Islam. Authentic Islam is not interested in pointing an unjustified finger at past wrongs nor does it remain silent about issues that need redress. Authentic Islam is a balanced middle path.

I knew, however, that writing papers about eighteenth-century jihad movements and Palestinian history were only a beginning. It could not replace the years I had spent marching around in an FOI uniform. On the other hand, I began to see that the NOI's misguided past strengthened me to establish a personal development strategy. My academic expedition paid off. I earned a bachelor's degree in the summer term of 1981 and enrolled in a master's degree program that September.

Blessed and Humbled

The summer before I started graduate school, I fried chicken at Kentucky Fried Chicken (KFC) and sold body oils. My job in the hot, small, greasy kitchen gave my self-esteem a partial black eye. My eye healed as I recalled NOI hard times. Work at the KFC kitchen made me feel like placing a label on my chef's hat that stated "college grad." The label, I mused, would heal my ego's black eye. However, KFC was a disguised blessing. The hot kitchen kept me humble, motivated and focused. KFC reminded me that commitment exacts a price and it was simply time to pay.

Graduating generated a flood of feelings. It brought back feelings about high school classmates. I felt vindicated and had proved many naysayers wrong. My graduation silenced those who had predicted I'd end up ruined. It silenced some who said I would die in a violent confrontation with white people. Graduation also brought up memories of my father.

I wanted him to see me in a cap and gown. I wanted that we could practice Islam together. I craved to celebrate Eddy's report that my father died as a Muslim even if there were major pieces of Islam he didn't understand. I wanted him to know that the clarity I gained from authentic Islam and the Sunnah (the Prophet's traditions) gave me the ability to worship Allah (God) without associating anything with him in my worship. I could also critique the social construction of race dispassionately. Authentic Islam cleared my head about marriage, having a family, and lifelong learning. Authentic Islam also gave me a genuine measure of self-confidence to remove whites as an excuse for failing.

I registered for fifteen hours in the first semester of my master's degree program. The courses required concentrated reading not limited to criminology. Degree requirements also stipulated studies in sociology and economics.

Graduate school, at first, unnerved me. I was anxious after the first couple of classes. NOI flashbacks kept me calm. Brittle NOI memories served me well as I came to grips with the fact that I had endured tougher times.

For sure, using NOI hard times as motivation became an odd paradox that shielded me from panic. One of the biggest NOI inspired lessons taught me how to persevere upon a fraction of good in spite of overwhelming misguidance. Also, throwing away a scholarship and a living stipend were not an option. I had a wife, a decent apartment, and a six-year-old daughter. I realized that much of my anxiety was self-imposed.

It didn't take long to see that graduate school was about making choices. I saw that deep learning, skill development, and, lastly, good grades came from faith in Allah (God), making the right decisions and taking action. When I embraced and faced the rigor and challenge of graduate school, I did so without trepidation. I was now comfortable with the things I used to ridicule as the white man's deception of the black middle class. My jitters dissipated. I made a habit of praying on campus to stay on top of things. It kept me balanced and protected. Prayer shielded me from harmful distractions and it kept me connected to my Creator. Regular prayer also operated to disconnect me from trivial, mundane pursuits. It redirected the inner self to higher life goals. The five obligatory daily prayers in Islam cultivate mindfulness. I used to draw on my steel mill job experiences as a frame of reference. The memories evoked strong feelings about the value and importance of prayer. On top of a hot coke furnace, I used to pause from work to pray. Prayers kept me focused. Prayer reinforced the hope of better days to come. I found comfort and resolve in prayer. Now prayer strengthened me to manage the rigor of academic requirements. It also helped me deal with family life.

CONNECTING THE FADED DOTS

I volunteered at one of Ohio's oldest medium security prisons once a month to give a one-hour talk to Muslim inmates. I spoke about Islam and self-improvement. I usually mixed in a good bit of personal development coaching with Islamic teachings. I would advise the inmates, "Brothers, it's never too late to turn your life around bit by bit. You can do this, with Allah's (God's) help, but don't forget to own up to your former thinking that got you here." I encouraged them to enroll in a GED program or attend college while incarcerated. Ohio ran several associate degree and bachelor's degree programs for eligible inmates.

"Find new friends and try to avoid your old hangouts. Do not forget to patch up the mess you made with your wife, your children, and other relatives and friends. You have to come face to face with your past. Join the twelve-step program if you have addiction problems. Their principles work." I covered different topics, but each of them migrated back to themes of self-assessment and personal development.

The hour and forty-minute drive from Cincinnati to the prison gave me space to reflect. It allowed me to think and review, with almost no regret, the bumpy road I had traveled.

I enjoyed gazing at the autumn-colored leaves cluttering the roadside. Nature, and especially the fall season, always filled me with serenity. I thought about how much I loved my daughters. I reflected on the bad and good in the NOI years. I contemplated my life during WD Muhammad's leadership as an important tipping point. WD Muhammad's break with the NOI ushered in practical and critical decisions for former NOI members. The transition proved to be liberating and debilitating.

I thought about my mother's help and support and how a binding love grew between us. She watched my transformation with patience. There were times I felt my life was too complex for her to understand. I once believed that black nationalism, religion, politics, and aggressive civil rights activities were beyond her grasp. I was dead wrong. She understood all of these issues as she had struggled to deal with life in America far longer than me.

She comprehended the inconsistency of America's claim to racial equality. She had stomached its broken promises for years. On top of all of this, her firm but gentle hand had assisted me through thick and thin. I tried to share authentic Islam with her. I told her it was not an NOI jaunt, and I explained my commitment to practice Islam as deserved. In her candid manner, she said, "Boy, what took you so long?"

PRECIOUS SOUL

Nafeesah, my second daughter, was born in October 1984. I watched the nurse remove the afterbirth from her face. My eyes filled with tears when the nurse showed her to me, and it hit me how strikingly she resembled my father's childhood pictures. My father had been dead four years, and my feelings about his life and death were strong. I also processed marriage issues that required immediate attention. I owed it to my two daughters to be patient and find a way to make it work. A semi arranged NOI marriage was at the root of my family problems. I doubted our compatibility after we left the NOI. My wife was navigating personal development issues as well. Our marriage suffered from poor communication and, sadly, I owned most of the blame. In addition to our communication woes, our vision for the future differed widely. I did not want the black middle-class promised-land trappings characterized by conspicuous spending and chasing material stuff. Moreover, I had learned over the years to distinguish living in comfort from being trapped by shallow values.

Financial challenges did not help either. We were always struggling to pay rent and take care of basic living requirements. I was unable to find a good paying job even though I nearly had a master's degree. Then, I got a break. My persistence and struggled started to pay off. A friend and classmate named Ronnie told me about a teaching job at a proprietary college at the Union Terminal building in Cincinnati. The school was a magnet for public assistance recipients. Ronnie happened to be a reformed "old head" from the streets. He had spent time in prison and finished his degree in my undergraduate class. He joined the master's program the same quarter as me.

He devoted most of his criminal life as a booster and fencing stolen merchandise. He ran the short con game with skill. He loved heroin. In fact, he was more dope fiend than criminal. Ronnie also possessed an agile mind.

He believed that all of society is a racket. He argued that crime is a political and social space managed by the rich and powerful. The shadows and gaps are leftovers for the hustler, pimp, and short con player. He believed the biggest criminals were invisible. Their opaque existence allowed them to manipulate events that most folks call reality. I understood his point of view of a larger manipulation of people and resources. Crime, in my opinion, is not the exclusive territory of a skillful invisible minority. America breeds crime from the lowest type to the most sophisticated. Street crime exists because street criminals make choices. He did have a point, however, given the nature of our employment at the business college.

The business college was founded in President Reagan's deregulation climate. Federal Pell grants offered businesses and investors a lucrative revenue source. The school made money, a lot of money. During the Reagan era, nimble-minded business people took advantage of soft government money and loosened regulations. Most of the students were young African American females on public assistance. All of them were required to make passing grades for ongoing support.

Grade inflation existed in every class. I realized that this job was temporary, but it opened a door to teaching. The effort I exerted to return to school to earn a degree paid off, even as I faced challenges. I needed to write a thesis since my graduate course work was already completed. I planned to write about my experiences in the NOI.

The NOI experience was a large part of the events that propelled me back to school. I would research and write about the NOI as an insider. My experiences in the NOI prepared me to tease out observations that eluded other researchers.

My path was fairly uncomplicated and straightforward. The two low-hanging fruit to pick were a thesis and a teaching job.

However, the business college was an academic setting in name only. Within eighteen months, the Federal Department of Education withdrew funding eligibility. The school closed amid claims of fraud.

Now without a job, I realized I could approach looking for another one with confidence. Before I obtained a degree, employment opportunities were like the rain; when it rained, it was fine. However, no one can make it rain.

Having a defined skill gave me self-confidence. It allowed mobility. I could move around to find rain. My attitude toward seizing opportunity came from within, and it came from coming to grips with the uncertainty of new experiences. When I learned patience, I found the power to change. I know this language sounds like an inexpensive self-help book, but practicing patience is a game changer.

Just because someone does not believe in gravity, his or her disbelief doesn't cushion a fall from a ladder. Natural law works for you or against you. It's an individual choice. A friend from WD's community, a bank manager and board member at a nonprofit, heard I needed a job. He recommended me as finance director at a human services organization. I brushed up on the principles of not-for-profit accounting. I explained my views about balancing the budget to the interview committee. I answered their questions about fund-raising. They liked what I said and, thanks to Allah (God), I got the job. The office building stood adjacent to Eden Park in the eastern section of Midtown Cincinnati.

The CEO of the organization was an African-American woman in her mid fifties, with a master's in social work. She came across as a middle-class professional who was also concerned timidly about racism and discrimination. She was aware of the organization's track record during Cincinnati's riots in the late 1960s that depressed Cincinnati's African American neighborhoods. Even with her timid approach to racial problems, I believe she wanted to make an impact. Her challenge to navigate the politics of compromise in Cincinnati had dwarfed many community-based organizations and its leaders before her. Securing funding in Cincinnati's conservative and racially biased climate did not come easily.

Her leadership style conveyed deference, a style I suspect she learned from Jim Crow hard knocks. Her approach appeared pliable as a palm tree bending in a storm.

Her acquiescence to conservative white board members and black ministers' fears made me uncomfortable. It hampered the agency's ability to assist poor black folks. She had little trouble articulating the plight of individuals. However, she dared not relate personal stories to broader trends of Cincinnati's stubborn racism.

This job was the first time I worked with whites from major corporations. Several well-positioned whites from Proctor and Gamble, General Electric, and local banks populated the board of trustees. A few board members from African American churches lent a measure of deniability that the organization was only a feel good façade. I watched the board of trustees with a fair amount of suspicion.

The board's timid approach to addressing thorny problems should have sobered the CEO. Perhaps she was sober, on the other hand, but had decided to play by the politically correct unwritten rules. Watching these events unfold, I came to grips with race, class, and how the business of sponsorship and 'minority patronage' operates in a corporate America. I realized many mistakes I committed over the years of confronting racism directly.

Some racist acts are played out as a mere function of the status quo. This tends to cause racist actors to give little thought to their behavior. They parcel out consequences but never experience them. A chance to engage them with reason vanishes when you confront them aggressively. At times, I realized that confrontation spoils the chances to educate as well.

I learned to listen and watch. Besides, I did not have an extensive social capital network, and I needed to hold on to my job. It just didn't make sense for me to fix every broken wheel, so to speak. I had just started to accumulate things like a car, bank account, and connections to so-called professional life. I didn't want to anger folks and lose my job.

Some folks in the NOI and in WD Muhammad's community had an abundance of this stuff. Many of them came to both experiences with expectations to accumulate an adequate income and even wealth. My three co-workers were homeowners and drove decent cars, and the contrast between our shares of social capital were wide. I owned a puddle jumper (my parent's favorite expression for a car that barely got by). It was a high-mileage Honda Accord on its last leg. The organization lent me a six-passenger van to drive when it died.

I was not naive about my life. I managed the work with a clear conscience. I put forth my best effort in a space I once considered as selling out. I was optimistic in spite of a modest salary, broken-down cars, and marital problems. I managed all of these challenges. None of them destroyed my peace of mind. I had two lovely daughters, and we lived in a duplex house with a wooden porch, and my neighbors were a quiet older couple. My years of struggling to find meaning and relevance reinforced my optimism. Allah's (God's) mercy reached me in spite of my mistakes and shortcomings. The hardship and tribulations in the NOI and WD Muhammad's community helped make me resilient to face adversity. I studied the dynamics of racial politics and learned how to contain my resistance to subtle racism. Graduate School helped me understand workplace expectations without excuses or complaint. My parents lived and taught workplace values long before I saw them operate in professional organizations.

My sister, Darlene, navigated the world of white folks before her teen years. She did not hide under a female Uncle Tom mask, as I once believed. She played to win. She dismissed the myth of racial incompetence by achievement. She defied local folklore that black folks could not compete with or outpace white folks. It took me years to understand the difference between selling out and working at peak performance.

My instinctive hatred of injustice and racism clouded my vision. It was hard for me to accept there was a difference. I rejected self-improvement on many levels because of my anger. I became convinced society's demand for black folks' self-improvement originated from a narrow mean-spirited place. It smelled like a bait and switch trick to keep black folk insecure. Self-improvement, unless established from ethnic pride and self-love, produces self-doubt. It could mutate quickly as the pretense my mother hated. I repaired parts of my cracked mirror, once again, by replaying my parents' lessons. Both of them were gurus of hard work, strong self-pride, and a firm work ethic. I came to realize that life for many African Americans was like a jagged mosaic of pieces in a puzzle. The professional, the janitor, the crackhead, and just normal folks all struggle day-to-day, fitting pieces together, to make life work. The challenge has not vanished in so-called postracial America. The ethnicity of President Obama has had near zero impact on the lives of African Americans.

We admire his presidency emotionally; however, I am sad to admit, his policies have done little to reshape the structure of race and class inequality.

President Obama speaks passionately about these structures, but he is powerless to make a dent in the fortress of institutional racism. On the other hand, most American presidents are errand boys for the formidable power centers of banking and corporate America. I should not hold President Obama to an unrealistic standard because of his mixed racial background. In the last thirty years, a significant amount of race-neutral economic marginalization affected the middle class in America. These trends placed many whites on the edge of a black economic experience.

Today, looking back at my thinking, I see it was not completely in error. The middle class struggles to hold life together in an economic climate where transnational banks move around investment capital and jobs and, thus, cripple middle-class economic opportunity.

Twenty-first-century racism has mutated and disguised its appearance but still plays a role in filtering economic opportunity, housing availability, and educational attainment. A so-called postracial black president has been unable to address this brand of racism.

It does not surprise me that President Obama has been unable to tackle racism of this sort. I expected he would not lean into the problem. Even his muted response has caused him trouble and the loss of political currency.

American presidents are only able to dance to the corporate music played. A few, like President Jimmy Carter, did not dance well. They served one term. I wrestled with these issues at work as I concluded that race and poverty are scary challenges to elected politicians. Champions of other causes also avoid a confrontation with those who use race and class politics to their advantage. When the sacred cattle of race and class are threatened, America's power elites will do whatever is required to maintain the status quo.

Organizations in Cincinnati stumbled for decades to oppose the social and economic trends that shape white privilege and black suffering. My employer feared aggressive racism with good reason. When I first moved to Cincinnati,

I noticed the unabashedly mean face of Cincinnati's working class whites. Some of them did not flinch from showing a determined stoic expression that seemed to say, "I am not ashamed for you to see that I don't like black people."

For many years, Cincinnati's police department earned an infamous reputation for shooting unarmed black men. Local courts rarely indicted police officers. Police misconduct came under scrutiny in 2003 when a federal consent decree imposed monitoring of the Cincinnati Police Department.[83] For many years, organizations and individuals in Cincinnati did little to challenge racism.

I watched these dynamics dispassionately. I could now keep my feelings about race and class in check with a detached emotional response. In light of my tenure at this social services agency, it was time for me to secure a better paying job.

DNA's Son

I had secured another job before I resigned as finance director from the social services agency. I was hired as a program director at a halfway house for men on probation and parole. The house operated as an alternative to institutional incarceration. The halfway house movement had gained popularity in Ohio as an alternative to state prison. A less expensive operating cost of halfway houses helped shape a different approach to managing community-based corrections. Instead of costing several hundred dollars per day, a halfway house cost the State of Ohio thirty-five dollars a day per occupant. The house I managed had seventeen beds. It grossed six hundred dollars per day. It grossed fifteen thousand to seventeen thousand dollars a month. Net revenue was nearly five thousand dollars per month.

Community-based corrections grew in Cincinnati and throughout Ohio at about 10 percent annually. The overall crime rate, the crack-cocaine epidemic, and the practice of disproportionately incarcerating black men for drug crimes fostered a classic supply and demand mechanism. The privatized corrections industry recognized the incapacity of state institutions to meet the increased demand for prison beds. A halfway house that cost seventeen dollars a day for each resident was far cheaper than the state prison costs of over a one hundred dollars per day. It is not surprising that Ohio and other states expanded the use of halfway houses in community-based corrections.

I supported Ohio's privatization of community corrections. I believe that the Muslim community should operate halfway houses. This would meet, at least, two needs in the broader community. First, a Muslim-managed halfway house could assist Muslim ex-offenders and non-Muslim ex-offenders to establish noncriminal community ties. I believed this would give them a second chance for crime-free life. Research shows that building noncriminal networks reduces the likelihood of recidivism. Second, a halfway house operated by Muslims could establish a best practices model in the community to promote Islam as an answer to stubborn social problems.

Unfortunately, the Cincinnati Muslim community was unprepared for this type of social entrepreneurialism. Yet the prospect of owning a halfway house intrigued me. I believed that blending social entrepreneurialism with community corrections would serve the community. It could also be profitable. But a venture of this nature would require financial capital. I grew up in a family business and my father's entrepreneurialism was always present in the back of my mind. As a friend said, "It is a cinch by the inch but hard by the yard." I needed to start small by saving money as start-up capital. Having a hustle on the side could move me in that direction. Opportunity hid in plain sight.

I had hired Ilyas Nashid, my friend from the Central State days, as Lead Counselor. Ilyas and I stayed connected during the NOI journey. Ilyas worked as a part-time night counselor at another halfway house facility. The promotion to Lead Counselor helped his career, and it reassured me the halfway house employed skilled people. Ilyas embodied the right disposition to counsel probationers. His maturity convinced me that young men would listen to him and respect him. Ilyas dropped out of Central State to join the NOI after I joined. He also transferred his Central State credits and enrolled at the University of Cincinnati. Within eighteen months, he earned a bachelor's degree in psychology.

Ilyas was one of the most gifted salesmen in the NOI. He could turn on his sales craft with efficiency and charm in the blink of an eye. We watched Ilyas sell a *Muhammad Speaks* newspaper that sold for fifty cents retail while he pounded the streets for twelve to fifteen hours. At the end of the day, he placed nearly one thousand dollars from his pockets on the tally up a table at Mosque No. 5.

His self-confidence and his instinct to understand people were near flawless. White folks were not spared from his sales savvy. He pioneered the science of squeezing people for big dollars. His technique was so effective that the FOI captain gave him center stage to teach sales techniques at FOI meetings. We imitated him and the coffers of Mosque No. 5 swelled. Both of us had clocked thousands of hours in direct sales experience in the NOI.

We discussed our mutual aspirations. Thus, we formed a partnership. We decided to sell earrings, assorted jewelry, and body oils. We purchased two vendor's licenses from the City of Cincinnati. We bought folding tables and set up our earrings, jewelry, incense, and body oils on a busy corner in a large black neighborhood. We took advantage of the popularity of big hooped earrings in the early 1980s made fashionable by the female hip-hop group Salt-N-Pepa. We bought twelve-karat and eighteen-karat gold-studded big hoop earrings for as little as twelve dollars a dozen from wholesale jewelry outlets. I had learned the earring hustle in the mid-1970s from Talib Deen Ahmad (aka Captain Willard) from Indianapolis. Sales were brisk. One incident stands out. I went out to sell on a Saturday afternoon at three o'clock. There was a nonstop flow of customers until about six and I had sold all but one bundle of earrings. I didn't count how much I made until the end of the day. I picked up this habit from Ilyas in the NOI days. I sat in my car and emptied my pockets and counted the money and discovered I made over eleven hundred dollars in three hours. Not all days were like this. Nonetheless, I could always rely on making several hundred dollars a day.

My return on investment was twofold. The first return was making a couple thousand dollars a month on an investment of fewer than five hundred dollars to purchase merchandise. The second return was psychological and emotional. I rehabilitated my outlook on the years of selling *Muhammad Speaks* as preparation instead of indentured servitude. I could now redeem those years with substantial financial benefit. The days and nights spent pounding sidewalks in the winters and summers paid off finally. I had gained critical knowledge about black folks' spending habits during those stressful NOI days. I developed the self-confidence to approach strangers and learned not to take rejection personally.

The key in street sales is to have a consistent sales approach based on customer type. Don't spend too much time closing a sale. Recognize rejection and move on to the next customer. Don't get played by the women that bat their eyes but are broke. Watch out for the stick-up boys. Be nimble with price and offer deals with discounts.

For example, if I paid sixteen dollars a dozen for earrings and I sold one pair for eight dollars I would often offer to sell two pairs for fourteen dollars. After selling four pairs, I would have eight pairs left. The eight pairs, even at eight dollars a pair, I considered as the unencumbered profit of sixty-four dollars. If you sell on average eight dozen a weekend, you make $512 before taxes. I didn't spend more than ten to twelve hours a weekend. I averaged forty-two dollars an hour.

I kept one thousand dollars in my pocket at all times. For years I longed for this type of financial security. Though initially satisfying, having a lump of dollars in my pocket grew old after a year of nonstop selling on weekends. My thesis was idle. I was not giving my best energies to my job or family.

Buying dress shoes, designer slacks, and dress shirts started to make me feel empty. I felt my father's DNA driving me after money nonstop. I also felt his ambivalence for placing money over everything. I thought if I acquired enough disposable cash it would settle the score of the penniless NOI days.

Chasing dollars leaves millions of people hollow and numb. I know, without question, that happiness does not live in the folds of a wallet or a purse.

Relevance Road

I decided to write my thesis on African American ex-offenders' conversion to the Nation of Islam. No NOI member at the time had researched and written about the organization academically. There existed, though, a considerable body of literature about the NOI by nonmembers. Malcolm X's autobiography with Alex Haley made millions aware of the NOI and Malcolm's life. Scholars, like C. Eric Lincoln, wrote about the organization as outsiders. [84] None of the fine pieces of scholarship like his unraveled the shades of NOI culture. These scholars did not have insights about the likes of Brother Kenneth X or Captain Brozier X. The primary focus of my thesis did not explain or relate personality nuance to the overall religious and organizational makeup of the NOI. Nevertheless, I could provide additional granularity about NOI conversion.

I understood the events that drove many to join the NOI. I decided to approach my research as an insider and explain and write why former criminals, social outcasts, and ex-offenders converted to the NOI. I also wanted to explain why Black Nationalists joined the NOI. My research focused on trends in conversion since the late 1960s, as black nationalism movements declined. I described an aspect of black people's history in America that was misunderstood widely.

My thesis advisor hinted mildly that my topic did not meet a traditional academic subject matter standard. I did not budge. I would research and write about the NOI, a subject I knew firsthand. I struggled, at first. I was anxious about research sources. I didn't know if my research could shed new insights.

I found some of the literature about the NOI laughable. It sounded like declassified FBI intelligence memos. Much of the stuff was pure rubbish.

Some of it contained racist innuendo. On the other hand, serious research existed and some of it was quite useful. Moreover, it supported my experiences.

One incident in the NOI served as a lens to frame an important parameter of my research. In the waning NOI days, a Muslim ex-offender came to Cincinnati. He requested parole transfer from New York to Ohio. Before prison, he lived a life as an angry country boy with a sharp knife. He paroled from New York's Attica Prison where he survived a shotgun blast during the Attica uprising in 1972. The NOI would have called him a Lazarus before he went to prison. He had no understanding of black history or black culture when he left the rural South to work in New York in his late teens.

I liked this brother immediately. He was "country as corn." Nothing about him felt contrived. His warm disposition shined through his massive physique.

He converted to the NOI while in prison and over the years in Attica he became a NOI bodyguard. He protected Attica's NOI inmate minister, one of the men convicted of the murder of Malcolm X. He stood in the prison yard in front of the minister when state troopers took aim and fired. He probably survived the blast because of his strong upper body physique. I would sit for hours and listen to his stories during the night-post duties at Mosque No. 5. I thought about these stories as I researched ex-offender conversion to the NOI.

Honestly, I can't blame academics that wrote about the NOI and black male prison conversion like an ornithologist studies birds. Many ornithologists devote a lot of their time developing models because they cannot experience life as a bird. Andrea Sullivan's work on religious conversion became one of the first studies in my literature review. Sullivan focused on the construct "conversion" and compared NOI ex-offender conversion with other types of religious conversion.[85]

Andrea Sullivan's research on black male conversion centered on religiosity. She defined the NOI conversion experience in prison as a "convenience" and a coping mechanism. She correctly identified why many converted to the NOI. She did not, in my view, explain the hidden redemptive aspects of NOI conversion. The NOI's nonpolitical approach to black identity appealed to large numbers of incarcerated African American males.

Sullivan also did not discuss how men like the Attica parolee overcame self-loathing and fratricidal violence. Her work was informative, nonetheless, and it supported my research.

I argue that the term "reversion" is a better measure to explain why many African Americans chose Islam. I believe the term carries natural and historical relevance that recognizes the fact that many enslaved Africans were Muslims.

The concept of reversion is also consistent with the creed of Islam. Islam holds that all created life is naturally inclined to recognize the oneness of Allah (God). Islam asserts the nature of life reverts (returns) to the Creator. I believe that Muslim captives from West Africa and Central Africa made into slaves provide a historical connection to today's African American Muslim revert.

African American Muslims did not find Islam in twentieth-century America. Many reverted to Islam, in spite of losing our Islamic identity and culture during slavery. A body of research suggests that nearly thirty- percent of Africans brought to America and enslaved were Muslims. Our connection to Islam was not recent.

My thesis dealt with a subject that had scientific merit, but the relevance was personal. I was pleased to contribute to the body of literature on African American Muslim ex-offenders. I completed my thesis and defended and I graduated with a master's degree November 1985.

Toward a Straight Path

I turned forty in October 1985. I was determined to mend big pieces of my cracked mirror. A significant mirror repair involved pursuing knowledge in the form of a terminal degree.

I longed for an academic environment after I finished my Master's. I missed reading and studying. I checked out a few Ph.D. programs in criminology and applied research. Every program required a Graduate Record Exam (GRE) score.

The requirement to take the GRE turns some students away from pursuing a graduate degree. Taking the GRE also made me nervous. I was anxious a low score would puncture my self-confidence and keep me from my goal of a terminal degree. Some of my fears came from rumors my UC classmates spread about the exam. They feared it. Some students of color complained the standardized aspects favored white people. I believed I could do well enough to apply to Ph.D. programs. A low score would make me feel bad, but I had felt bad before and I could deal with the exam.

I took the exam and walked away feeling good. After waiting nervously for a month, the results came. I tore open the envelope on a chilly Saturday afternoon. I watched the postal worker climb back in the mail truck and drive to the next house. I said quietly, "OK, read it, Zaid." My combined GRE score stood out higher than the national average, but not by much.

I applied to three schools. I received two rejections and one acceptance. Florida State University offered a scholarship and a living stipend, and they ranked among the top five Ph.D. criminology programs in the country. The living stipend was $250 a month and the cost of University housing was $150 a month.

After rent had been paid, I had only one hundred dollars a month to support a wife and two daughters. This was a significant decrease from a job paying $2,000 a month and $2,500 a month from earrings sales.

I did not tell anyone the amount of the Florida State stipend. I painted a rosy picture for everyone, including my mother. I selectively told a few people that I planned to leave Cincinnati for Tallahassee to attend graduate school.

I borrowed my mother's well-kept 1967 Chevy Nova and loaded a few things for the road and drove to Tallahassee. I registered for classes, secured graduate student housing, drove around Tallahassee sightseeing, and then drove back to Cincinnati to return my mother's car.

I bought a one-way bus ticket and returned to Tallahassee alone a couple of days later. I thought about being broke and struggling in graduate school at forty years old. It was not easy to deal with. I realized that I had to find a way to have more than a hundred bucks after paying rent.

I had about eight hundred dollars worth of earrings and other merchandise tucked away in an old suitcase, so I looked for a place to sell. Then I learned that the university's Auxiliary Services Office opened space in the outdoor FSU Mall every Tuesday to vendors for ten dollars. I hesitated. I was a full-time Ph.D. student. How would that look?

I swallowed my pride and set up a table. I was broke and my family would be joining me soon. I was anxious about not having money, and on top of that, I carried five time-consuming courses. I felt trapped and surrounded by the fear of a stiff academic challenge and the nostalgia for my former lifestyle of working, selling, and financial security. I only committed about 60 percent of my mental and spiritual energy to study. I fought off self-talk that whispered, forget this Ph.D. and get serious about building a strong sales business.

I could not study. My thoughts drifted. I sat in front of my living room window and watched the sun's rays skip back and forth between cars.

I felt like Richard Pryor must have when he set himself on fire to get a grip on his life. Fear paralyzed me. My limp motivation grabbed me by the collar and screamed in my face, "Wake up, Zaid. Stop playing dead." I earned two Bs, a C, and an F. It felt like a failure.

Guidance comes, at times, when hardship is at your doorstep and you can no longer run. I walked the rotten planks of denial the first six months at Florida State. I heard the wood crack beneath my feet and ignored the sound.

I rekindled a desire to "buckle down"—my father's expression rang true in my heart. I needed to be a drill sergeant over myself. Returning to basics turned my situation around. I rebounded as I did from the NOI days. No amount of self-recriminations could make me study hard. It had to come from a curiosity for knowledge. I dropped my pitiful excuses and stop whimpering.

My temporary emotional and spiritual paralysis turned out to be a disguised blessing. It forced me to take a sober assessment. I believe that people tend to see change when intention shifts. A repositioned intent produces firmness. Intention and resolve move things. Movement occurs, but not by itself. The intention is a means, not a cause. Faith in Allah (God) produces the change.

My alignment with the will of Allah (God) opened a door to new possibilities. A milestone occurred like my exodus from the NOI.

My new paradigm pushed the fear away. It gave me a lens to see life's constant uphill battles. I started to comprehend the wisdom of patience. I realized that mundane, seemingly simple acts begin a process. A process of meaningful change is shaped by patience and completed by unwavering faith. Patience and faith are like two wings. Flight occurs when they move together.

I abandoned an autopilot, knee-jerk reaction to life's challenges and I confronted my shortcomings. I reflected on a concept in Islam that means "man proposes but Allah (God) disposes." Good things started to happen. My wife found a job in the emergency room of Tallahassee Memorial Hospital. The threat of being homeless abated. My worry about slipping into the black middle-class trap that I tried to avoid since my days at Central State no longer hung over me like a dark cloud. I now accepted that a lot of black folks and white folks embraced the same values. They could live without giving into crass impulses of materialism, racism, and shallow thinking. They work hard to get ahead. They also want to live in comfort. They want their children to have a decent life. They are not sellouts. I could be concerned about the principles of racial justice without going overboard. I found an emotional and practical balance, at last. I reconciled both urges that my biography fashioned.

Nevertheless, full reconciliation remained beyond my reach by the middle of the 1980s. As I adopted this attitude, things took a turn for the better. My wife told me that her coworker, a Ph.D. student in music, resigned as Night Manager in the Florida State Student Union. He would mention me to his supervisor if I wanted and, of course, I did.

His name was Deen. This spelling, oddly enough, gave me hope that Allah (God) had guided me to this job. His name was spelled like the trans-literation of the Arabic word for the religion of Islam, "Deen." I took it as a sign from Allah (God). The Night Manager job signaled a revival. I could commit fully to self-development. I could achieve concrete goals. The job offer came in mid-December. The pay was good and it afforded me a lot of time to study.

My duties as Night Manager started in January, the beginning of a new year and new possibilities.

As I waited for the new year to start, I noticed that I harbored a history of ill-feeling for breaks between semesters and I hated sitting idly. I felt isolated and it affected me like an odd depression.

I first noticed this feeling at Central State when buses lined up for winter break. I'd watch my friends, already inventing lies about sexual exploits, par-ties, and Reefer, as they boarded buses for the big cities.

I only traveled down the back road from Wilberforce to Yellow Springs, and as Antioch students left for the break, Yellow Springs felt empty, as well. Those days were gone, and those feelings as well. Some of this retrospective anxiety came from my rapid identity journey. I had made a speedy transition from colored boy to black man by the mid-1960s. Hardly anyone from Yellow Springs traveled as quickly as I moved. The transition was hurried and bumpy and years passed like months. I had not lived in Yellow Springs for over thirty years, but the village still stirred my heart with good memories.

I remembered a few poignant images. The sound of our station wagon in the driveway made me feel safe. It meant my parents were home. My mother's kitchen produced marvelous smells. The aroma gathered us as a family. Small flashes of Yellow Springs inspired memories that blunted the sting of Emmett Till's America.

When the new semester started, I retook the class I failed. I made a B-plus. I made As in other classes. My study routine was thoughtful and disciplined. People took notice. I felt assured and no longer terrified. I embraced a determined mindset without swagger. By the end of spring semester, my advisor asked me to teach undergraduate classes in summer school. I couldn't get "yes" out fast enough. I wasn't even thinking about additional pay.

To everyone's surprise, the state legislature raised the graduate fellows' stipend from $250 a month to $500. I made $750 a month as student union Night Manager and $600 a month as a teaching assistant. The additional money didn't feel bad at all.

I had no connection with WD Muhammad's community when I left Cincinnati for Florida, but a spiritual void existed. Nonetheless, I wanted Muslim community involvement, but not organizational participation. For too long African American Muslims were challenged to choose an Islamic organization over religion or vice versa. Often the goals of the organization conflicted with core values of authentic Islam.

There were two masjids in Tallahassee. The Muslim Student Association-affiliated Masjid stood on a corner just a few blocks from campus. The WD Muhammad-affiliated masjid was nestled in an African American neighborhood on the south side of town. I lived near the MSA Masjid and the location made it easy for me to pray there and take part in the weekend activities. I confined my involvement to the MSA Masjid. My decision to avoid the WD Muhammad community in Tallahassee stemmed from an informal credo, "the Imam said." It shaped the community's activities and behavior. I saw enough of that in Cincinnati.

Participation in the student-based Tallahassee Muslim community made me a bit anxious. Most of the students at the masjid were barely over twenty; a few were in their early thirties and a couple was over forty. However, they welcomed me warmly. Some were happy to see an African American Muslim in a Ph.D. program.

Florida State enrolled a significant number of immigrant Muslim students during the years I attended (1986–1990). The largest group came from the Kingdom of Saudi Arabia, followed by Kuwait, Oman, and Libya.

A smaller number represented other Muslim countries. It did not take long for me to develop cordial relationships with them.

The fact that I came to Florida State to earn a Ph.D. did not overshadow a need for community involvement. I knew the engagement with Muslims would help me develop strength as a father and as a husband. It would also help me to become a better Muslim.

I interacted with students in the Department of Criminology as well. Most were white and only a few were from the South. There were two black males in the department. One of them had nearly finished his dissertation. Two black females joined the program with me.

I noticed right away how easy the white students joined mentoring networks with professors in the department. Early graduate student mentoring and academic support is a well-known factor that supports dissertation completion, the most formidable hurdle in a Ph.D. program. I got off to a bumpy start and I thought faculty avoided me. I retreated into a defensive shell. I just knew they rebuffed me because of my age and race. The problem was my attitude. There, I said it. My attitude was awful.

My attitude was so off balanced that it became a hinderance to embrace some very simple facts regarding one of the brightest and best professors in my department at Florida State. I remember going to his office and noticed a Sierra Club Foundation poster on his wall. I nodded to affirm my suspicion that he was a John Birch Society card-carrying member, a survivalist, and an undercover racist probably raised in Montana or Idaho. I thought he was a conservative neo-libertarian out to get me. He was neither. I was off base and dead wrong. He gave me an F in research methods class because I earned an F.

I took an advanced statistics class from him the following year with my head on straight. I had a good attitude, and the resulting grade was an A.

My body language said, "I am not here to critique you. I am here to learn." The first time around, in his class, I was insecure and expected to experience Southern racism. I was defensive and didn't trust faculty.

I tried to prove I belonged, yet I displayed a stern, moody expression. I should have worked harder to make my mark and earning an F was a fitting dose of medicine.

I remember Jesse Jackson once said, "It's not your aptitude that determines your altitude, it's your attitude." That described me. Personal engagement requires dropping concocted assumptions. This is not selling out or being an Uncle Tom. On the contrary, dropping concocted assumptions is antithetical to jaundice racism.

I learned this lesson the hard way and it has helped me maintain balanced relationships. My contact with people of any race, those I love and trust, is free from reacting to racism and other trivial stuff.

After approximately two years, I finished coursework in the spring of 1987. I spent the next nine months preparing for three comprehensive exams.

I also continued as student union Night Manager and taught undergraduate classes. I played basketball to reduce stress as I prepared for exams. I probably do not need to mention it (but I will) that I have used basketball to assess self-worth. I played to get in touch with my deepest feelings. I started this when I left the Black Nationalist movement.

Florida State's basketball team was a NCAA playoff contender and I was an avid fan. I was not content to watch their games on TV. I purchased discounted student tickets and went to the sports center to see them play.

I also found pickup games on a basketball court near my apartment. We would play hard until dark and then go our separate ways.

I navigated my middle age transition by playing basketball because I couldn't afford a Porsche! Seriously, though, playing basketball helped me maintain a strong mind-body link.

Once again, at forty-two years old, I was obsessed with dunking. I needed to dunk, just one more time. I ran several miles every evening to lose weight. I regained enough strength in my legs to touch the rim. I dunked softballs. Next, I dunked volleyballs. I waited one evening just before dark. The court was near empty. I had been playing for about one hour. I was sweating and I felt loose. I started my approach toward the rim at the foul line. I relaxed, jumped and slammed the basketball through the hoop. Both of my wrists extended inside the rim. I had a small patch of gray in my beard. The younger men I played with called me Bill Cartwright, the former Chicago Bulls center. He had strands of gray in his goatee. A comparison to him meant "this older brother can play." They paid me a nice compliment. The basketball habit opened up practical and spiritual insights.

It proved to be a crucial stage to fix pieces of my cracked mirror. It affirmed a principle that overall wellness stems from a major mind-body component. I cannot stress too much the importance of keeping fit. It helped me traverse the uneven highway to personal development. I believe being fit helped me excel in the challenging subjects as I worked hard to master statistics.

I completed the department's nine hours requirement for statistics courses with As. I also enrolled in several elective statistics courses and made As or Bs in each course. I spent long hours in a statistics lab writing syntax in a popular statistical software application. Then, out of nowhere, other students sought my help.

Their requests affirmed my new skill. Many students offered money for my help, and they kept me busy as word spread I was good at statistics and understood a popular statistical software package.

Khalid, a communications major from Saudi Arabia, often asked me for statistical coaching. I coached him often as he finished his course work and prepared for the comprehensive exams. Most of the brothers admired his fair-minded openness. Even when my coaching did not consume a lot of time, he compelled me to accept payment. His generosity became his trademark and, because of this, he became a masjid board member and helped the masjid organize activities. His family, then and now, are prominent business owners in Saudi Arabia.

Coaching statistics opened a door for involvement in masjid activities and broadened my contacts. I also developed a connection with an older student, Ali from the Sudan. Ali turned out to be as warm and engaging as anyone I have ever met. His friendly nature rang true to the reputation of the Sudanese people. In Arab countries, Sudanese are often hired in sensitive roles because of their trustworthiness and honesty.

Ali served as president of the Masjid; an office created from the charter with the Islamic Society of North America (ISNA). ISNA emerged, as an organization, in the 1960s to accommodate immigrant Muslims enrolled in American and Canadian universities. It is worth pointing out that two basic types of immigrant Muslim students attended Florida State during the years I attended. One group or type planned careers in government or business in their native countries after graduation. The other group cast an eye on staying in America. The latter group, it seemed to me, wanted to live the American dream. It was the policy of some majority Muslim governments to invest heavily in educating a class of nonpolitical leaders abroad.

Some of these governments supported students in undergraduate and graduate programs. After students had graduated, they were required to return home to work in government or fill midlevel positions in the private sector.

However, there were problems inherent in some of these policies. Some of the oil-producing states feared the emergence of an independent middle class. Some of these states told returning students bluntly to leave democratic ideas where they found them. This policy resonated with some students. Others rejected it in silence.

In some countries placing graduates in meaningful jobs proved to be challenging. It seemed some countries would rather import technocrats from the West instead of hiring their graduated nationals from Western universities. These policies took on political and social consequences.

However, this should not surprise anyone who knows the recent history of these countries. Foreign occupation and colonialism influenced leaders in Arab, Indo-Pak, and African countries. The policies of nineteenth-century colonialism set the stage in many Muslim-majority societies for future leaders to mimic the West.

Some of the young Muslims at Florida State were keen to align their career aspirations with policies in their country. Sometimes the policies supported foreign interest above the long-term well-being of the country. The so-called Arab Spring of 2011 reflects the misdirection in many of these policies. Many countries in North Africa and in the Gulf Region have large numbers of degree students. These countries do not have a defined mechanism that leads to employment. Some of these countries are ruled by autocratic and dictatorial regimes that talk about development but repress activities that would support development.

Some of the Florida State Muslim students sought to combine intellectual curiosity with a desire to have prestige and earn six-figure salaries. These values dominate most students in graduate school irrespective of religion or national origin. I witnessed a lot of immigrant Muslim students experienced pressure during the comprehensive exam period leading up to Ph.D. candidacy. One of the factors that shaped pressure for them was the finality of student life along with peer pressure and prestige expectations from relatives and friends back home. My challenges were quite different. No government job waited for me. I faced only stiff competition in store, so my drill focused on the next hurdles of the comprehensive exam and a dissertation.

I passed my comprehensive exams and anticipated what came next. My financial aid did not cover writing a dissertation, so I needed to either find additional support as a graduate assistant or find a job. Both possibilities worried me and underscored the reality that my days in Tallahassee were numbered.

Then, like rain from heaven, the department chair at the University of Cincinnati called me and asked me if I was interested in an assistant professor position. I traveled to Cincinnati and interviewed. They made an offer two weeks later of thirty thousand dollars and, what a relief, thirty thousand seemed like a lot in 1990 as a starting salary.

Even though things seemed to usher forth improvement, I felt unprepared to navigate departmental politics. After I left Florida State and resettled in Cincinnati, it did not take long to figure out I loved academia but didn't like the culture of the academy. One of the most troubling barriers was that I didn't socialize well. I just didn't like the ceremony and the pretending. I felt uncomfortable with my colleagues drinking. I loathed their jokes, even the innocuous ones. I avoided their squabbles given the fact I tend to be naturally guarded.

Sometimes their squabbles were skirmishes that stemmed from a long history over theory or an academic perspective. Pay inequalities made old scores even worse.

I filled a position that an African American professor vacated. I inherited the "black job." I soon realized why higher education was an ivory tower. It inspired hubris and elitism.

I felt the urge to return to Florida State after the first six months. I longed for intellectual honesty. Intellectual honesty and cordiality seemed more important than promotion or tenure and infighting. I experienced joy at Florida State when I thirsted knowledge. It felt wonderful to "leave it all on the floor" as basketball players do in a tough game.

At UC, I grew tired of being anxious and worried about dodging peer critique and unwarranted criticism from a few students who did not want to take classes from an "affirmative action hire." At Florida State, I framed a picture of what intellectual honesty and curiosity looked like. My life at UC didn't match. A political economy class at Florida State shaped my view of intellectual honesty. The course clarified a perspective on the market economy, society, and how the interplay of these structures shaped economics, race relations, and crime.

Dr. Rubinstein, a sociologist, taught the course. He turned out to be an extraordinarily thoughtful scholar at the top of his field in research and publications. He was not a Marxist, nor a capitalist for that matter. He unraveled the arguments of both dialectics and teased out the impact of culture and politics on market mechanisms, along with crime. Empirical evidence supported his research. He did not exonerate the hardened criminal as a mere pawn of a corrupt capitalist system like some so-called critical criminologist. He discussed the mechanisms in culture and society that shaped individual choice.

The class far exceeded a typical graduate seminar where a midterm and final grade underscored effort. We wrote papers weekly and defended our arguments in class. I did well in his course.

The course sparked my interest in political economy. It provided me with answers to perplexing questions that had troubled me for years. A book used in the class, Polanyi's *The Great Transformation*, illuminated the rise and fall of the market system and the evolution of the market pattern in a refreshingly explicit fashion. I read the book in one setting. Polanyi's arguments engaged me so much that I could not set the book down until I finished.

The class represented the type of intellectual honesty that should constitute the driving forces in an academic career. One should be passionate about finding answers to tricky issues and to perplexing questions with candor and honesty. The class prepared me to think beyond textbook Criminology.

I became more interested in how the interplay of politics, economy, and religion shaped criminal behavior than buttonhole theories. Modern criminology is dominated by traditional textbook explanations. Mainstream theory is accentuated by a dichotomy: (1) Crime is the result of naturally disposed bad people, or (2) Crime is the result of naturally disposed bad places. I believed that competing theories were required. These theories should explore the impact of culture, the market economy, and the impact of American slavery on crime.

Theories were also needed to clarify how the criminal justice system operated with respect to African Americans. Research needed to go beyond simplistic models and politically convenient explanations. Robust models needed to examine the historical criminalization of African Americans. These models should combine microeconomic and macroeconomic analysis of society and crime.

I argued that analysis should begin with measures of historical periods. A history of African American crime from slavery through Jim Crow needs exploration. Research should also examine preindustrial and postindustrial incarceration rates of African Americans.

It is widely known that during slavery resisting enslavement or attempting to escape from bondage was defined as criminal. Jim Crow policies denied free black people voting rights, employment, and unrestricted participation in public life. Is it not reasonable to explore and critique the mechanisms that supported and shaped definitions of criminality because of ex-slaves' and their descendants' quest for freedom and full citizenship?[86] A historical examination of the status of African Americans in society and how the criminal justice system has responded to black folks must form the basis of this type of analysis.

American institutions have advanced racism and the criminalization of black people and other people of color. These institutional patterns retard social justice and economic development among people of color and negatively impact American society. I felt then, as I do now, that crime in America couldn't be explained without deconstructing systematic biases that operated based on ethnicity, religion, or social class.

Has America learned anything about crime and social justice since the end of slavery? I think not.

Any time a systematic exclusion of labor force talent occurs there are bound to be negative ripple effects at every level of society. Structural racism has stymied black folks' economic participation, and as rational-choice theory suggests, high rates of black crime occur because choice and opportunity mechanisms have been narrowed. This narrowing of choice also applies to the problem of childbirth, education, and health care.

For example, crime rates increase when rational actors weigh their options to work at low paying jobs versus high-risk and high-income criminal activities. The choice is an explained by a systematic process that makes choosing, often the wrong choice, too easy.

The rational-choice crime model is not exclusive to black folks. Several groups of American immigrants passed through a crime opportunity rational-choice funnel. Most of these groups were integrated into the larger Anglo-American white society because they fit inside of a broader definition of whiteness or were not considered black. The US government's categories of racial classifications give a glimpse of how an irrational selection funnel operates. Black people do not enter the integration funnel because of unofficial or official definitions based on color. Currently, anyone from any region in Sub-Saharan Africa is "black." This classification scheme excludes black people from North Africa, black folk from the Middle East, and large numbers of black people from the Caribbean and South and Central America.[87] The stigma of slavery is maintained as a governmental definition and this keeps the descendants of slaves forever excluded from the rite of passage.

The rite of passage from crime to a race-based barrier-free legitimate opportunity, as a rational choice, is blocked for scores of African Americans. Persistent structural racism blocks this rite of passage.

There is enough blame shared over time by people and institutions. Blame, however, does not resolve the problem of social inequality, economic instability, racism, and crime.

Novel solutions are required. Government and corporate support need to be in place. Historically black colleges and universities, especially the larger ones, should lead research and develop models to address crime in African American communities.

Over one hundred twenty-five historically black college and universities (HBCUs) exist. These schools should lead the way to champion social change in America. Informal and formal Jim Crow racism made these institutions a necessity. African American access to majority white institutions was restricted systematically until recently.

I believe that employing HBCUs to tackle social inequality, economic instability, racism, and crime would become a best practices model. I also believe that timid responses and politically correct nice talk will not break the chains of structural racism. It is clear that America's political and educational institutions refuse to face a history that created killing fields of Native Americans and a slave empire from African Americans. I still find public school history textbooks that describe slavery as a time black people were not treated well. Loaded understatements make it nearly impossible to have a candid dialog about the lingering effects of slavery in America. America fails as a model of democracy and moral authority as long as American institutions deny the fact that enslaving African Americans and the mass murder of Native Americans continues to have damaging effects. The institution of slavery damaged a broad range of actors and a diverse cast of supporting roles. Slavery scarred America deeply. The profound nature of the injuries continues to infect the country with social, economic, and political illnesses. I am convinced that the civil rights movement shook the earth under the feet of white people. The shaking was caused by guilt from the deep scars. The ghosts of dead slaves have evoked too many echoes for America to deny.

America's brutal history still packs a wallop on the jaw of public conscious when race, class, and injustice is discussed. I still have to coach myself away from anger every time I hear some pretentious know-it-all telling me not to play the race card.

The authentic texts of Islam helped me frame an intellectual and spiritual roadmap about slavery. I explored the historical and political economy of race and crime from a fresh angle. An unexpected set of events propelled me in that direction during my final months at Florida State.

THE TRUTH IS NOT TRYING TO FIND YOU

Tony Brown's Journal invited me to talk about Malcolm X in September 1992.[88] I flew to New York, spent nearly one hour with Mr. Brown, and then flew back to Cincinnati the same evening. I went to my office at the University the following Monday morning. I had received over fifty voice messages. The recordings were diverse and the messages ranged from invitations to speak to a simple thank you. One message was from a dear childhood friend.

I had taught at the University nearly four years. The thought of teaching criminal justice students as a career saddened me. Criminology offered no answers to address persistent crime in America. I was no longer willing to ignore economic inequality and historical racism. Both issues, I believed, were correlated significantly with high crime rates.

Academic Criminology relegates economic inequality and historical racism to critical criminology or Marxist scholarship. Critical criminology comes close to unraveling the nexus between economic inequality and historical racism. It falls short, however, because it is inflexible. Also, the age of grand theory was dead.

I wrote an article about this nexus my second year at the University of Cincinnati. The article appeared in a *Critical Criminology* publication.[89]

In many universities, the radical and Marxist professors do not have the same footing of respect as a traditional criminologist. They also do not mentor significant numbers of students. It was obvious to me that economic inequality and historical racism was the big nasty elephant in the room. Traditional criminology paid no attention to obvious contradictions. It bothered me that my profession refused to deconstruct how the corporate plutocrats operate as criminals. I became equally concerned that we didn't attempt to unravel how the American middle class is marginalized under the color of law.

I realized that laws, both criminal and civil in any society, were designed to advance the public good.

People who wield money and influence also manipulate laws. Corporate lobbyists dominate American politics.[90] This observation is factual. I stopped believing that teaching lies and half-truths was just a hazard of an academic profession. I thought what if the medical profession taught surgical procedures that were well-known killers! The same rigor for truth and a complete examination of fact should also govern the social sciences.

I knew I needed to think about earning a living outside of academia. I realized that it was possible to earn a living without teaching half-truths about crime and injustice in America.

I had developed some program evaluation contracts with human service agencies and drug treatment programs over the years in Cincinnati. I turned my attention to consulting and speaking engagements. The speaking venue emerged first.

My friend Hussein moved to Gary, Indiana, after graduating from Central State. He too went back to college as an older student. When he became Muslim, he returned to finish his degree. He became the business manager for the Gary Masjid and invited me to come lecture on a subject of my choosing.

I spoke about the life of Malcolm X (El-Hajj Malik Shabazz). I called the talk "Malcolm X: A Yardstick for African American Manhood."

Several Muslims and a few non-Muslims attended, including a reporter from one of Gary's newspapers. I spoke about Malcolm X on the eve of Spike Lee's movie *Malcolm X*. Hussein introduced me as a criminologist and an expert on the Nation of Islam. The talk went well and subsequently, a recording of my talk, made its way on to a well-known Islamic website in Chicago.

I described Malcolm X's early life as typical for many African American males. His early life shaped him to become a public enemy. It landed him in prison. His circumstances reflected the momentum of slavery that propels African American men toward the snare of crime.

However, Malcolm transformed his past when he joined the Nation of Islam. The NOI's discipline, hard work, and clean living supported his reformation. Malcolm X left the NOI after a very public dispute with the leader, Elijah Muhammad.

Malcolm X grew as a leading spokesperson for African American human rights and justice. He then emerged as the leading symbol of African American manhood. Before his transformation, he sold drugs on the streets of Roxbury. After the NOI transformation, he lectured at Harvard University and Cambridge University. He demonstrated what any black man could accomplish by embracing an uncompromised ideology of black excellence and self-respect. I believe, Malcolm X, as a model and symbol of transformation, threatened white cultural hegemony to its core.

I discussed slavery and the economic undercurrents of surplus slave labor. I depicted Malcolm X as an example that modeled how black men are sidetracked and prevented from entering so-called legitimate labor markets. Black competition and black participation in labor markets became the tip of the spear of a racist rationale to marginalize black folk throughout the Jim Crow period. This dynamic created a clear path for black men from slavery to crime. I concluded my talk by discussing reversion narratives of black Muslim men. These stories described how they escaped a criminal lifestyle. The common thread in their stories was learning about a preslavery identity.

When they changed the picture of themselves, they changed their behavior. They learned what every engineer knows: design informs function. If you shape and fashion a structure to suppress economic prosperity for black men (black people), don't be surprised by their property crimes. If a society discourages personal responsibility and compels black men to survive in a Darwin-like world of survival of the fittest, don't complain about the crime rate.

At the same time, also teach these men how to make moral choices regardless of external circumstances. Teach these men how to overcome adversity.

African American slavery, as a structural mechanism to extract free labor, mutated into a criminal justice system with respect to African Americans.

Profits were a byproduct of social control over black folks' freedom and labor. Slavery justified and legalized the exploitation of black labor. If black folk resisted or escaped, it became a criminal act.

Since Africans arrived in America, they wanted personal freedom and unrestricted free labor. These two aspirations were criminal and antithetical to the so-called American dream of freedom and liberty white people enjoyed and preached to the world. There is no polite way to get around these stark facts. America taught one thing and behaved another. In his book *Seven Habits of Highly Effective People*, Stephen Covey said, "You cannot talk yourself out of what you behaved yourself into."[91]

Covey's statement reinforces an accusing finger black leaders point to America's structural patterns of racism and moral negligence. This finger still merits wagging. I realized that there were four hundred years of empirical evidence that linked the black freedom struggle to a structural definition of crime.

The structural definition is a craft to extend black oppression. Its experts fashioned persistent patterns of political and economic warfare against black folks. It defined protest as criminal; other types of resistance were illegal. Rosa Parks refusing to relinquish her seat on a public bus was illegal. These structural norms and the social conventions they held dear disrupted black family life. They restricted economic life and curtailed other forms of freedom.

Malcolm X connected the critical, political, and historical dots. He explained how black folks' struggle to obtain freedom collided with America's historical and political structure and interest. He did this in his 1965 speech "The Ballot or the Bullet." For my money, Malcolm X's speech delineated where criminology should have focused its grand theories regarding race and crime. The dynamics of slavery and crime deserved attention instead of analytic models describing bad people or bad places (nature versus nurture). Author and law professor Michelle Alexander builds a compelling argument about prison warehousing as neoslavery. She presents evidence for her findings in her book *The New Jim Crow*.

Alexander's well-documented analysis exposes the myth that black males are an inherent public enemy. Her work underscores the practice of racial profiling and aggressive policing as an invading occupation in black communities. She describes how the criminal justice process prelabels black men as criminals and then justifies the label by over policing black communities. She also documents how selling marijuana became a cynical justification to lock up scores of black men for long prison terms. Today many whites are making fortunes selling legalized marijuana. Academic Criminology rarely considers these observations.

My dissertation grew cold, but I was not bothered. I was intrigued by the prospect of giving talks on the lecture circuit. I planned to explain how Islam answered many of the social and spiritual contradictions related to society, race, and crime. A good friend, Herbert Muhammad, (May Allah have mercy on him), who died in his late forties, said, " If a black man with a master's degree cannot make a job for himself, he has wasted at least six years of his life".

Herbert Muhammad's reminder reinforced my conviction that I was on the right path. I left teaching criminal justice because I could not teach what I didn't believe. The half-truths and lies were too big to justify, but I did realize that there was no such thing as living with 100 percent conviction in an academic profession. Most of us do as best we can. I was trying as best I could to find a meaningful way to earn a living and take care of my family. Either run your part of the world or run from it. I had done the latter far too long. I needed to take charge of my life, both academically and personally.

My personal life was also in transition, and I had to face the ugly truth that my marriage was dead. I refused to continue to fool myself and contribute to an unhappy climate of discord. I moved out just before I decided to leave UC.

A nasty divorce ensued, however, I committed myself to remain close to my daughters as much as I could. At times, I had to jump through hoops to see them, but I kept my cool. I dealt with financial hardship for several years. Looking back, I felt that no financial hardship would force me into avoiding child support.

I tried to figure out, in the meantime, what I wanted in a relationship. Trying to find someone "just right" caused me stress and a lot of self-recriminations. I made several hasty and stupid decisions as I stood on the threshold of mending a major mirror crack as I attended a New Year's Eve dinner party. I went to dinner with a much younger woman recently graduated from the University of Cincinnati. She was beautiful, talented, and artistic. I hoped she would revert to Islam, and if she reverted, I'd ask her to marry me. She focused on other things in her life more important than marriage. Besides her unwillingness, I feared the leap across age and religion. We both moved on.

Of course, drinking alcohol dotted the New Year's Eve party. I asked myself, "What the hell are you doing here?" I did not drink. Just the smell of alcohol and the sound of others slurring their words turned my stomach. I would not secure change until I changed within. My resolve to practice Islam with knowledge, and without compromise availed me to abandon attempts to marry a non-Muslim. I had enough compromise. I decided to exercise patience.

Love and relationships are important. They are also hard to find and maintain. Many men and women abandon their core principles to find love. In my view, true love is supported by core values. Personality synergy comes later.

Most people, black, white, and others lack patience and faith. After banging my head against the brick wall of these fundamental values, I chose patience. I waited for a spiritually grounded relationship to occur.

I found the resolve to act in accordance with the Quran and the authentic Sunnah, the verified traditions of the Prophet (prayers and salutations upon him). I continued to visit my daughters on weekends. Dark times can be spiritual medicine. It can remove shortcomings, moral lapses, and return one to worship Allah (God). My spiritual renewal was not a "road to Damascus" experience. I took a sober gaze at my cracked mirror.

Being part-time to myself and part-time to authentic Islam was over. I said enough is enough. Next morning, the first day of the New Year, I dusted off Sayeed Sabiq's book of Islamic jurisprudence. I read it from cover to cover. At times, I soaked the pages with tears.

THE LAKE

I traveled once again to Gary to visit my friend Hussein in early spring of 1995. I arrived around three in the afternoon. I knew Hussein worked until five so I walked to a beach near his house on the Gary, Indiana, side of Lake Michigan. I paused at the edge of the sand and watched the choppy waves tossing a few light boats. I felt a strong urge to write, and as I gazed at the litter on the beach, I found a torn piece of cardboard and a burned charcoal chip. I wrote without thought. My feelings gushed forward like a thawed spring from a winter snow. Within minutes, I'd finished a poem. I scribble a title at the top: "The Lake."

Important as it is
My vision of the eventual demise of self-seekers flickers dimly
As we all somehow manage to drown ourselves in the billowed waves
of doubt
About that which is doubtless.
Our fleeing from the Almighty, like a madman's dash from insects he
believes will devour him
Punctuate the futility of our narrow sense of balance.
By this, our fears have now become organic and the wild imbalance
of our noblest feelings produces remorse.
The tempest wolf watches and waits for sadness to wrinkle my brow
as I journey on the back of trials.
Allah (God) is Eternal. The highest reward in life is to seek Him—a
Guidance Sure, and A Love Supreme.

I tucked the poem under my arm and walked back to Hussein's house. Writing it had a cathartic effect but it also airbrushed insecurity.

Leaving the University left me with an unambiguous direction of wanting to earn a living with dignity. I also wanted to get married again. The last aspiration of getting remarried seemed like a big leap. This would not be easy. There were very few eligible Muslim females in Cincinnati or in the surrounding communities. Then, unexpectedly, a prospect for marriage unfolded. I met Hudayfah, a blind Muslim brother. He needed transportation for kidney dialysis twice a week. I told him I would take him and pick him up. I insisted. After several weeks, we became close. After we had broken the ice of getting acquainted, he asked me if I had a family. I told him I divorced a couple of years before. He then asked me if I wanted to get remarried. I told him yes and he laughed and made a motion with his head some sightless people make from side-to-side. He said, "Brother, I got just the sister for you. You are not scared of young sisters, are you? You still in good health?" We both laughed aloud. I knew what he meant.

"Brother," I said. "I am ready, Insha'Allah (God willing)." The following week, he introduced me to a twenty-one-year-old recently divorced Muslim sister. He acted as her guardian. In Islam, women are represented by a male guardian, usually a family member. If the guardian is not family, then the guardian can be a respected male in the Muslim community.

We talked a couple of times on the phone. We also had dinner at Hudayfah's house. Afterward, her interest grew cold. I felt uncertain as well. I had just turned forty-seven and she had turned twenty-one a few months before we met. She worried about marrying me and we both sensed it could be a challenge if we married. Moreover, we looked for excuses to make a last minute exit. Nevertheless, we were married on a Tuesday evening in March of 1996. I had eleven dollars to my name.

I expected a check from an evaluation contract to come in a couple of weeks. We ate tuna casserole until then. We still faced lean times even after I picked up my check. The early days were happy times in spite of the little money and getting used to one another. She had a young daughter three years old and a son just a shade over a year. My two daughters grew to love her. We were a family. I believe that most of us can sense tragedy and many times we avoid confronting it head on. In our marriage, we dealt with good and bad for ten years.

After we had settled in the Bay Area of California, she told me, after an argument, she did not love me as a wife should. I played a psychologist. I told her she did, but she could not express her feelings. I should have listened. She was right, but I didn't want to hear it. I loved her and wanted to keep my family together. Her rejection hurt and looking back, some of the blame belonged to me. I developed a need for order. Some of it goes back to how I grew up. I think my father's drinking scared me and it robbed our house of order. I needed order to feel less anxious. Love for me even required order. I also had acquired my father's penchant for work. I worked hard at most things. Pushing a work ethic too hard troubled her and I didn't leave much wiggle room for mistakes. To strain things even more, I cannot count the times I called her a lazy N-word under my breath but I am sure my faced showed it. She was far from lazy yet her lack of urgency to perform trivial tasks irritated me.

When she asked me for an annulment, it hit me hard, but it didn't shock me. I recovered, bit by bit, over the next year as I struggled to take a hard look at myself. Even now it is not easy to write about. For sure, it saved me from a journey far worse as her departure helped me focus on interpersonal self-awareness. I really sucked at this for a very long time. I'll leave it here. There is not a lot more to say without making myself into a pincushion.

Perspective matters. Experience matters. Both make us who we are. Both should help us examine how we treat others. How we handle golden moments. How we love. Physical intimacy, as important as it is, will not carry the day.

Marriage requires connecting on many interlocking levels. It requires connections of the intellect and of the disposition. It requires having fun. I made myself "scratch what itches." I scratched the chill of being aloof. I scratched my emotional rope-a-dope defenses. I scratched feeling vulnerable. I knew where my detachment came from. I knew how it started. For years, I lived like a madman fleeing from insects (my poem "The Lake"), from trivial concerns I feared would devour me. I heard a voice from within whisper, "Next time you get married, know that love can come without order. Just let it come." I remarried after two years. We remain married for nearly twenty years.

WEATHER REPORT

I thought about the Cincinnati Muslim community. I knew I would not find meaningful involvement in WD Muhammad's community, and I also realized that there was no point in trying to fit in with elitist immigrant professionals.

A new masjid opened in one of the toughest neighborhoods near downtown Cincinnati, Over-the-Rhine. It was an old neighborhood with plenty of violence and drugs. A University of Cincinnati graduate, Brother Bilal, founded the masjid. He grew up in Over-the-Rhine and believed Islam could penetrate the fortress of crime and drugs by inserting the stability of a neighborhood masjid. He was a realist, though. He knew it would take time to challenge the mandate of the streets. His plan set forth a straightforward goal. If neighborhood people embraced Islam correctly, life would improve. The prospect inspired him to act by walking the talk. His gift to the 'hood' meant establishing a masjid. It would stave off violence and chaos in the lives of residents, and it would make the streets safe. He picked his former turf because the people deserved better. I searched for the same thing. I drove over to the building and parked my car, and I walked over to Bilal and greeted him. "Salaam Alaykum (Peace be upon you), my brother," I said. He looked up while painting the new masjid and replied, "Wa Alaykum Salaam, (Peace be upon you) Zaid. "Hold tight and let me finish this spot so we can talk."

I stood there and watched him paint for a couple of minutes. The early summer morning reddened the sidewalks with sun along with the smell of summer. As Muslims and non-Muslims passed, everyone spoke and wished Bilal well. He turned to me after a few minutes and said, "Brother Zaid, Allah inspired me to do something down here. It didn't occur to me until you parked your car and walked over. Zaid, you are supposed to be the imam of this masjid," he said.

My mind froze. I stared at him, and he looked at me and said, "Think about it, Zaid."

I swallowed and caught my breath. "Akhi (my brother), I can't do this. It's too much for me," I said. We both laughed.

I said, "I am not built for this, Brother Bilal."

He said, "OK, at least come to the masjid now and then, you know, to hang out with the brothers." His face lit up with a mischievous grin.

"I can do that. I'd be happy to," I said.

I returned the following week in work clothes. When I arrived, a few Muslims were working. Bilal stopped painting and turned to us and said, "Brothers, I asked Brother Zaid to be an imam, but he says he can't. What do you brothers think?"

No one answered. Bilal turned to me and said, "Brother Zaid, you can give good talks. You read Arabic, and the brothers and sisters respect you. You were a professor at UC. Folks will listen to you. You know how black folk are. We respect teachers. At least give a talk now and then when the masjid opens."

I grinned. Bilal was trying to run a short con game on me. The short con starts when the mark (that was me in this case) is taken in little by little. After several small steps, the mark is then asked to take the big step. I agreed to give a couple of talks. After a week, I gave in and took the big step of becoming the imam of Masjid Ar-Raheem. Ar-Raheem is one of Allah's (God's) names. It means "recurring mercy." I suggested the name because the masjid would be a mercy for residents in the neighborhood. It did not take me long to notice how the role of race and class operated among Muslims in Cincinnati.

The masjids in Cincinnati were not immune from a "monkey see, monkey do" syndrome regarding African Americans and America's class structure. Many immigrant Muslims viewed African American Muslims in a similar fashion like white Americans saw African Americans, with a jaundiced racist slant.

In Cincinnati, African American Muslims experienced racism from many quarters. Several masjids cast a blind eye on income inequality and social disadvantage. I experienced attitudes that seemed to proclaim that "the poor Muslims are not my problem" because they brought it on themselves. This attitude sickened me. Masjids also faced the challenge to assist homeless Muslims. Request from homeless individuals and families to stay in the masjid were typically denied. Homelessness affects Muslim families, in the same way, as non-Muslims. The underlying causes are chronic unemployment, mental health issues, drug and alcohol dependency, and an ex-offender's status. Masjid Ar-Raheem's members were poor. A few were homeless. Many did not feel like second-class Muslims at Masjid Ar-Raheem as they felt at majority immigrant masjids. I recruited a masjid board of trustees who could embrace coaching, helping, and counseling. I encouraged them to give emotional support to those in need. I tried to explain to board members why shaming and blaming did not solve problems. These services made me proud to be imam. As Imam, I gave talks a couple of times a week.

I prepared the Friday talk ("jum'ah" or "the gathering") carefully. After a brief lecture, a congregational prayer is held. Men are required to attend and women attend as well but are not obliged. I used the text of the Quran and the authentic Sunnah to convey a message to strengthen balanced decision-making, mindfulness, and faith in Allah (God). I tried to practice, as best as possible, these virtues. Within months masjid attendance increased. Students from UC visited along with African American Muslims from other masjids, and a modest number of immigrant Muslims and a few non-Muslims. Masjid Ar-Raheem established a welcomed presence in the community.

I struggled as an imam in spite of several positive developments. I learned to listen carefully, not take criticism personally, and study regularly. I came to the masjid daily, several times a day. I got to know and understand the brothers that came for prayers. I saw them when they were happy and depressed. I counseled couples with marital issues. The climate of the masjid, like a weather report, changed daily. Some days produced bright conditions. On other days, a cloudy overcast produced storms. I began to face grumbles and distractions after a year as Imam. One board member pressured me to allow a propagation group to dominate masjid activities. I refused and decided to resist Tablighi Jamaat (the propagation group) when I became an imam.

Masjid activities must follow the fundamentals of the Quran and Sunnah, as understood by the first three generations of Muslims, the Pious Predecessors. I realized that adherence to the authentic creed, the Quran, and practices of the companions of Prophet Muhammad (prayers and salutations upon him) made Islam practical and meaningful.

I resisted extremes of all types based on my belief in the stability of Quran and the authentic Sunnah (prophetic traditions). During this time period, I changed jobs as all of these events occurred. I took a job as a research coordinator at Central State University after a year as Imam. Central State is sixty-one miles north of Cincinnati. Central State became the birthplace of my spiritual awakening in the 1960s. Now, due to my new work requirements, I did not come to the masjid daily. My job also required travel to conduct evaluation site visits at other universities. Disputes with Masjid Ar-Raheem's board came to a head when I invited a well-known imam for a weekend seminar. He advocated adherence to the Quran and authentic Islam. He believed that the Quran and the verified sayings of Prophet Muhammad (prayers and salutations upon him) should shape masjid activities.

We both considered sects and groups that emerged in Islam after the end of the third generation, over twelve hundred years ago, altered the explicit teachings of authentic Islam. These groups innovated newly invented additions. They also instituted critical deletions. Some of these groups were ultra spiritual Sufi sects, race-focused groups like the NOI, and men who use terror in the name of Islam.

Authentic Islam emphasizes balance and moderation. My ongoing dispute with a couple of board members weighed heavy on my heart. I resigned as imam of Masjid Ar-Raheem in spring 1997.

Actions and Intentions

The composition of Islamic organizations in America has lacked vitality for many decades. My background in the civil rights movement, Black Nationalist groups, and the Nation of Islam shaped my expectations about community-based activities. I believe that Islamic groups should take the lead to confront injustice, restore social equity and compassion, and develop mechanisms to promote income equality.

For the most part, immigrant Muslim organizations failed miserably to embrace these activities. Some immigrant Muslims were aware they should play a more significant role in the community. However, too many immigrant Muslim organizations were content to function as weekend social clubs.

After I had departed from WD Muhammad's community, it seemed the community made a deliberate effort to distance itself from the authentic Islamic creed. It would be unfair to heap all of the blame upon Imam Muhammad. I believe his community will emerge eventually to embrace authentic Islam according to the understanding of the first three generations of Muslims during the time of the Prophet Muhammad (prayers and salutations upon him). I also believe that WD Muhammad fell victim to the burden of history and family pressures.

WD Muhammad's community is not alone in distance from authentic Islam. Many Muslim organizations in North America do not promote the beliefs or implement the methodology of authentic Islam. A few well-known Muslim organizations exist and perhaps most visible of these groups is the Islamic Society of North America (ISNA).

ISNA is mostly membered with professional Muslims. Many of them are second-generation immigrants. The organization attempts to meet the needs of immigrants and a few nonimmigrant professionals. The bulk of their activities occurs on the weekend. The organization's leaders and many of the general membership are secularized American-Muslims in dress, economic aspirations, and career pursuits. Other organizations are single-purposed like Hamza Yusuf's Zaytuna College.

Hamza Yusuf and Zaid Shakir founded Zaytuna in 2009. Hamza and Zaid are visible prominently as spokespersons for what the media calls Moderate Islam.[92] Both Hamza and Zaid seemed fond of the idea Muslims should have a place at the table of American pluralism. I personally do not endorse their position on some matters of Islamic creed and Islamic methodology. On the other hand, Hamza and Zaid have established organizational capacity. They also seemed to understand how to use social capital. They have used it to advance Islamic higher education. They denounce terrorism as well, as it should be denounced. The concept of terror is alien to the authentic teaching of Islam. Many in the West know this implicitly. Nevertheless, certain political groups and political and financial interest insist on blaming Islam. Their habit of blaming Islam for the behavior of some Muslims is like a man pointing to the sun. The one being asked to look at the sun refuses. Instead, he stares at the pointing hand. The hand and the sun should not be mistaken. Promoting or condoning terrorism in Islam is just wrong. No authentic Islamic classical text sanctions terror. Most Muslims denounce terrorism regardless of ethnic origin, class status, or family income. It is sad that many immigrant Muslims do not denounce prejudice and class bias like they abhor terrorism.

However, I believe that one must concede that the same structural forces that shape class bias for white Americans operates in a similar way to fashion class bias for immigrant Muslims.

These powerful forces influence how they interact with African American Muslims. The stranglehold that social class biases have on many immigrant Muslims is shameful, but not surprising. Thousands of Muslims immigrated to America to blend in and assimilate. Many came to pick the fruit of the good life. A good number of them became wealthy. I admit these groupings are not comprehensive or exhaustive. Other Muslim groups have a significant presence in America. There are organizations like WD Muhammad's community, Imam Jamil Al Amin's[93] (formerly H. Rap Brown, SNCC leader). Also, there is the Jammat Tabliq, the Quran and Sunnah Society, and the various organizations QSS nurtured and mentored. Other groups exist like the Ansar Group and its leader, Dr. Malachi Z. York[94] and his various alias and reincarnations are in a class of its own. His organization evolved from street hustling for donations in New York to building pyramids and obelisk-like structures in rural Georgia. They occupy the distinction of being at the extreme end of esoteric African American groups that claim Islam. Farrakhan's NOI and the rival NOI groups that also claim Islam are like Dr. York's group. A majority of Muslim scholars consider the latter two outside of Islam. Both groups is not Muslim, according to Islamic jurisprudence. A lot of Muslims were drawn to the Quran and Sunnah Society (QSS) of North America in the early 1990s.

QSS attracted about ten thousand Muslims. QSS's appeal was attractive because of its clear message, objectivity in the creed, and sound methodology of following the traditions of Prophet Muhammad (prayers and salutations upon him).[95] I was happy, beyond words, to find an organization based on theological clarity and textual proofs. One month after I resigned as imam, QSS moved its headquarters from Austin, Texas, to Cincinnati, which was perfect timing for me.

QSS was founded in 1986 and was chaired by Mahmoud Murad from 1986 to 1991. Dr. Muhammad Al-Jibaly chaired QSS from 1991 to 1997. Dr. Jibaly, the QSS president, was educated as a physicist at the University of Florida in the 1980s. He was a graduate student at the University of Florida while I was in graduate school at Florida State University. He knew some of the Saudi students from Florida State that visited the Gainesville campus for religious gatherings. However, I do not remember meeting him during my visits to Gainesville. QSS's impact in North America was one of the most significant developments in the American Muslim community, after the death of Malcolm X.

QSS was influenced strongly by Shaykh Muhammad Nasir Din Al Albaanee (may Allah (God) have mercy on him). Shaykh Al Albaanee spurred a revival of Islam in the West and elsewhere. He was the major hadith scholar in this century. May Allah (God) grant him abundant mercy and a generous reward!

The QSS message was: "Invite people to Islam; to help them understand it; practice it; and purify themselves with it, all in accordance with the blessed Manhaj (methodology) of the Salaf" (Pious Predecessors). The Dawah (call and mission) of QSS comes from Allah's Book and the Sunnah of His Messenger (prayers and salutations upon him).

It's hard to estimate the impact the QSS website, their weekly newspaper, *Huda,* and the QSS bookstore had on Muslims in North America. QSS books were in no small measure a significant source of accurate Islamic literature. Dr. Al-Jibaly's books were popular and widely read. He also translated some of the important works of Shaykh Al Albaanee.

Shaykh Al Albaanee's book *The Prophet's Prayer Described* was a game changer for the average Muslim. It focused not on just the prayer. The book advanced learning the methodology of the authentic Sunnah. The book placed a strong emphasis on adherence to authentic statements of the Prophet (prayers and salutations upon him) to guide Muslims in all matters.

Then, Dr. Muhammad Al-Jibaly, the QSS President and Abu Khaliy, a talented translator and long-standing QSS staff member left Cincinnati in 1997. They relocated the QSS office to Detroit. However, QSS only stayed in Detroit for a little more than a year when Dr. Al-Jibaly left America for Lebanon while Abu Khaliyl took a job as an editor and translator for a publishing company in Saudi Arabia. I was disappointed that Dr. Al-Jibaly and Abu Khaliyl left QSS, and thus, I saw no reason to remain in Cincinnati.

SELF-MASTERY WHISTLE STOP

I applied for a job as a researcher in San Francisco. I interviewed twice and, after a couple of weeks, the company offered me a position as a senior research associate. The job seemed like a good opportunity, but I was concerned about leaving my mother. She had not been feeling well and complained about a pain just below her left rib cage, but she told me not to worry. She wrote it off as old age or a stomach virus. I faxed an appeal to a Masjid in downtown San Francisco and explained I needed to rent a room. "I can pay," I said. "Please call if anyone can help." I got a call the following day from a Yemeni expat. He had lived in San Francisco several years and invited me to sub rent.

I asked my wife and children to remain in Cincinnati until I could afford to bring them. I prepared to leave Ohio for California and flew from Cincinnati to San Francisco in the third week of September 1997. I lived with the Yemeni brother six months. I slept, with humility and pride, in a large walk-in closet when the floor space became too crowded with other sub-renters. I spent my days and nights reflecting that no sacrifice would prevent me from relocating my family as I searched for a place after I saved enough, even though I felt overwhelmed. The dot-com boom made Bay Area rents sky-high. Even though I earned a decent salary, I was hard pressed to find a livable place in a suitable neighborhood. I prayed on how to move forward. Shortly afterward, a friend gave me a business card for a residential motel in Vallejo, California, owned by an immigrant Indian Muslim. Vallejo ranked as one of the least expensive places in the Bay Area. When the family arrived, we settled into the Vallejo hotel. The hotel was not as run-down as I had feared, so I rented a room two weeks in advance. My wife arrived on an Amtrak train two days later.

We had lived in the hotel for a few weeks before I found an affordable apartment, and moreover, I was happy that the organization paid for the shipping of my belongings. At work, I started with small research projects, coordinating data collection and evaluating program activities. The organization was doing well financially. In just one year, the organization's state and federal contracts increased by thirty percent.

At the end of the calendar year, the organization's president arranged bonuses for staff. My supervisor resisted my raise. Red flags went up. The president told her to stand down. It caught both of us by surprise. Eventually I got the ten percent raise but she did not forget the snub by the president. She launched sortie after sortie at me, but I didn't have the energy to fight back. I was too preoccupied with real life issues.

I felt numb after I learned that my mother's gastric irritation turned out to be lung cancer. I flew out to Ohio to be with her. I prayed for her recovery as she underwent an operation, but the cancer metastasized as her death drew near. I had used all of my leave time and returned to San Francisco. My dear friend, my mother, struggled to hold onto life three thousand miles away. I recalled her wisdom, her direct and candid way and her soft heart and gentle eyes. I thought about how she chided, guided, and urged me to be strong: "Zaid, God has your back. If it didn't kill you, it just got your attention. Handle it. That's all." She started reading an English translation of the Quran in 1996. She said the Quran comforted her and she believed its message. She used to remind me to read a surah (chapter) when I struggled with various issues. I thought about her several times a day, every day. I just didn't have the will or time to worry about my supervisor's micromanaging, her hovering, and her faultfinding. I didn't feel at my best personally or professionally. Maybe her anger stemmed from something in me that threatened her on an emotional level.

I have experienced, like others have, that some people dislike us immediately. Once I asked a friend why someone we knew mutually didn't like me. He never gave me a clear answer. One friend told me that it seems I gave a poker face look too often and my emotions are hard to read. Anyway, I wasn't sure why my supervisor had it in for me and didn't care. My mother's health preoccupied my every thought.

Maybe my supervisor didn't realize how much of her rage I felt. At first I thought it was job performance—maybe I sucked. However, even if I sucked, why did it feel so personal?

Then I said, well, maybe I offended her. I thought about every possible interaction. "Nope, that's not it either," I said. It made me sick that she sized me up and then grew an attitude the size of Jack's beanstalk. Her demeanor puzzled me and I did not fathom the depth of her visceral feelings until I accidentally brush against her arm. She jerked away and said, "Yuk."

"Yuk?" I thought. I do not rub off. Damn lady, what is your problem? I knew it would be just a matter of time before she fired me. The ax fell a month after my mother died, just a few days shy of her eighty-third birthday in 1999.

Getting fired did not surprise me. Racial bias operates as an intentional bad guy and an unintentional bully. A characteristic of American racism and social class bias shapes individual actors and molds institutional structures into a complex web of racial and class-based emotions that defy rational thought. Sometimes the actors smack you in the eye without realizing they threw punches. At other times, the hatred cannot be hidden. It would be more just if they would simply say the reason was "I don't like you and your race."

But don't hold your breath for that level of candor. American culture fashions people to conceal the truth in the name of political correctness.

I packed a few belongings to leave my small office feeling both dismay and fatigue while most staff avoided eye contact with me. Nonetheless, a couple of people wished me well as I walked out the office door. I caught the East Bay train to the last stop and then took a bus to Vallejo. When I walked into our townhouse, my wife asked me nervously how would we survive. I told her the organization gave me three months severance pay. I sent out scores of resumes. Two and a half months had passed before I heard anything, then in the following week, I received two interviews and two offers. The first offer was for a data analyst position. The second offer came from a local university as a research associate.

I accepted the University job offer and started work just as my severance pay ended. Allah (God) is ever watching, kind and merciful. The department's physical and organizational location at the University illustrated the marginal role it played. It was not because it lacked value, but times had changed. The building stood at the very edge of the campus in a single large room. Perhaps its location symbolized its nebulous status in the University. The department did good work in the heyday of grants and soft money, but in the late 1990s, "pickings were slim," as my mother used to say.

Now, I stood face to face with the fact that my mother's death separated me from her spiritual and emotional support. Her death demonstrated some mistakes that I had made. Her ears had safeguarded many of my secrets for years, and I had turned to her in hard times. Instead of turning to her too often, I should have relied on Allah (God). Reliance means to put forth every effort possible and then trust in the outcome from Allah (God). Effort is a means, not an outcome. Moreover, the outcome is not always linear.

At times, results show no straight path. Reliance on Allah (God) requires insight and faith and firm trust. Sometimes we pray for things and strive as best we can to make things happen but have no idea how things will turn out. An instance of this observation stands out. While I drove down a busy street before I left Cincinnati for California, a young woman ran in front of my car. I hit her—bam! I didn't have time to apply my breaks. She rolled across my hood, hit the sidewalk, and jumped up. She started running to catch a bus. The street was filled with white faces. Stoic white Cincinnati faces that I have described previously. I stepped out of my car and expected drama. A police car pulled up. Between the police officer and me stood three or four older white folks. Before I could say a word, a couple of them said, "It was not his fault. She ran right in front of his car. He had no choice." We all turned to the hurried woman. She shook visibly.

"Are you OK?" I asked.

"Yes," she said nervously.

The policeman asked me, "Can you take her to the hospital up the street?"

I glanced at her. She nodded to agree. I turned my car around, she got in, and we drove to the hospital. Now in my car she said, "You know, this comes as a blessing that you hit me. I am going through a divorce and my mind is all over the place. I am not aware of myself like before. Getting hit was a wake-up call. My prayers are answered. Thank you, sir."

I got out of the car, walked to the passenger side, and opened the door. She got out and walked into the emergency room. As I watched her walk into the emergency room, I thought about the incident and reliance on Allah (God). It showed me that things are not always as dreadful as they first appear. Her dash in front of my car helped her snap out of not being present in her life and it demonstrated to me that I shouldn't airbrush all Cincinnati's white people as racist.

My life on the west coast unfolded with spiritual and personal development lessons. I spent precious time with family and used the surplus for intellectual and religious pursuits. Since I had no friends in the Bay Area and my prospects for socializing were slim, I started giving lectures at a rented storefront to a small group of local Muslims.

A local branch of Jamaat Tabliq, the same group I resisted in Cincinnati, controlled the Vallejo Masjid. They invited me to give talks at the masjid from time to time. I also reviewed a book on the creed of Islam with a small group of Muslims in Vallejo, as well as a few Muslims from surrounding North Bay Cities. Abdullah, one of the young men who attended my talks, lived in a less affluent section of Marin City, and he looked up to me as a big brother, if not a father figure. I ran into Abdullah years later, and he reminded me that my talks helped him make an important life change. His words echo a well know tradition in Islam that one should never discount good deeds, even if they are small.

Given the pattern of my life, I realized that I would struggle with near poverty, flashes of prosperity, and pauses between joy and sorrow. I came to realize that Allah's (God's) plan for me of varying grades of joy and pricks of sorrow turned out to be a trusted teacher of faith and patience.

I spent four years in the Bay Area. I believe the nature of adversity is always medicine for what ails us. I experienced trials and tests of my faith and it grew me in important ways. Nevertheless, once again, it was time to move on. My inclination to leave remained unhobbled by the illusion of job security, an apartment, or other so-called traditional security markers.

I browsed the web for jobs in the winter of 2000 and landed two interviews. I interviewed at Georgia Tech University in Atlanta in March 2001 and
at Charles Drew University of Medicine and Science in Los Angeles in May
2001. I received offers from both schools. I accepted the Georgia Tech offer
and started my plans to leave for Atlanta.

On my journey to Atlanta, I stopped at a Los Angeles masjid and Muslim
school to visit friends. My old companion, Muhammad Madany, made arrangements for me to spend the night in a masjid guest room. I rested well and
prayed in the Masjid around five o'clock in the morning. After prayer, I rested
a while longer, and then drove over to the school to meet Muhammad. At the
school, I watched Muhammad make a phone call. The phone call facilitated a
critical decision that would connect me to people and places I longed to know
more about. Muhammad called a friend at a money transfer network. As he
spoke with him, I sat at his desk, ate a breakfast roll, and sipped a cup of cof-
fee. Muhammad transferred several hundred dollars to his wife thousands of
miles away in the Republic of the Gambia. The transaction required no Western
Union fee and no pin numbers. This event rested in my mind. Money transfer networks are not new to West African and East African communities in
America and Europe. The informality and trust intrigued me. It operated seam-
lessly. It tied people together as an extended family. I longed to live that type of
cohesion and trust that creates social capital.

Social capital is the human 'super-glue' that holds healthy communities
together. It is an interlocking mutual dependency of shared values, shared
resources, and being committed to "walk the talk."

I bid farewell to Muhammad and pulled onto the interstate and headed east
to Georgia. I drove my Plymouth van to Atlanta in three days, arriving Friday,
June 8, 2001. I put social capital to work yet again in Atlanta. I stayed with a
close friend and business associate, Mikhail, in a basement apartment of his
home, located in an older upscale Atlanta neighborhood. I found it necessary to
force him to accept money from me to stay in his very comfortable home.

We had been friends years before when we both lived in Indianapolis. I started
work at Georgia Tech the following Monday. Life in Atlanta began with a genuine
feel of home. The buildings, topography, and people reminded me of Ohio.

A masjid opened a few years prior to my arrival on a street minutes from Mikhail's home, Masjid As-Salaf As-Salih. The masjid building used to be a thrift store. I had high expectations that life in Atlanta would be all I had hoped: affordable housing, a large number of African-American businesses, an established Masjid, and social contacts with good Muslims. I felt my family would find Atlanta suitable as well. Over fifty masjids populate Metro Atlanta, a number of Muslim operated schools, and several Muslim-owned businesses. I saved enough money in June to lease a house and purchase airfare for my family. They arrived in late July. Georgia Tech paid for the shipping of my household belongings and we spent the month of August unpacking. By September, I settled at work and I developed a routine of domestic life.

I drove to work September 11, 2001. When I walk into my building, none of my coworkers was present. After about five minutes, our secretary returned from an office in an adjacent building. She asked me if I heard the news. The expression on her face told me that she thought I knew. I told her, "No, I just arrived and I didn't hear a thing. Why, what happened?"

She said someone crashed hijacked passenger jets into the World Trade Center. Thousands of people were dead and injured.

Two thoughts came to mind. I hoped an accident caused the crash and I hoped Muslims were not involved. It appeared that both hopes proved wrong.

I walked over to the adjacent office building to watch the TV with other staff. A hush covered the room as I watched the second plane crash. A woman from the provost's office started to cry while others shook their fists angrily. Two people turned to me and searched my face with their puffy red eyes, looking for a response, and then my supervisor asked us to return to our office.

Within an hour, Georgia Tech closed. By evening several Muslims in Atlanta and across America had been attacked, some fatally. America's foreign policy response to invade Iraq because of the planes that crashed into the twin towers resembled the racist rebel yell "Get them niggers!" It reminded me of the race riots from 1920 to 1930 when angry white folks attacked communities over single incidents where black folks were involved.[96] The race riot in Tulsa is famous where an entire black community was victimized because of some actual or perceived event that involved an African American. I must say, I only repeat the term 'race riot' to be consistent with how history books describe the incident. It was not a riot. Rather, it was an attack by whites, and while some black people tried to defend their lives and property, does not make the incident a riot.

It doesn't take much tugging to peel off America's xenophobic mask and the events on September 11, 2001, proved to be more than enough.

After 9/11 many things changed for me and other Muslims. On the one hand, Muslims had to examine why and how some Muslims fell into carrying out acts of violence against symbols of Western civilization and killing innocent people. On the other hand, several Muslims have failed to confront America's xenophobic and racist reaction to Islam. To speak out against xenophobic racism is threatening for many Muslims.

Trusted Islamic scholars should clarify Islamic religious and public affairs. These issues are not appropriate for mouthpiece hacks, despots, or half-studied advocates to offer violent solutions to problems real or imagined. No one would accept a legal ruling from an auto mechanic on corporate income tax. Thus, it is improper for unqualified individuals to justify extremism or terrorism that is contrary to the clear principles of Islam. When this happens, doors open for people to act out suffering and oppression in an inappropriate manner.

Some Muslims accepted a rationale that America was justified in carrying out an aggressive war against Islam, the so-called War on Terror. The lynch mob hysteria following the 9/11 attack became a foreign policy rationale for the invasion of Iraq. The myth surrounding the fabled weapons of mass destruction was exposed as a fabrication. Then it mutated into a rationale called Operation Enduring Freedom. Following this, America's war machine went into high gear to prosecute an all-out war against an insignificant Iraqi leader, Saddam Hussein. Tens of thousands of Iraqi citizens died. Many Americans died needlessly as well.

America should have never prosecuted this war. America claimed that Iraq posed threats to world order with weapons of mass destruction. No weapons of mass destruction were found. It does not matter if clever neocons or Jim

Crow racists cooked up the rationale for war. There is no excuse for this type of betrayal of public trust. I am disappointed by the American Government's litany of paranoid lies and distortions regarding threats from enemies it created and nourished. Let us not forget that Iraq became a partner in an American-supported war against Iran and as a proxy for American interest in the Persian Gulf. America supported Iraq when it suited America's interest, and then within years, America invaded Iraq. Policies and practices like these are imperialistic.

The claim that America is justified to attack other nations in the name of America's interest is neoimperialism and gunboat diplomacy. America's interest and its double-standard support for friendly despotic regimes are appalling. I believe that America's maintenance of double standards as domestic and foreign policy are the main reasons America has lost moral authority.

America cannot preach to the world about justice and democracy while flaunting such blatant double standards.

My job at Georgia Tech went smoothly for the next year. Then, in November of 2002, my supervisor's department underwent reorganization. My position disappeared. I applied for a job as a statistical analyst at Morehouse College, the alma mater of Martin Luther King, Jr. After I had interviewed at Morehouse College, they made an offer within a week. I accepted the offer, but the job didn't begin until January. I said to myself, "Man, I have free time, some money, and a passport." I decided to visit my ancestral home, the Republic of the Gambia. Allah (God) protected me once again.

The Gambia

Every day there are things that connect our past to the present. It may not be clear to us why various life events unfold in the manner they do. Sometimes the connections that link us to places, people, and events we learn later were a part of Allah's (God's) guidance. It is then we have an 'aha' moment of certainty. I did not realize how a small event could generate far-reaching changes. Watching Muhammad Madany that morning in the LA Muslim school access an informal but powerful social capital network made me think. I thought about the problems I encountered growing up. Many problems African Americans face could have been solved if only our communities tapped into our natural networks of social capital. We could have resolved many issues that confronted African Americans. Our use of social capital would have made seeking integration unnecessary.

The African American community's need to cultivate a culture of strong social bonding was characterized by the NOI expression "word is bond." Social capital thrives by keeping promises as the expression 'word is bond' captures the essence of social capital. Words and actions deserve follow-through and require unshakable trust. Africa's underdevelopment is stubborn to alter, and the absence of social capital supports intractable underdevelopment. The habit of not keeping promises, not being on time for appointments, and not paying attention to detail in business and personal affairs makes for building trust and social capital difficult.

In Africa, weak social capital comes from tribalism and neocolonial economic structures along with the lack of principled connections between people across ethnic lines.

Social capital is frail also when African governments allow international development banks to manufacture debt and suppress local production and exports. On the other hand, weak social capital encourages imports and dependency and nudges weak states in the direction of dependency of failed states.

Migrating to an African Muslim majority country appeals to many African American Muslims. I promoted the Gambia to anyone that would listen. I found two Muslims who wanted to visit the Gambia. They wanted to reconnect with a distant African pass. They felt what I felt. I told them about the Gambia one night as we sat in my minivan in a supermarket parking lot. I described what took place as I watched Muhammad Madany at the Muslim school. I told them stories about other African American Muslims in the Gambia. Months after I arrived in Atlanta from California, Muhammad left Los Angeles and returned to the Gambia. I had e-mailed him several times before we left for the Gambia. Now, I would e-mailed him to rent a bungalow on a small plot of land near the rear of his main house. Over the next few weeks, we got immunizations, purchased international mobile phones, budgeted our expenses, and made flight arrangements.

We bought standby airline tickets for a trip to Paris, and then planned to fly to Dakar, Senegal. From Dakar, we planned to take a short flight to the Gambia. We attempted to leave on a Friday night and I could not wait to depart.

We hit a hitch because full-fare passengers occupied all seats. We returned home and successfully flew Saturday night, landing in Paris Sunday morning to catch a transfer flight to Dakar. Once again, those pesky full-fare holiday travelers filled every seat. We thought standby would give us an inexpensive hassle-free bargain. We anticipated being a step ahead of holiday travel in the first week of December.

We had no idea that the traditional holiday break in France began two weeks earlier than the holiday break in the United States. We huddled in the visitor's lounge, discussed our situation, and decided to find an inexpensive hotel. We found one in South Paris.

We caught the subway to check out the infamous Paris suburbs and also to see downtown Paris. As we rode the train, we were shocked to see that the Paris suburbs were actually worse than the housing projects on the south side of Chicago.

As we walked through one of the downtown mall areas, I remembered a dream I had several years before. In my dream, I was wandering around downtown Paris with two other Muslims, who I didn't know well. It was a vivid, colorful dream. We were looking for a place to pray and now, in the downtown area, walking around, I recalled the dream. I told myself just let the dream unfold. If my dream foretold anything, it said that divine guidance comes with prayer. I just needed to chill. We ate at a McDonald's in the downtown mall area and then we looked for a Paris version of an American economy hotel. We were exhausted, but hard hotel mattresses didn't rob us of a good night's sleep. The following morning we hopped aboard a train to the airport.

My two traveling partners wondered if we should go back to America and try after a month. "Nope," I insisted. "We will make it. Allah (God) is with us." My desire to reach Africa remained unshaken.

Then reality hit us. We realized that standby tickets are near worthless in the holiday season. We decided to purchase full-fare tickets on Moroccan Airlines to Dakar. When the plane began to descend over Senegal, it made a wide approach to the east. I looked out of the window and saw Dakar surrounded by green-blue water. Its white buildings nestled together against a blue December sky caused my heart to race with joy.

As we prepared to land, I noticed one of my traveling companions sobbing. He moved his head from side to side while wiping tears from his eyes.

In a whisper, he kept repeating, "We are home, we are home!" His outpouring of joy reached the depths of my heart. Yes, finally, I had arrived home. A bliss filled me that was impossible to express with words. My feelings caused me to remember the title of the book *I Know Why the Caged Bird Sings*. The building takeover thirty-five years before at Central State came to mind. Ok, I thought, the events that compelled me to reject the black middle-class promised land, actually, stemmed from the reality that I craved to experience Africa beyond African Studies. The dots of the near past and a distant past connected me to Africa and I was thrilled to remove the romance of Africa and accept its gritty reality. I knew it would not look like America or Europe and there would be practical and emotional challenges to deal with. Nevertheless, the adage "There's no place like home" was the best expression to match my feelings.

It saddens me, however, that millions of African Americans have no visceral connection to Africa. Many African Americans continue to carry around denial and shame about an African past. It prevents us from owning our biological, ethnic, and historical connections to Africa. The brutality of the trans-Atlantic slave trade endures. It inflicted a horrible aftermath in our minds and our emotional makeup. Dr. Joy DeGruy called this aftermath post-traumatic slave syndrome.[97]

We began our journey the previous Saturday and we arrived in the Gambia on Thursday. We stepped off the plane into customs and proceeded to pick up our luggage. During a four-hour layover in Dakar, each of us exchanged US dollars for Senegalese Francs and sidestepped the airport short con artists. "Welcome home to Africa, my brothers, let me help you," they said.

"Yep," we laughed among ourselves. "Game knows game" and it only differs in Africa as an accent.

We bought tickets to Banjul, Gambia, and after a short delay, we were on our way. As I mentioned before, I had arranged with Muhammad Madany to rent his bungalow, a "boy's house" as the Gambians call it, before we left Atlanta. Now in Africa, I did not think about a restful visit, taking back great stories, and colorful pictures. I sought after a way to make a living, build a house, and make Gambia my home. I wanted to live in a Muslim society with decent Quran and Arabic schools for my children. During the first week, Muhammad Madany introduced us to some of the Americans that lived in the Gambia. Most of them had lived in the Gambia for a number of years. Some were remnants of a group of Muslims from Los Angeles that migrated to Brikama, the country's second largest city in the late 1980s.

The LA Muslim group had purchased a modest-sized plot of land and had built several houses and a school. A group of Muslims from London had built several houses, a masjid, and a school in an area dominated by the Jola tribe, a few miles south of Brikama. Both communities attracted a number of Western Muslim families. The President of the Gambia, Yahya Jammeh, adopted a friendly policy toward American and British expats. I was also thrilled to reconnect with a man from the Bahamas, Latif Johnson, I knew during the QSS days in the mid-1990s.

By the second week in the Gambia, Latif told me about two plots of inexpensive land on the north side of the Gambia River. We crossed the river on the state-run ferry to the portside village of Barra. We took a taxi to Mayamba, a small Mandinka village a few miles from the border of Senegal. We hiked through the bush to meet the village chief (the "Okalla") to negotiate the purchase of two plots of land. Both plots were ideal for building compounds. Our purchase cost less than one thousand US dollars.

The small plot of land is the only place on earth that I own. Allah (God) blessed me to do what millions of African Americans have not yet been blessed to do. The dream was to reconnect personal biography with history and land. Sadly, the African diaspora is a history lesson that many are not interested in learning full circle. The lesson is about African people and the way the world has perceived us, both in Africa and in scattered lands. It was important for me to return to Gambia for two reasons. The first reason was to practice my religion without a concern of being misunderstood or maligned. The second reason was to embrace a neglected past. I knew that both reasons were important. I removed my sandals and dug my toes into the warm rust-colored soil and felt the heat from the ground rush up my legs to the rest of my body. With a couple of deep, joyful sighs, I held back tears. I owned a piece of Africa and it made me feel complete.

In the third week of my visit, time ran out. I had to return to America and start my job at Morehouse College. I was nearly out of money and I did not want to go back to America empty-handed. I was on the doorstep of desperation. I even thought about applying for jobs at the UN or with an NGO.

As a last attempt to secure an opportunity in the Gambia, I bought a local newspaper in the parking lot of a petrol station. I browsed the classified section. My eye was drawn to a request for funding proposal (RFP). It was for a survey of radio and television consumer habits. A week remained until the deadline. I typed a proposal on an old computer at Muhammad Madany's house. The next day I phoned an American expat from New York, Abdul Malik, I knew from my street merchant days. He had lived in the Gambia for over fifteen years. Abdul Malik had social connections to several government officials.

He made a few calls and arranged an appointment for me with the Gambia Radio and Television Service's (GRTS) general manager.

I presented a practical qualitative research approach of training local workers to collect data, managing the language diversity in the Gambia by hiring Wolof, Mandinka, Fula, and Jola speakers. I planned to analyze the data using a multistage complex survey design. I included state-of-the-art procedures in my proposal. My budget of forty-five thousand US dollars covered six months of data collection, administrative work, and a report of the findings. The deadline for submission closed in two days. Only one proposal was submitted. Sure thing I thought. But not so fast, Zaid, more surprises were in store. I waited for a call from GRTS. I planned to go to their office, sign the contract, work out the logistics, and start my life in the Gambia. No call came. I called my old friend, Abdul Malik and the sound of his voice alerted me he knew why I called. He told me the contract went to another bidder. "What other bidder?" I asked him. Another bidder won the contract, that's all he could tell me. I called the GRTS director several times without success. Muhammad Madany and Abdul Malik advised me not to protest or make accusations.

"Zaid, don't push the Western transparency argument too far," Muhammad said. "America doesn't even work like that. In Africa, it is common. Don't take it personally."

I remained angry nonetheless. I emailed the department head at Morehouse College to say I would start the following week. Mustafa and I caught the ferryboat to Barra, not far from where I bought my land. We then caught a bus to Dakar. Abdul Aziz, our traveling partner, traveled with the Gambian pilgrims to Mecca, Saudi Arabia, for the hajj pilgrimage. The government of Saudi Arabia leases an aircraft to several African countries every year to accommodate African pilgrims.

I felt ill when I boarded the airplane in Dakar because I had contracted stage one malaria. I dreaded a layover in Paris and I could not afford a hotel.

When I ticketed in Paris for New York, an upgrade landed me in business class. This was a blessing from Allah (God) and it eased the discomfort of a seven-hour flight. There was light snow when I landed in New York. As I took in a few breaths of the cold winter air, I felt sad, and I repeated to myself, "Failure is an event, not a person." It sounded good, but the reality of returning to America without accomplishing my main migration objective was tough to accept. I struggled to remember that events that feel like failure are not necessarily a failure, after all. I arrived in Atlanta at seven-thirty in the evening, caught a train to a stop near my house, and after a short wait, my wife picked me up. I hoped that the job at Morehouse would turn out fine. I prayed for contentment, but it did not take long to see that Allah's (God's) plan for me was better than being in the Gambia.

After a year at Morehouse, I became director of institutional research. My job at Morehouse gave me a chance to sharpen my professional skills and I benefited in meaningful ways with African Americans in higher education. I also regained self-confidence as the threat of a racist critique vanished. The times I messed up did not warrant race-tainted finger pointing. I took corrective steps and moved forward. Working at a majority African American institution gave me the personal security that white people must feel at majority white institutions. Thousands of African American academic professionals start and end their careers at African American schools. One significant factor for this security, without a doubt, is that the phantom of racism no longer lingers in the shadows. Excellence and failure are assessed free of race.

I worked at Morehouse five years. Working at a HBCU felt like what many white people must experience with white privilege as a result of race-neutral performance assessments.

Morehouse College had opened in 1867. It earned a reputation for excellence under President Benjamin Mays from 1940 to 1967.[98] Beginning in the Reconstruction Era, historically black colleges and universities (HBCUs) have constituted a safety net for African American students, faculty, and employees. Some in the African American community believe HBCUs are outdated and unimportant. I disagree with this view. Since the Reconstruction Era, HBCUs played a significant role to stem the effects of slavery. It would be a grave mistake to believe that America's educational institutions are postracial. Racial divisions in America have widened over the past twenty years and some efforts to maintain racial inequalities are mean-spirited and violent. It is one of the many paradoxes of having an African-American President. On one hand, many whites are comfortable with President Obama's performance, net of race. Other whites, and there are many, hate President Obama because of race, net of performance.

My work at Morehouse turned out to be a bittersweet final scene to a thirty-five-year journey. I watched Morehouse gain recognition for its leadership. I also watched the institution drift from a culture of deep learning and community development to a culture focused on career success. Morehouse and other HBCUs did not create this trend. The trend is an outgrowth of misplaced priorities and economic insecurity. The drift from deep learning to jobs and money was not race specific. I believe that a society's dignity comes from a distribution of social opportunity and economic justice. Collective success will emerge when the playing field is leveled and masks of pretense are discarded. African Americans can, then, calmly reject race-driven double standards. If you chase the world, it flees from you.

If you approach obtaining wealth with purpose and dignity, it runs toward you. This concept once lived in the heart of the African American freedom struggle. Even when confronted by a few negative events and attitudes, it felt wonderful to work at Morehouse.

It saddened me, however, that my generation failed to provide young African American men and women with a critical lens to examine our history. We failed them. The giants of the past like Fredrick Douglas, W. E. B. Dubois, Marcus Garvey, Malcolm X, and others were not hamstrung by the lure of living good over principled lives. If HBCUs focused on a sober assessment of the African American freedom struggle, these institutions would be capable of creating the capacity to reduce high rates of violence and graduate more students. They could reduce risky sexual behavior and divert young black males from glorifying "thug life." A focus of this nature would also produce a climate that promotes ambition, innovation, a vibrant business community, and strong family life. These institutions could also help majority white institutions escape from a morally bankrupt atmosphere of sexual assault, binge drinking, drug use and Greek organization-inspired racism and bigotry. I used to stare at a statue of Dr. King at Morehouse College that rises about twenty-five feet upward between two walkway entrances to the campus administration building. The statue is a symbol of dignity and the resolve that

Dr. King exemplified. The statute of Dr. King should promote critical think-ing, not sentimentality. HBCUs were not founded as middle-class country clubs for an African American elite. Many HBCUs drifted from a focus on the well-being of "a people" to the success of individuals. Adult visitors, grade school students, middle school students, and high school students often pose in front of Dr. King's statue for pictures. But are they connecting with what this image represents? I have watched them stare at Dr. King's likeness with a mixture of awe and reverence.

It seems to me that if the walls of the buildings around King Chapel could speak, they would tell us stories about a freedom struggle. They would not narrate how to turn a start-up business into a publically traded company.

The pieces of brick and mortar would unravel stories about men and women who put their lives and their reputations on the line. It would not tell stories about selfish leaders who destroyed their reputations resulting from greed and moral lapses. The walls of the buildings would reflect how these men and women pressured America to live what it preaches without selling out for crumbs from the dining table of status quo. The walls would also echo how Dr. King and Malcolm X critiqued a war in Vietnam and resisted FBI plots to destroy them.[99]

Both men shared a vision of human rights, not merely civil rights. They did not succumb to cynical hedonism. Both men rejected the rationale that material prosperity trumps ethics. Many of today's African American estab-lishment leaders have abandoned these principles. I could mention names, but I won't. I listened to Dr. King's speeches and I pondered the "I Have a Dream" speech. Little black children and little white children are not holding hands. They will not grow up respecting each other until America abandons its obsession with white privilege or being a world power and an empire. Both men rejected predatory capitalism and they denounced an economic system mired in greed and inhumanity. I believe their stance lead to both men's as-sassination. When Dr. King denounced the war in Vietnam, he refashioned the civil rights movement in the context of a human rights struggle. He advo-cated support for labor movements on the eve of his assassination. Dr. King lost the bulk of his support when he publically opposed the war in Vietnam.

The mainstream press and former civil rights supporters abandoned him. Formidable black voices, like that of Dr. King and Malcolm X, were capable of influencing millions to rethink life in America.

These two voices unnerved the white power structure as both men threatened the power elites with a race-neutral narrative about economics, ethnicity, politics, and social class. The narrative rings true today. Taylor Branch and others have documented that Dr. King remained isolated and marginalized until his assassination because he ventured beyond civil rights. Dr. King echoed the voices of W. E. B. Dubois and Paul Robeson. Both of these men began as moderate Negroes. As they matured, they denounced America's hypocrisy. The critique from Dubois and Robeson angered elements in the white power structure and these fears were evident in the behavior of yesterday's FBI.

J. Edgar Hoover, the long-standing head of the FBI, feared a black Moses.[100] Hoover had an obsession to destroy black leaders as America's chief law enforcement officer. He spoke for the American government when he declared Malcolm X, Dr. King, and Elijah Muhammad as dangerous troublemakers and subversives.[101] All three men were freedom fighters. For too long white leaders depicted authentic African American freedom as trouble for white America. This is a structural definition and it underscores the depth and breadth of racism in America. My work at Morehouse recapped three deadly trajectories for African Americans: (1) we could remain surplus laborers, even as professionals; (2) we could be left adrift in the criminal justice system or; (3) we could join the military to fight America's many aggressive wars.

The first two paths of the trajectory began in slavery and the third came from America's ongoing wars. The issue of surplus slave labor has always been the basis for violence against African Americans. Black folk did not come to America to enjoy the fruits of their labor. The denial of just compensation has not disappeared over time. African American male unemployment remains shamefully higher than the national average for white men. I recognize that many black men are voluntary actors in a cycle of economic backwardness.

This cycle is kept alive from the residue of slavery. I also understand how African American backwardness evolved. Many African Americans suffer from a variety of post-traumatic stress disorders. Some experience these disorders by making wrong choices. Other African Americans are smothered by the burden of dysfunctional families and chaotic neighborhoods. A combination of these factors has influenced high African American incarceration rates. The incarceration levels have increased recently geometrically. In the past black folks were controlled by lynching, Jim Crow segregation, and grinding poverty. Mandatory sentencing laws, mostly for drug offenses, have only aggravated these past injustices. These laws have exploded black incarceration rates.

The broken promise by the US government during the Reconstruction Era to give former slaves forty acres and a mule never became policy. Even as a popular metaphor, the broken promise underscored the necessity for an economic vehicle to reconstruct African American family life. Slavery left African Americans with no foundation on which to create wealth. Even today there are significant structural economic barriers African Americans face that stem from age-old constraints borne during reconstruction. Some of these barriers prevent African Americans from wealth creation. Research shows that a significant percentage of individual and family wealth creation comes from generational property ownership. Freed slaves had zero opportunities to own property. There has never been an initiative like the Marshall Plan (officially the European Recovery Program) to assist African Americans. I believe the aftermath of nearly three hundred years of slavery was more harmful to African Americans than was five years of war in Europe to the European economy.[102]

I calmly came to these conclusions in light of my work at Morehouse College. It began thirty-five years after the student revolt at Central State University and just a few months after my first visit to Africa. Both of these events helped me reorder pieces of my cracked mirror. Morehouse introduced a defining chapter in my life. I lived in Atlanta for six years and worked at Morehouse for five years. Four of my children were born in Atlanta. Africa beckoned once again.

AFRICA IS MORE THAN A STATE OF MIND

I returned to the Gambia for the second time to improve my chances to live and work in Africa and the Muslim world. I flew from Baltimore to the Gambia in the summer of 2004 and planned to stay for one month to see if a permanent transition to the Gambia could happen. I arrived in Banjul around 11:30 p.m., but my luggage continued on to Accra, Ghana. I was very happy when my bags returned after a few days. I stayed with a group of local and expat Muslims. The building doubled as a teaching center for children and adults. After I had relaxed enough, it was time to find business opportunities.

My old friend Abdul Malik invited me to his house for a shrimp dinner. As I sat with him in the "majlis" (living room), I overheard him ask his wife to take out a couple of shrimp and prepare dinner. She agreed and I said to myself, "A couple of shrimp?" Man, I thought, two shrimp is not enough for two grown men. I did not say anything in a desire not to be rude. I also thought, "Well, I'll just buy some good old fried chicken from a Gambian restaurant owner who used to live in the Bronx since his place was close to the apartment."

When Abdul Malik's wife brought out the dish of shrimp, smothered in traditional Gambian jasmine rice, I noticed that the two shrimp were each as large as a man's fist. I had no idea Gambian shrimp were so big and some of the finest in West Africa. The seafood export trade in the Gambia is underdeveloped compared to the principal exports of mangoes and peanut products. I figured I could make a go at exporting shrimp and promised myself not to repeat the mistakes I made three years earlier. To make a go of this, I needed connections with insiders in government and I stubbornly refused to waste time with barriers I could not overcome.

The first thing I noticed was that Gambian fishers did not have the capacity to catch large yields of shrimp. That was the first obstacle. The second obstacle to overcome came from the government's invisible deep-sea fishing policy. I also worried that the Lebanese-Gambian merchants dominated this sector like other businesses in the Gambia. I did not become discouraged, though. This time, I understood the reality of doing business in the Gambia. Without key government officials endorsing a fast track, finding significant investment capital, and working through export arrangements in foreign markets, it did not take me long to figure out I couldn't export shrimp. I had to suck it up and move on.

My trip was expensive and I didn't want to return home without something to sell. I hired a local tailor to make thirty shirts with matching pants in a traditional Islamic style with a distinctive West African flavor. Each garment cost me seven US dollars and I intended to resell them for forty dollars a set in Atlanta. I needed a suitcase for the garments, so I went out to purchase a bag in a big open-air market in the town of Serekunda. I took with me a Fula friend, Mahmoud. When we entered the store to buy a suitcase, we found the owners, an old man and his adult son, at work with other customers. The old man took one look at me, turned his head away in disgust, and walked away to the rear of the store. I was stunned. I asked Mahmoud why this old man didn't like me. Since Mahmoud spoke the Fula language, he could find out. Mahmoud and the old man's adult son walked to the back of the store. When they returned, both were laughing. Mahmoud said, "Zaid, Baba (slang for father) is convinced you are his brother's eldest son, the son that went to study and live in England many years ago. He believes that you think you are too educated to speak Fula."

"Just tell him who I am!" I said, exasperated.

We did. "He insists you are his nephew," Mahmoud said, looking at me with a broad smile, showing his natural white teeth. "I told you you're a Fula." We smiled and laughed about Baba's take on me. This incident underscored the importance of African American identity. We are Africans. Others know it, but many of us do not.

Many African Americans experience the absence of specific ethnic and a historical identity as an unarticulated pain. We don't know the details of the impact of slavery has had on us and many of us don't wish to know. It remains buried as a collective trauma. We seldom comprehend the essence of our biological and cultural connections with scores of Africans. Baba's reaction became a poignant reminder of who I am. My DNA spoke loudly. My encounter with this skeptical Gambian-Fulani storeowner taught me an important lesson about misplaced identity. Many African Americans have little knowledge about the African continent. What we know for sure is that some distant ancestor was from some place in Africa and became a slave. This reality comes with the stigma that many African-Americans live on the edge of personal and racial insecurity regarding Africa. The insecurity occurs when the assumptions are accepted. It is easy to see how this vicious cycle took root. It was a crime for slaves to accumulate wealth or have full control over their lives. Unless one is favored with a good education, athletic ability, or entertainment talent, the adverse effects of the wealth worth mythology are hard to shake. We have struggled to define our best selves without the bondage of antiblack racist definitions. We have overcome many shades of injustice and oppression. Nevertheless, many African Americans have lost the historical perspective of how and why we live in America. The same forces that stymied Africa's potential still prevent African Americans to acknowledge our disconnected roots.

Some African-Americans' problems also stem from cultural practices to deal with racism that, over time, became dysfunctional. My mother believed that the source of most black folks' dysfunctional adaptations came from wearing a pretense mask. I think my mother hit the nail on the head. Other problems come from a misguided insistence we are Americans without an African hyphenation. Many African Americans only see Africa on the evening news when a famine or epidemic is reported. No doubt, formidable problems exist in Africa. The continent is racked by senseless ethnic wars, chronic disease, famine, and infrastructure backwardness. Nevertheless, Africa has enormous potential. Africans came to America to work as slaves. We should embrace this reality by making our existence in America a vindication of survival and excellence. Many problems in African American communities stem from a rejection of our African identity.

The personal position of my elder Fula distant relative did not matter. My kinsman, by a default of history, genetics, and a striking physical resemblance, helped me reassemble important pieces of my cracked mirror. It cemented my connection to Africa practically and emotionally.

I prepared to leave and packed a few gifts with the garments. The brothers who accommodated my visit dropped me at the airport around midnight. The line to board did not wind its way outside of the terminal as I have seen previously. I thought, well, OK, the trip back to the United States should not be stressful if they do not lose my bags again.

Then, just as we boarded the plane, an airport official announced our flight from the Gambia to Baltimore would travel to Accra, Ghana, for a short layover. OK, a brief layover in Ghana would be fine. In the airport in Accra, I witnessed a near riot of disgruntled white Christian missionaries. Elderly women were screaming at Air Ghana officials shaking their fists.

They had been stranded for several days and the last excuse they received was the last straw. They pushed back, hard. When our layover lasted longer than expected, we nearly rioted. However, the Air Ghana staff took us to a decent hotel not far from the airport after a couple of hours. We spent two days in Ghana.

I arrived in Baltimore and then flew to Atlanta. The next three years passed quickly at Morehouse. I revised plans about Gambia. Living in the Gambia, or anywhere in underdeveloped Africa, needs long-range planning. It requires capital and it needs family buy-in. It is not for everyone. Living in Africa takes faith in Allah (God) and loads of patience to deal with ethnic and cultural diversity. Take my word. I shifted my focus to finding a job in one of the Gulf States. I cranked out several resumes to universities in the United Arab Emirates, Qatar, and Saudi Arabia. I was shortlisted three times. A couple of times the committee members expected to interview a South Asian given the fact that there are many Indians and Pakistanis who have the same name as me.

One time for sure, the interview ended before it started when they saw I was an African American. During a video interview with a University in the UAE, the campus provost, a retired American, and I connected professionally and personally as we agreed on several issues during the course of the interview. We hit it off. He urged the selection committee to make an offer. Three members seemed onboard. Two were reluctant and both were Egyptians who lived in the United Arab Emirates.

The provost told me to have patience. I would get a written offer over the weekend. No offer came. I was on the verge of giving up.

Doors Opened

By mid-May 2007 I decided to suspend my job search, but not before I thought, "Wait—make one more stab." I saw an announcement on an international jobs website for the director of institutional research at an American university in the United Arab Emirates (UAE). It sounded perfect, but disheartened, I said to myself, "What's the use? These Arabs won't hire a black American Muslim."

As I sat there, lost in my frustration, the phone rang. It was an American Muslim brother calling from the UAE. We had met online and he wanted me to put him in contact with an American Muslim woman he wanted to marry.

After I had hung up the phone, I was overcome with a feeling his call was a sign to apply. It was a strong encouragement to apply, that night.

I believe that Allah (God) answers prayers and provides us with tangible cues of his guidance. Sometimes these signals are not known or visible to anyone except the one who prayed. When a supplication removes barriers, a believing person is never surprised. Supplication is one of the core elements of Islamic worship. It is a two-step process. First, it informs us to use every lawful and tangible means and resource to achieve our goals. Second, I realized that regardless of how diligent our striving, how sharp our intellect, and how substantial our resources, the means alone do not make a successful outcome. The result is from Allah (God). Relying on Allah (God) combines worldly means with faith in Allah (God) for a beneficial outcome. Implementing reliance ("tawakaal" in Arabic) increases one's faith. I sent a resume immediately. Within two days, I interviewed with the campus vice president and four other staff.

I braced myself for another disappointment. Instead of a rejection, the campus vice president made an offer twenty thousand dollars less than what I made at Morehouse.

I countered the offer. I wrote that it would take an additional fifteen thousand dollars if they wanted me. The following day I received an e-mail with an offer of twenty thousand dollars plus incentives.

I processed passports for my wife and all the children and prepared the family to leave by August. We sold everything except our laptops and clothes. I literally wrestled our George Foreman grill from my wife's hands and made a solemn promise I would buy one in the UAE. We flew from Atlanta to Frankfurt, Germany, on Lufthansa Airlines. My children were beside themselves with the thought of international travel and living near Dubai. After a two-hour layover, we boarded our flight to Dubai.

RAS AL KHAIMAH ("THE HEAD OF THE TENT")

When we arrived at the Dubai Airport, a University driver picked us up and drove us fifty kilometers north of Dubai to the emirate of Ras Al Khaimah (RAK). The University provided us with twelve days in a local hotel and meals. Two full-time staff arranged getting visas and a residence in Ras Al Khaimah. Daily temperatures in Dubai and Ras Al Khaimah reach 115 degrees Fahrenheit in July and August. Every day my oldest daughter declared she was at the point of dehydration and near death.

After two weeks, we moved into a townhouse seven minutes from campus. I came to RAK to work at George Mason University's branch campus as Director of Institutional Effectiveness. The majority of faculty and staff were Arab, Indian, and Pakistani. Many of them were educated in America or Canada.

It took me a while to realize how many American universities in the Gulf region had opened. By the end of the decade, several prominent American universities had opened campuses in Qatar and the United Arab Emirates. American-styled universities also were established in Kuwait and Lebanon.

Typically, a local nonacademic management team ran the administrative side of many universities. Expat faculty had oversight of curriculum and the academic operations.

George Mason University's academic curriculum was robust. They also maintained an English language exam requirement that proved to be too difficult for most students in the region to pass.

Zaid Adib Ansari, Acting Vice President, with two Emirati
nationals during a press conference in 2008.

The language requirement affected the number of students willing to apply. The university's experiment in the Middle East was beset with challenges from the beginning.

George Mason hired several campus vice presidents in five years. The campus vice president who hired me faced the same nature of challenges previous vice presidents had faced. I started work in August 2007, and by February 2008 George Mason's provost reappointed the campus vice president to work on the US campus after faculty and staff expressed deep dissatisfaction.

In the days leading up to the VP's reassignment, the provost queried staff for a candidate to replace her. The majority of faculty and staff nominated me.

The provost alerted me what would occur on the day her reassignment took place. The following day I became acting vice president.

I thought about the irony. I was ready to hold a campus president hostage thirty-five years before at Central State and I now held the office. Allah (God) alone is worthy of praise!

The need to increase enrollment was the number one problem for the University. It had always been the biggest challenge since the University's inception. It was a perennial problem. I struggled to convince George Mason's decision makers to lower the English entrance requirement. I also wanted to recruit more American and Canadian second-generation Arab students and Southeast Asian and Indian students. I visited three large American cities to recruit students. Interest was good, but my efforts were too little too late. The local board of trustees hired a hatchet man to cut the budget by 70 percent after eighteen months of stagnant enrollment and the same level of expenses. The new director's draconian measures forced George Mason's provost to suspend the university's relationship with the Ras Al Khaimah Emirate. George Mason closed in June 2009 while a new incarnation, The American University of Ras Al Khaimah, emerged from the closure.

George Mason University did all it could to establish a top-notch University branch campus in the United Arab Emirates. It would be unfair to blame George Mason or the RAK emirate for the failed aspirations. The University's closure was rooted in the 2008 financial crash along with the cultural obstacles that proved to be too formidable to overcome. I cannot remember being as disappointed over a job ending. I looked for a job in the UAE after the 2008 financial crises and the economy was weak and thousands were leaving Dubai and other Emirates. I broke the news to my family. My children were devastated. They feared the loss of friends and the comfort of their familiar surroundings. They felt at home in Ras Al Khaimah and they had learned the local Arabic dialect rapidly. Ras Al Khaimah felt like home and we loved living there. My choices were limited, but I was determined not to return to America.

imHowever, I gave in to fears of not having a job and interviewed for a dean's position at a two-year college in suburban Washington DC. I did not hear from them after the interview. I was a finalist for a position in Dubai, but it, too, failed to pan out. I had nearly twenty thousand dollars from a combination of a payout settlement and personal savings. I thought about settling in Egypt. Instead, I decided to take the entire family to the Republic of the

Zaid Adib Ansari, Acting Vice President of George Mason's UAE branch campus is with the Crown Prince of the Emirate of Ras Al-Khaimah, Shaykh Saud Bin Al Saqr, in the summer of 2008.

Gambia. I arranged a shipping container, gathered all of our belongings, and left for Dakar, Senegal, through Addis Ababa, Ethiopia, in the third week of June 2009.

With a family of ten and no job, I moved my family to one of the poorest countries in Africa. My reliance on Allah (God) sustained me and gave me peace of mind.

Goree Lessons

The Ethiopian Airlines flight to Dakar had been uneventful except for a slight fuss between my wife and a Senegalese woman. The Senegalese woman told my wife to adjust the seat belt for one of my sons. My wife was offended and snapped at her, as she was unaccustomed to the direct and candid manner of Wolof women. I attempted to tell the woman with my scant knowledge of the Wolof language that I planned to visit Goree Island. She laughed and told me in perfect English that her aunt owned one of the hotels on Goree Island and gave me a number to call. She reminded me warmly to tell her aunt that she sent us and I agreed.

We found our way to the Goree Island ferry and boarded with nearly thirty pieces of luggage. We arrived on the island after sunset, just in time to make our evening prayers.

We ate a traditional Senegalese dinner of fish and rice with a cold hibiscus drink.

After dinner, we set off back to the hotel following dimly lit twenty-five-watt lights that hung outside the small cement houses. In front of us, local men and women walked with handheld flashlights because electricity service was sporadic, which was common in most parts of West Africa.

Saturday morning we ate breakfast in a small outdoor garden restaurant. We then set off to see the slave-holding fortress that my ancestor's experienced nearly three hundred years ago. I tried to imagine how my ancestors felt when they were dragged away in chains and then forced onto boats and packed in like sardines for the new land of capitalism, America. The main slave castle on Goree Island is a museum and a reminder of the horror that Europeans and Americans inflicted on Africans. I tried to picture how dark and hopeless it must have felt for thousands of Africans as we walked in and out of each of the holding rooms.

I envisaged that even the sunny blue Senegalese sky must have felt like a blanket of darkness. The blue water and sandy beaches must have stimulated remorse as they bid farewell.

I returned to Africa to reclaim my endowment of history and ancestry. Standing on the shore of Goree Island, facing the Atlantic Ocean, I understood why thousands of African Americans embraced the religion of Islam. It became abundantly clear as I watched my children walk in and out of the slave-holding rooms. A verse from the Quran helped increased my certainty. Allah (God) said:

"Who, when disaster strikes them, say, 'Indeed we belong to Allah, and indeed to Him we will return'" (Surah Al-Baqarah, verse 156).[103]

The disaster of slavery struck millions of Africans, Muslim and non-Muslims. However, the tragedy of slavery was always under the merciful care of Allah (God). Three centuries of slavery in America left the slave nothing but Allah (God) to call on for freedom and justice. The affliction of slavery was a teacher of monotheism and reliance on Allah (God). The inhumane treatment and unprovoked violence that slaves endured for centuries are crimes Allah (God) will judge on the Day of Final Accounting. The unrepentant will regret what they did.

I am sure that man's intended relationship with his Creator and Sustainer is consistent with the nature of man, as taught by Islam. Islam teaches that human beings crave one Creator for worship and devotion. I have observed this unpretentious natural disposition in every race. The natural disposition of all of the creation is called "fitrah" in Arabic. Fitrah is the comfort the heart feels seeing a beautiful sunset. Fitrah is felt hearing the sound of the sea's rhythmic tapping on the shore.

Understanding this concept removes the myth of race as an advantage. Biological determinism is irrelevant. One day my children will find the pictures and video of Goree Island. I pray they will grasp the essence of what they saw. I trust they will save room in their hearts for their heritage.

They will see Goree Island as a testament of possibility borne upon my cracked mirror. They will experience that day as a painting on the canvas of my life.

That evening, I hired a twelve-passenger van to drive our family from Dakar, Senegal, to Banjul, the Gambia.

Mirror Mended

My cracked mirror is almost mended. It has taken over fifty years to find the pieces and fit the jagged edges together. I found fragments in diverse places. At times, the pieces hid in plain sight.

My childhood memories are fresh as to why my mirror cracked. I am saddened to hear the braying voices of bigots and racists proclaim that African Americans and Latinos are ruining America and that Muslim terrorists will strike at any time. It is a sobering reality that white supremacy is active in America. There are aspects of America's claim of freedom and justice that the country is unwilling to reconcile. Among these fissures is the promise that all men are "endowed by the Creator with inalienable rights" of equality before God.

The sentiments and the behavior of some white Americans are inconsistent with the values they parade around the world. Many in America have launched an open attack on the Office of the President. It exposes a reality that some whites long for a time when African American leaders did not lead whites folks in anything. Race continues to be a significant relic of American life for those who cling to it, as it reveals a naked immorality of American culture. The murder of Emmett Till was a brutal and defiant affront to humanity. The residue of Till's murder, even now, inspires acts of violence directed at African Americans. Racism is a spiritual disease that lives in the heart. Emmett Till and Barack Obama are born of the same cosmic substance and both men symbolize primal fears that terrify some white people.

Emmett Till was sacrificed on the altar of American race mythology. Barack Obama is now the American President and, ironically, he preserves the mythology, as high priest, that America is an exceptional, blessed land. He represents exceptionalism, even though America's exceptionalism is a myth.

America has ignored the opportunity to dismantle the shrine of racism and xenophobia. Instead of tearing it down, large segments of America choose to dishonor her high priest, President Obama. The disrespect President Obama experiences is a public display of aggressive racism. Many people in the media and politics, as well as ordinary white folk, do not hesitate to disrespect President Obama. Disagreement over ideas and policies is expected. Racist disrespect is shameful. The culture of white supremacy fuels a primal fear and a primitive hatred of African Americans. The ghostly shadows of racism that haunt and taunt President Obama share the same violent impulses that killed Emmett Till. My mended mirror reminds me that these fears cannot be subdued easily. The best cure for the disease of racism is the belief in the Oneness of Allah (God). This principle of oneness of belief ("Tawheed" in Arabic) and what Tawheed requires will give a proper burial to a social construction of race and racism. The Quran says, "O mankind! Indeed, we created you from a male and a female and we made you nations and tribes that you may know one another. Indeed, (the) most noble of you near Allah (is the) most righteous of you. Indeed, Allah (is) all-knower, all-aware" (Surah 49–13).[104]

Racial reconciliation will not be achieved unless this fundamental reality is understood and practiced. This principle must become a reality and live in the hearts of human beings.

Recommended Readings

African American Culture

Christopher Booker, *I Will Wear No Chain: A Social History of African-American Males* (Westport, CT: Greenwood Press, 2002.).

Christopher Bracey, *Saviors or Sellouts: The Promise and Peril of Black Conservatism, from Booker T. Washington to Condoleezza Rice.* (Boston: Beacon Press, 2008).

Haley, Alex, and Malcolm X. *The Autobiography of Malcolm X (As Told to Alex Haley).* New York: Grove Press, 1965.

Colin Grant, *Negro with a Hat: The Rise and Fall of Marcus Garvey* (New York: Oxford University Press, 2008).

Cornel West, *Black Prophetic Fire.* Edited by Christa Buschendorf (Boston: Beacon Press, 2014).

David Davis, *The Problem of Slavery in the Age of Emancipation (*New York:: Knopf, 2014).

Robert Fogel, and Stanley Engerman. *Time on the Cross: The Economics of American Negro Slavery* (Boston: Little, Brown 1974).

Eugene Genovese, *The Political Economy of Slavery: Studies in the Economy and Society of the Slave South* (New York: Random House, 1967).

Gwendolyn Hall, *Slavery and African Ethnicities in America* (Chapel Hill: University of North Carolina Press, 2005).

Black Power and Black Nationalism

Joshua Bloom and Waldo Martin. *Black Against Empire: The History and Politics of the Black Panther Party* (Berkeley: University of California Press, 2013).

Stokley Carmichael and Charles Hamilton. *Black Power: The Politics of Liberation in America*(New York: Vintage Books, 1967).

Karl Evanzz, *The Judas Factor: The Plot to Kill Malcolm X* (New York: Thunder's Mouth Press, 1993).

Jeffrey Ogbar, *Black Politics and African-American Identity* (Baltimore: Johns Hopkins University Press, 2005).

Arthur Smith, *Rhetoric of Black Revolution* (Boston: Alan & Bacon, 1969).

Civil Rights Movement

Taylor Branch, *Parting the Waters* (New York: Simon & Schuster, 1998).

Taylor Branch, *Pillar of Fire* (New York: Simon & Schuster, 1988).

Taylor Branch, *At Canaan's Edge: America in the King Years 1965–68* (New York: Simon & Schuster, 2006).

John Blake, *Children of the Movement* (Chicago: Lawrence Hill Books, 2004).

Racism and White Supremacy

Edward Baptist, *The Half Has Never Been Told: Slavery and the Making of American Capitalism* (New York: Basic Books, 2014).

Elliot Jaspin, *Buried in the Bitter Waters: The Hidden History of Racial Cleansing in America* (New York: Basic Books, 2007).

Randal Kennedy, *The Persistence of the Color Line: Racial Politics and the Obama Presidency* (New York: Pantheon Books, 2011.

Tim Madigan, *The Burning: Massacre, Destruction, and the Tulsa Race Riot of 1921* (New York: St. Martin's Press, 2001.

John Potash, *The FBI War on Tupac Shakur and Black Leaders* (Baltimore: Progressive Left Press, 2007).

Stephen Whitfield, *A Death in the Delta: The Story of Emmett Till.* (New York: Free Press, 1988).

RELIGION OF ISLAM
Nasir Deen Al Albaanee, *Prophet's Prayer Described.* Translated by Usama Bin Suhaib Hasan (Riyadh, Saudi Arabia: Darussalam Publisher, 2003).

Fadl Al-Ilaahi, *Kindness and Gentleness.* Translated by Tarik Preston. (Walthamstow, UK: Invitation to Islam, 2003).

Muhammad Al-Jibaly *Eemaan Made Easy.* 6 vols. Madinah, Saudi Arabia: Al-Kitaab & as-Sunnah Publishing,2008).

Aminah Assami trans. *The Quran.* Jeddah, Saudi Arabia: Abul-Qasim Publishing, 1997.

Ahmad Farid, *Purification of the Soul: According to the Earliest Sources.* Translated by Ashraf (London: Al-Firdous, 2008.).

Bilal Philips, *The Fundamentals of Tawheed (Islamic Monotheism)* (Riyadh, Saudi Arabia: International Islamic Publishing House, 2006.

CITED WORKS

Michelle Alexander, *The New Jim Crow: Mass Incarceration in the Age of Color Blindness* (New York: The New Press, 2010).

Zaid Ansari, "The Characteristics of Conversion by Ex-Offenders and Non-Ex-Offender Black Males." Unpublished thesis manuscript, (University of Cincinnati, 1985).

Zaid Ansari, The Muddled Methodology of the Wilbanks NDT Myth Thesis." *The Critical Criminologist* 2, no. 1 (1990), 13.

Edward Baptist, *The Half Has Never Been Told: Slavery and the Making of American Capitalism* (New York: Basic Books, 2014).

Amiri Baraka, *Tales of the Out & the Gone*. New York: Akashic Books, 2007).

Hans Bare, *The Black Spiritual Movement: A Religious Response to Racism.* (Knoxville: University of Tennessee Press, 1948).

Lerone Bennett, *Before the Mayflower: A History of Black America* (London: Pelican B & B, 1964).

Taylor Branch, *At Canaan's Edge: America in the King Years 1965–68*. New York: Simon & Schuster, 2006).

Tom Burrell, *Brainwash: Challenging the Myth of Black Inferiority* (New York: Smiley Books, 2010).

Stokley Carmichael and Charles Hamilton, *Black Power: The Politics of Liberation in America* (New York: Vintage Books, 1967).

Hundred Years of Yellow Springs, ed. Diane Chiddister et al. (Yellow Springs: Yellow Springs News, 2005).

Ward Churchill and Jim Vander Wall. *The COINTELPRO Papers: Documents from the FBI's Secret Wars Against Dissent in the United States* (Boston: South End Press, 1990.).

David B. Davis, *The Problem of Slavery in the Age of Emancipation* (New York: Knopf, 2014).

Basil Davison, *The African Slave Trade* (Boston: Back Bay Books, 1961).

Leary, Joy DeGruy. *Post Traumatic Slave Syndrome: America's Legacy of Enduring Injury and Healing* (Portland, OR: Uptone Press, 2005.

David DeLeon, *Leaders from the 1960s: A Biographical Sourcebook of American Activism* (Westport, CT: Greenwood Press, 1994).

Cheik Anta Diop, *Cultural Unity of Black Africa* (Westport, CT: Lawrence Hill, 1962).

Allen Ginsberg, *Howl* (San Francisco: City Lights Books, 1965).

Ralph Ginzburg, *100 Years of Lynching*. Reprint, (Baltimore: Black Classic Press, 1996), First published in 1962 by the author.

William Grier and Price Cobbs. *Black Rage* (New York: Basic Books, 1968).

Alex Haley and Malcolm X, *The Autobiography of Malcolm X (As Told to Alex Haley)* (New York: Grove Press, 1965).

Richard Hofstadter, *The American Political Tradition and the Men Who Made It* (New York: Vintage Books, 1948).

Charles Eric Lincoln, *Black Muslims in America* (Lagos, Nigeria: Kayode Publications, 1964).

Jeffrey Ogbar, *Black Politics and African-American Identity* (Baltimore: Johns Hopkins University Press, 2005).

Nell Erin Painter, *The History of White People* (New York: W. W. Norton, 2010).

William Pepper *An Act of State: The Execution of Martin Luther King* (London: Verso, 2003).

David Pilgrim Curator of the Jim Crow Museum of Racist Memorabilia: Jim Crow Museum of Racist Memorabilia. http://www.ferris.edu/jimcrow/who.htm.

Karl Polanyi, *The Great Transformation: The Political and Economic Origins of Our Time* (Boston: Beacon Hill Press, 1944).

Fabio Rojas, *From Black Power to Black Studies: How a Radical Social Movement Became an Academic Discipline* (Baltimore: John Hopkins University Press, 2010).

Martin Duberman, *Paul Robeson* (New York: New Press, 1995).

Jerome David Salinger, *The Catcher in the Rye* (Boston: Little, Brown, 1951).

Arthur Smith, *Rhetoric of Black Revolution* (Boston: Alan & Bacon, 1969).

Andrea Sullivan, "Politicization: The Effects of the Nation of Islam on Prison Inmate Culture." Unpublished Dissertation, University of Pennsylvania, 1976).

Ekwueme Thelwell, *Ready for Revolution: The Life and Struggles of Stokely Carmichael (Kwame Ture)* (New York: Scribner, 2003).

Cornel West, *Black Prophetic Fire* (Boston: Beacon Press, 2014).

Eric Williams, *Capitalism and Slavery* (Chapel Hill: University of North Carolina Press, 1944).

Stephen Whitfield, *A Death in the Delta: The Story of Emmett Till* (New York: Free Press, 1988).

Carter G. Woodson, *The Mis-Education of the Negro* (Washington, DC: Associated Publishers, 1933).

Richard Wright, *Native Son* (New York: Harper Perennial, 1940).

Howard Zinn, *SNCC: The New Abolitionists* (Brooklyn: South End Press, 2002).

INDEX

ENDNOTES

1. Edward E. Baptist, *The Half Has Never Been Told: Slavery and the Making of American Capitalism* (New York: Basic Books, 2014).

2. Karl Polanyi, *The Great Transformation* (Boston: Beacon Press, 1944). I was introduced to Polanyi's work in graduate school. He describes with a great deal of detail how the rise of the market economy supported mercantile capitalism. He explains the political and economic forces that supported the trans-Atlantic slave trade beginning in the seventeenth century.

3. David B. Davis, *The Problem of Slavery in the Age of Emancipation* (New York: Knopf, 2014).

4. Edward E. Baptist, *The Half Has Never Been Told: Slavery and the Making of American Capitalism* (New York: Basic Books, 2014).

5. Professor Glenn Hinson of the University of North Carolina at Chapel Hill says in an article in the *New York Times*, "The song ['Kumbayah'] in white hands was never grounded in faith. Its words were simplistic; its tune was breezy. And it was simplistically dismissed." Samuel G. Freedman, "A Long Road From 'Come by Here' to 'Kumbaya,'" *New York Times*, November 19, 2010. http://nytimes.com/2010/11/20/us/20religion.html?pagewanted=print.

6. Stephen J. Whitfield, *A Death in the Delta: The Story of Emmett Till* (New York: Free Press, 1988), 23.

7. Stephen J. Whitfield, *A Death in the Delta: The Story of Emmett Till* (New York: Free Press, 1988).

8. Tom Burrell, *Brainwashed: Challenging the Myth of Black Inferiority* (New York: Smiley Books, 2010).

10. Chiddister, E. ed et al *Two Hundred Years of Yellow Springs* (Yellow Springs, OH: Yellow Springs News, 2005). Site Staff http://www.warof1812.ca/tecumseh.htm, 2012

11. Chiddister, E. ed et al *Two Hundred Years of Yellow Springs* (Yellow Springs, OH: Yellow Springs News, 2005), 7.

12. Chiddister, E. ed et al *Two Hundred Years of Yellow Springs* (Yellow Springs, OH: Yellow Springs News, 2005), 23, 24.

13. David Pilgrim, "Who Was Jim Crow," Jim Crow Museum of Racist Memorabilia. http://www.ferris.edu/jimcrow/who.htm: (March, 2015).

14. David Pilgrim, "Who Was Jim Crow," Jim Crow Museum of Racist Memorabilia. http://www.ferris.edu/jimcrow/who.htm: (March, 2015).

16. Michelle Alexander. *The New Jim Crow: Mass Incarceration in the Age of Color Blindness* (New York: New Press, 2010).

17. Ralph Ginzburg, *100 Years of Lynching* (reprint, Baltimore: Black Classic Press, 1996. First published in 1962 by author).

18. Ginzburg, *100 Years of Lynching.* 18.

19. Alex Haley and Malcolm X, *The Autobiography of Malcolm X (As Told to Alex Haley)* (New York: Grove Press, 1965).

20. William Pepper, *An Act of State: The Execution of Martin Luther King* (London: Verso, 2003).

21. "In Berry's case, the Mann Act charges stemmed from what Berry contended was his offer of legitimate employment in his St. Louis nightclub

to a girl he had met in a bar in Juarez, Mexico. Three weeks after being fired from Berry's nightclub, fourteen-year-old Janice Norine Escalanti took a different story to the St. Louis police, and Berry was arrested two days later, on this day in

22. Retrieved from http://www.pbs.org/unforgivableblackness/knockout/ mann.html: (March 2015)

23. Billie Holiday's song "Strange Fruit" was a stinging critique of Jim Crow terrorism. Few people in later generations know the lyrics, so I present them here: (March 2015).

> Southern trees bear a strange fruit,
> Blood on the leaves and blood at the root,
> Black body swinging in the Southern breeze,
> Strange fruit hanging from the poplar trees.
>
> Pastoral scene of the gallant South,
> The bulging eyes and the twisted mouth,
> Scent of magnolia sweet and fresh,
> And the sudden smell of burning flesh!
>
> Here is a fruit for the crows to pluck,
> For the rain to gather, for the wind to suck,
> For the sun to rot, for a tree to drop,
> Here is a strange and bitter crop.

David Margolick, "Strange Fruit: Billie Holiday, Café Society, and an Early Cry for Civil Rights." https://www.nytimes.com/books/first/m/margolick-fruit.html.

24. Nell I. Painter, *The History of White People* (New York: W. W. Norton, 2010).

25. David DeLeon, *Leaders from the 1960s: A Biographical Sourcebook of American Activism* (Westport, CT: Greenwood Press, 1994).

26. Rojas, *From Black Power to Black Studies: How a Radical Social Movement Became an Academic Discipline* (Baltimore: John Hopkins University Press, 2010).

27. "Birmingham Church Bombing," History.com. http://www.history.com/topics/black-history/birmingham-church-bombing: (January 2015).

28. Dr. Cornel West's discussion of Ida B. Wells is one of the better accounts of Wells's mission and character:

> Ida B. Wells is not only unique, but she is the exemplary figure full of prophetic fire in the face of American terrorism, which is American Jim Crow and Jane Crow, when lynching occurred every two and a half days for over fifty years in America. And this is very important, because Black people in the New World, in the Diaspora, Brazil, Jamaica, Barbados, were all enslaved, but no group of Black people were Jim Crowed other than US Negroes. *Black Prophetic Fire*, (Boston, MA: Beacon Press, 2014), 140.

29. "A police and FBI investigation of the murder quickly unearthed a prime suspect: Byron De La Beckwith, a white segregationist and founding member of Mississippi's White Citizens Council. Despite mounting evidence against him—a rifle found near the crime scene was registered to Beckwith and had his fingerprints on the scope, and several witnesses placed him in the area—Beckwith denied shooting Evers. He maintained that the gun had been stolen, and produced several witnesses to testify that he was elsewhere on the night of the murder." ("Medgar Evers," Biography.com. http://www.biography.com/people/medgar-evers-9542324#tragic-death-and-aftermath.): (March 2015).

30. "On December 4, 1969, Chicago police raided Fred Hampton's apartment and shot and killed him in his bed. He was just 21 years old. Black Panther leader Mark Clark was also killed in the raid. While authorities claimed the Panthers had opened fire on the police who were there to serve a search warrant for weapons, evidence later emerged that told a very different story: that the FBI, the Cook County State's Attorney's Office and the Chicago police conspired to assassinate Fred Hampton…Noam Chomsky has called Hampton's killing 'the gravest domestic crime of the Nixon administration.'" ("The Assassination of Fred Hampton: How the FBI and the Chicago Police Murdered a Black Panther," Democracy Now. http://www.democracynow. org/2009/12/4/the_assassination_of_fred_hampton_how.): (March 2015).

31. John Potash: *The FBI War on Tupac Shakur and Black Leaders* (New York: Progressive Left Press, 2008), 88.

32. William Jennings Bryant, Populist: Richard Hofstadter, *The American Political Tradition and the Men Who Made It* (New York: Vintage Books, 1948).

33. Richard Wright, *Native Son* (New York: Harper Perennial, 1940) and J. D. Salinger, *The Catcher in the Rye* (Boston: Little, Brown, 1951).

34. LeRoi Jones (Amiri Baraka), "The Revolutionary Theatre," *Liberator*, July 5, 1965, 4–6.

35. LeRoi Jones (Amiri Baraka), *Home: Social Essays* (New York: William Morrow, 1966).

36. Allen Ginsberg, *Howl and Other Poems* (San Francisco: City Lights Books, 1965).

37. LeRoi Jones (aka Amiri Baraka) had a significant impact on the Black Arts Movement. His sharp lyrical talent for poetry, essays, and stories influenced many black people to write and think critically about America:

The Black Arts Movement helped develop a new aesthetic for black art and Baraka was its primary theorist. Black American artists should follow 'black,' not 'white' standards of beauty and value, he maintained, and should stop looking to white culture for validation. The black artist's role, he wrote in *Home: Social Essays* (1966) is to "aid in the destruction of America as he knows it. "Amiri Baraka," Poetry Foundation. http://www.poetryfoundation.org/bio/amiri-baraka. (April 2015).

See also Amiri Baraka, *Tales of the Out & the Gone* (New York: AKASHCI Books, 2007).

38. David DeLeon, *Leaders from the 1960s: A Biographical Sourcebook of American Activism* (Westport, CT: Greenwood Press, 1994).

39. Stokely Carmichael and Charles Hamilton, *Black Power: The Politics of Liberation in America* (New York: Vintage Books, 1967).

40. "Race Relations Under Theodore Roosevelt," United States History. Accessed [date], Retrieved from http://www.u-s-history.com/pages/h943. html: (March 2015).

41. The Brownsville Affair is one of the ironies African-Americans faced serving in the military—defending the country abroad but in need of defense at home:

In the summer of 1906, the first battalion of the 25th Infantry Regiment, all blacks, was transferred from Nebraska to Fort Brown near Brownsville, Texas. Despite a splendid record in the Spanish-American War and the Philippine Insurrection, the African-American soldiers were not welcomed into their new community. Many white residents of the south Texas community were fearful that the newly arrived blacks might ally with the large Mexican-American community and upset the carefully maintained racial balance. Letters were sent to Washington asking for the removal of the soldiers, but all such appeals were turned down.

In the early morning hours of August 14, a melee broke out near the fort and shots were fired. Casualties included a dead bartender and a seriously wounded policeman. Brownsville citizens immediately stepped forward and blamed the soldiers, some claiming to have actually seen the soldiers firing shots and others asserting that they heard black voices during the skirmish. On the strength of these allegations, plus the finding of several discarded army rifles and shell casings, twelve members of the 25th were imprisoned. "Race Relations Under Theodore Roosevelt," United States History. http://www.u-s-history.com/pages/h943.html: (March 2015).

42. Howard Zinn, *SNCC: The New Abolitionists* (Brooklyn: South End Press, 2002).

43. C. Eric Williams, *Capitalism and Slavery* (Chapel Hill: University of North Carolina Press, 1944).

44. Examples here: "What He Said Archive," Brother Malcolm.net. http://www.brothermalcolm.net/mxwords/whathesaidarchive.html: (February 2015).

45. Basil Davidson, *The African Slave Trade* (Boston: Back Bay Books, 1961).

46. Chiekh Anta Diop, *Cultural Unity of Black Africa* (Westport, CT: Lawrence Hill, 1962).

47. Lerone Bennett, *Before the Mayflower: A History of Black America* (London: Pelican B & B, 1964)

48. See Senate Joint Resolution No. 20 honoring Charles Flowers: "WHEREAS, Dr. Flowers held many leadership positions during his distinguished career as an educator and administrator, including as dean

of students at Central State University and associate professor of education, department chair, and director of student personnel services at Fisk University…" https://leg1.state.va.us/cgi-bin/legp504.exe?081+ful+SJ20. (March 2015).

49. In Dr. Ibram Rogers's lecture entitled "The Black Campus Movement and the Reformation of Higher Education, 1965 to 1972, "Dr. Rogers mentioned that Central State University was one of the first universities to stage a campus take over:

The activism at HBCU's had traversed over to white institutions in the fall of 1967 with the first known protest to diversify a white college, occurring at San Jose State. Black students also went protest at semester at Grambling in Louisiana, the University of Texas, Central State in Ohio, and San Francisco State. The local and national media began to notice the Black Campus Movement, as 1967 was ending. (http://www.loc.gov/today/cyberlc/transcripts/110119klu1200.txt.) : (March 2015).

50. I refer to Nat Turner here to underscore that Unity-for-Unity perceived our campus takeover similar to the slave rebellion of Nat Turner. Even though our reference to Nat Turner was inaccurate, it served as an important reference in the heydays of the 1960s Black Nationalist fervor. http://www.history.com/topics/black-history/nat-turner/print Nathanial "Nat" Turner (1800-1831) was a black American slave who led the only effective, sustained slave rebellion (August 1831) in U.S. history. Spreading terror throughout the white South, his action set off a new wave of oppressive legislation prohibiting the education, movement, and assembly of slaves and stiffened proslavery, anti-abolitionist convictions that persisted in that region until the American Civil War (1861–65): (June 2015).

51. Dr. King is quoted to have said, "I want to be the white man's brother, not his brother-in-law" in the *New York Journal* on September 10, 1962. "Civil Rights Quotes," History Learning Site. http://www.historylearningsite.co.uk/civil%20rights%20quotes.htm.

52. Ekwueme Michael Thelwell, *Ready for Revolution: The Life and Struggles of Stokely Carmichael (Kwame Ture)*, (New York: Scribner, 2003), 660-662. Thelwell describes the relationship between Huey P. Newton and Stokely Carmichael as cooperative. He wrote that Huey respected Stokely and acknowledged he could learn how to organize the Black Panthers by following many of the lessons SNCC learned. Thelwell relates that Huey agreed with Stokely that the Panthers needed to move away from the armed resistance image if they wanted to reach adults in the black community. This relationship deteriorated when Eldridge Cleaver informed Stokely that he could no longer visit Huey in jail as he awaited trial.

53. Thelwell, *Ready for Revolution*, 660-662.

54. Peniel Joseph, *Stokely: A Life* (Philadelphia: Perseus Books, 2014).

55. Ekwueme Thelwell, *Ready for Revolution*, 660-662.

56. "Stevens was a graduate student at Tuskegee and Editor on his student newspapers. And he wrote the first coherent and detailed ideological foundation of the Black Campus Movement at HBCU's. He asked, "How long will it be before black leaders and educators take hold of Negro colleges and transform them from training schools for Negroes into universities designed to fit the real needs of black people in this nation?" Rogers, "The Black Campus Movement and the Reformation of Higher Education, 1965 to 1972." (March 2015). http://www.loc.gov/today/cyberlc/transcripts/110119klu1200.txt.

57. Howard Zinn, *SNCC: The New Abolitionists* (Brooklyn: South End Press, 2002).

58. My instinct about the grittiness of Stax was no accident. It seems the record label created a down-home and soulful brand to distinguish its music from Motown's drift toward the mainstream:

Stax Records is critical in American music history as it's one of the most popular soul music record labels of all time—second only to Motown in sales and influence, but first in gritty, raw, stripped-down soul music. In fifteen years, Stax placed more than 167 hit songs in the Top 100 on the pop charts, and a staggering 243 hits in the Top 100 R&B charts. It launched the careers of such legendary artists as Otis Redding, Sam & Dave, Rufus & Carla Thomas, Booker T. & the MGs, and numerous others. Current Stax recording artists include Ben Harper, Booker T. Jones, and others. "About," Stax. http://www.staxrecords.com/about. : (March 2015).

59. Lauren Araiza, *To March for Others: The Black Freedom Struggle and the United Farm Workers*, (Philadelphia: University of Pennsylvania Press, 2013). Hundreds of Black Panthers adopted the Bitter Dog as the organization's official drink.

60. William Grier and M. Price Cobbs, *Black Rage*, New York: Basic Books, 1968).

61. "Did you know that Bob Marley's 'Get Up, Stand Up' was inspired by WAR's ('Slippin' into Darkness'? A young and rising Marley toured as WAR's opening act in the early seventies, and often sat on the skirt of the stage groovin' to WAR's jam of their hit 'Slippin.'" Mtume ya Salaam and Kalamu ya Salaam, review of *All Day Music*, by WAR. http://www.nathanielturner.com/warslippinintodarkness.htm: (March 2015).

62. In President Obama's speech "A More Perfect Union" he said, "Just as black anger often proved counterproductive, so have these white resentments distracted attention from the real culprits of the middle class squeeze—a corporate culture rife with inside dealing, questionable accounting practices, and short-term greed; a Washington dominated by lobbyists and special interests; economic policies that favor the few over the many. And yet, to wish away the resentments of white Americans, to label them as misguided

or even racist, without recognizing they are grounded in legitimate concerns—this too widens the racial divide, and blocks the path to understanding." *Wall Street Journal*. http://blogs.wsj.com/washwire/2008/03/18/text-of-obamas-speech-a-more-perfect-union/: (April 2015).

63. Rudyard Kipling, "The White Man's Burden: The United States & The Philippine Islands, 1899." Rudyard Kipling's Verse: Definitive Edition (Garden City, New York: Doubleday, 1929)."A straightforward analysis of the poem may conclude that Kipling presents a 'Euro-centric' view of the world, in which people view society from only a European culture's point of view. This view proposes that white people consequently have an obligation to rule over, and encourage the cultural development of, people from other ethnic and cultural backgrounds until they can take their place in the world by fully adopting Western ways. The term 'the white man's burden' can be interpreted simply as racist, or taken as a metaphor for a condescending view of non-Western national culture and economic traditions, identified as a sense of European ascendancy that has been called 'cultural imperialism.' A parallel can also be drawn with the charitable view, common in Kipling's formative years, that the rich have a moral duty and obligation to help the poor 'better' themselves whether the poor want the help or not until, according to Europeans, 'they can take their place in the world socially and economically.'" Jane Thomas and Rudyard Kipling, *Victorian Literature, 1830–1900* (N. P: Bloomsbury, 1994) 1092–93: (March 2015).

64. Elijah Muhammad, *A Message to the Black Man in America,* (Chicago: Nation of Islam, 1965).

65. Muhammad, *A Message to the Black Man in America.*

66. Hans Bare, *The Black Spiritual Movement: A Religious Response to Racism* (Knoxville: University of Tennessee Press, 1948).

67. Elijah Muhammad, *A Message to the Black Man in America*.

68. Elijah Muhammad, *A Message to the Black Man in America*.

69. The FBI waged a relentless war from the late 1950s through the 1970s and beyond against black organizations. The language "outside agitator" always amused me with its racist overtone. It implied "don't come here and upset our docile Negroes with an objective examination of our local racism." See Kenneth O'Reilly, *Racial Matters: FBI's Secret File on Black America* (New York: Free Press, 1991).

70. Retrieved from http://www.ciphertheory.net/supremewisdom.pdf: (April 2015).

71. Elijah Muhammad, *Fall of America*, (Chicago: Nation of Islam, 1973).

72. Karl Evanzz, *The Judas Factor: Plot to Kill Malcolm X* (New York: Thunder's Mouth Press, 1993).

73. Saeed Sabiq, *Fiqh us-Sunnah* (Indianapolis: American Trust Publications, 1970).

74. "Throughout his controversial career, Elijah Muhammad was the nation's most potent preacher of black separatism. Yet when he died last week at seventy-seven, he was mourned as a statesman. Proclaimed Chicago's mayor Richard J. Daley: 'Under his leadership, the Nation of Islam has been a consistent contributor to the social well-being of our city for more than forty years.' A New York Times editorial noted his movement's success 'in rehabilitating and inspiring thousands of once defeated and despairing men and women.'" "Religion: The Messenger Passes," *Time*, March 10, 1975. http://content.time.com/time/magazine/article/0,9171,917218-1,00.html :(March 2015).

75. Elijah Muhammad, *How to Eat to Live* (Chicago: Nation of Islam, 1970).

76. Taylor Branch, *At Canaan's Edge: America in the King Years 1965–68* (New York: Simon & Schuster, 2006).

77. Taylor Branch, *At Canaan's Edge.*

78. www.merrian-webster.com/dictionary/hadith: (June 2015).

   1. A narrative record of the sayings or customs of Muhammad and his companions.
   2. The collective body of traditions relating to Muhammad and his companions.

79. Eiichi Shimomissé "The Philosophies of Enlightenment." http://www.csudh.edu/phenom_studies/western/lect_8.html. : (March 2015).

80. "The Al Mahdi is commonly referred to in non-Arabic literature as the forerunner to the return of the Jesus, Son of Mary (peace be upon them)." Shaykh Muhammad Salih Al-Munajjid, "Is the Mahdi Real or Not?" Islam House. http://islamhouse.com/en/fatwa/407635/. : (March 2015).

81. Nasir Deen al Albaanee, http://shaikhalbaani.wordpress.com/innovation: (June 2015).

82. See comments by Dr. Abdul Hakim Quick on the jihad of Uthman Dan Fodio at http://www.africa.upenn.edu/Articles_Gen/Uthm_Fodio.html.

83. "There are only a few documents in Middle Eastern history that have as much influence as the Balfour Declaration. The Balfour Declaration was sent as a sixty-seven-word statement contained within the short letter addressed to the British Foreign Secretary, Lord Arthur Balfour

on November 2, 1917. The declaration acknowledged the establishment of a Jewish home in Palestine. The statement of the Declaration read as:

> His Majesty's Government view with favor the establishment in Palestine of a national home for the Jewish people, and will use their best endeavors to facilitate the achievement of this object, it being clearly understood that nothing shall be done which may prejudice the civil and religious rights of existing non-Jewish communities in Palestine, or the rights and political status enjoyed by Jews in any other country."

"The Balfour Declaration," Palestine Facts. http://www.palestinefacts.org/pf_ww1_balfour.php: (March 2015).

84. "In 2001, Cincinnati was forced into a consent decree after a police shooting ignited three days of rioting. The city's extraordinarily powerful police union was vociferous in its opposition to the decree, and the rancor between the Cincinnati PD and the court-appointed outside monitor became so pronounced that on at least one occasion the monitor was actually kicked out of police headquarters. It took seven years for Cincinnati cops to finally come into compliance." Joe Domanick, "Police Reform's Best Tool: A Federal Consent Decree," *The Crime Report*, July 15, 2014. http://www.thecrimereport.org/news/articles/2014-07-police-reforms-best-tool-a-federal-consent-decree. : (March 2015).

85. Charles Eric Lincoln, *Black Muslims in America* (Lagos, Nigeria: Kayode Publications, 1964). Professor Lincoln's work is one of the first objective analyses of the Nation of Islam.

86. Andrea Sullivan: Politicization: The Effects of the Nation of Islam on Prison Inmate Culture." Unpublished Dissertation, University of Pennsylvania, 1976.

87. Michelle Alexander, *The New Jim Crow: Mass Incarceration in the Age of Color Blindness* (New York: New Press, 2010).

88. https://apps.carleton.edu/campus/ira/fed_race_ethnic/. Racial classification of whites, as noted on a site at Carlton University' Department of Institutional Research, illustrates the arbitrary nature geographically driven racial classification in as much anyone from non-Sub Saharan Africa is. : (June 2015).

89. Zaid Ansari, *Tony Brown's Journal*, PBS, 1993.

90. Zaid Ansari, "The Muddled Methodology of the Wilbanks Non-Discrimination Thesis (NDT) Myth" (Thesis, Eastern Michigan University, 1990), *The Critical Criminologist* 2, no.1. In this article, I critiqued Wilbanks methodology. He argued that when controlling for other factors, race had no impact in disadvantaging African-Americans in the criminal justice system.

91. Teachout Zephyr, *Corruption in America: From Benjamin Franklin's Snuff Box to Citizen United* (Cambridge: Harvard University Press, 2014).

92. Stephen R. Covey, *Seven Habits of Highly Effective People* (New York: Free Press, 1989).

93. http://www.nytimes.com/2006/06/18/us/18imams.html?pagewanted=all&_r=0. The establishment media have identified Hamza Yusuf and Zaid Shakir as leaders of so-called moderate Islam. In this article, author Laurie Goodstein, *US Muslim Clerics Seek a Moderate Middle Ground*, appeared in the *New York Times*, June 2006: (June 2015). Many observers, myself included, have surmised that Islam does not need to advocate an extra stance of moderation because its' teaching espouses a balance and moderation in all matters, both temporal and spiritual.

94. Jamil Al Amin has been in prison since 2003. http://www.workers.org/ articles/2014/09/05/support-jamil-al-amin/. Author Kathy Durkin described Imam Jamil Al Amin's struggles in article *Support Jamil Al-Amin* that appeared in the *Workers' World*, June 2014: (June 2015).

95. A historical and biographical description of Dwight York (also known as Malachi Z. York, Issa Al Haadi Al Mahdi, or Dr. York) can be found at http://www.mtv.com/artists/dr-york/biography/.

96. For more information on the Quran and Sunnah Society of North America (QSS), see http://www.qss.org/aboutus.html.

97. Tim Madigan, *The Burning: Massacre, Destruction, and the Tulsa Race Riot of 1921.* St. Martin's Press (2001).

98. Joy DeGruy Leary, *Post Traumatic Slave Syndrome: America's Legacy of Enduring Injury and Healing* (Portland: Uptone Press, 2005).

99. Edward Jones, *Candle in the Dark: A History of Morehouse College* (Valley Forge, PA: Judson Press, 1967).

100. Curt Gentry, *J. Edgar Hoover: The Man and the Secrets* (New York: W. W. Norton, 2001).

101. Ward Churchill and Jim Vander Wall, *The COINTELPRO Papers: Documents from the FBI's Secret Wars Against Dissent in the United States* (Boston: South End Press, 1990).

102. Churchill and Wall, *The COINTELOPRO Papers.*

103. Greg Behrman, *The Most Noble Adventure: The Marshall Plan and How America Helped Rebuild Europe* (New York: Free Press, 2008).

104. Aminah Assami, trans., *The Quran* (Jeddah, Saudi Arabia: Abul-Qasim Publishing, 1997), 22.

105. Aminah Assami, trans., *The Quran* (Jeddah, Saudi Arabia: Abul-Qasim Publishing, 1997), 522.

www.ingramcontent.com/pod-product-compliance
Lightning Source LLC
Chambersburg PA
CBHW072245310526
45795CB00011B/73